Cardinal Newman in His Age

CARDINAL
NEWMAN

IN HIS AGE

*His Place in English Theology
and Literature*

Harold L. Weatherby

Nashville
Vanderbilt University Press
1973

Library of Congress Cataloguing-in-Publication Data

Weatherby, Harold L   1934–
   Cardinal Newman in his age.

   Includes bibliographical references.
   1. Newman, John Henry, Cardinal, 1801–1890.
I. Title.
BX4705.N5W4   262′.135′0924 [B]   72–1347
ISBN 0–8265–1182–1

Printed in the United States of America by
Kingsport Press, Incorporated, Kingsport, Tennessee.

In memory of my father

Contents

Acknowledgments

My thanks are due to the editors of *Victorian Studies* for allowing me to reprint here several passages from my article, "The Encircling Gloom," which appeared in volume XII (Septemer 1968) of that journal. I also owe a particular debt of gratitude to Vanderbilt University, which not only aided me financially but also allowed me a leave of absence for the completion of this book. I am grateful to many friends for help and advice, especially to the Reverend C. S. Dessain of the Birmingham Oratory for many courtesies, to the staff of Pusey House, Oxford, for the use of their library, and to Milo B. Howard, Jr., and the staff of the Department of Archives and History of the State of Alabama for their hospitality while I was writing the final draft of the manuscript.

Abbreviations Used in Footnotes

Abrams   M. H. Abrams, *The Mirror and the Lamp* (New
                York: W. W. Norton & Company, 1958).

Ap.   John Henry Newman, *Apologia pro Vita Sua*,
                ed. Martin J. Svaglic (Oxford: The Clarendon
                Press, 1967).

AR   S. T. Coleridge, *Aids to Reflection* (London:
                George Bell and Sons, 1904).

Arians   John Henry Newman, *The Arians of the Fourth
                Century*, in the uniform edition of Newman's
                works (London: Longmans, Green & Co., 1874–
                1921) forty volumes.

Auden   W. H. Auden, *The Enchafèd Flood* (New York:
                Random House and Alfred A. Knopf, Vintage
                Books, 1967).

AW   John Henry Newman, *Autobiographical Writ-
                ings*, ed. Henry Tristram (London: Sheed and
                Ward, 1956).

Bigg   Charles Bigg, *The Christian Platonists of Alex-
                andria, The 1886 Bampton Lectures* (Oxford:
                The Clarendon Press, 1968).

BL   S. T. Coleridge, *Biographia Literaria*, ed. J.
                Shawcross (London: Oxford University Press,
                1958), two volumes.

Boekraad   A. J. Boekraad, *The Argument from Conscience
                to the Existence of God* (Louvain: Nauwelaerts,
                1961).

Callista   John Henry Newman, *Callista, A Tale of the
                Third Century*, in the uniform edition.

CG	St. Thomas Aquinas, *Summa Contra Gentiles* (New York: Doubleday & Co., Image Books, 1955–1957), five volumes.
Clement	Clement of Alexandria, *The Miscellanies* (or *Stromateis*), trans. William Wilson, in *The Writings of Clement of Alexandria* (Edinburgh: T. & T. Clark, 1869).
Cosin	*The Works of . . . John Cosin,* ed. J. Sansom (Oxford: John Henry Parker, 1843–1855), five volumes.
DA	John Henry Newman, *Discussions and Arguments on Various Subjects,* in the uniform edition.
Devotions	*The Private Devotions of Lancelot Andrewes,* trans. John Henry Newman (New York: Abingdon-Cokesbury Press, 1950).
Devel.	John Henry Newman, *An Essay on the Development of Christian Doctrine,* in the uniform edition.
DI	C. S. Lewis, *The Discarded Image* (Cambridge: Cambridge University Press, 1964).
Diff.	John Henry Newman, *Certain Difficulties Felt By Anglicans in Catholic Teaching,* two volumes, in the uniform edition.
Divine Poems	John Donne, *The Divine Poems,* ed. Helen Gardner (Oxford: The Clarendon Press, 1959).
Essays	John Henry Newman, *Essays Critical and Historical,* two volumes, in the uniform edition.
Exhortation	Clement of Alexandria, *Exhortation to the Greeks,* trans. G. W. Butterworth, in Loeb Classical Library (Cambridge: Harvard University Press, 1960).
Finney	Claude Lee Finney, *The Evolution of Keats's Poetry* (Cambridge: Harvard University Press, 1936), two volumes.

First Principles Origen, *On First Principles*, trans. G. W. Butterworth (New York: Harper Torchbooks, 1966).

GA John Henry Newman, *An Essay in Aid of a Grammar of Assent*, ed. Charles Frederick Harrold (London: Longmans, Green & Co., 1947).

Gilson Etienne Gilson, *The Christian Philosophy of St. Thomas Aquinas*, trans. L. K. Shook (London: Victor Gollancz, 1961).

Harrold Charles Frederick Harrold, *John Henry Newman* (Hamden, Conn.: Archon Books, 1966).

Herbert *The Works of George Herbert*, ed. F. E. Hutchinson (Oxford: The Clarendon Press, 1959).

Hooker *The Works of . . . Mr. Richard Hooker*, ed. John Keble (Oxford: The Clarendon Press, 1888), three volumes.

Houghton Walter E. Houghton, *The Art of Newman's "Apologia"* (New Haven: Yale University Press, 1945).

HS John Henry Newman, *Historical Sketches*, three volumes, in the uniform edition.

Idea John Henry Newman, *The Idea of a University*, in the uniform edition.

Laud *The Works of William Laud*, ed. W. Scott and J. Bliss (Oxford: John Henry Parker, 1847–1860), seven volumes.

Lectures *Keble's Lectures on Poetry, 1832–1841*, trans. Edward Kershaw Francis (Oxford: The Clarendon Press, 1912), two volumes.

Letters and Diaries *The Letters and Diaries of John Henry Newman*, ed. C. S. Dessain (London: Thomas Nelson and Sons Ltd., 1961–).

Merton	Clement of Alexandria, Selections from *The Protreptikos*, ed. Thomas Merton (New York: New Directions, 1962).
Miracles	John Henry Newman, *Two Essays on Biblical and Ecclesiastical Miracles*, in the uniform edition.
Mozley	*Letters and Correspondence of John Henry Newman During His Life in the English Church*, ed. Anne Mozley (London: Longmans, Green & Co., 1911), two volumes.
MW	Lancelot Andrewes, *A Pattern of Catechistical Doctrine and Other Minor Works* (Oxford: John Henry Parker, 1846).
Nédoncelle	Maurice Nédoncelle, *La Philosophie Religieuse de John Henry Newman* (Strasbourg: Société Strasbourgeoise de Librairie, 1946).
On Kingship	St. Thomas Aquinas, *On Kingship*, trans. Gerald B. Phelan (Toronto: The Pontifical Institute of Mediaeval Studies, 1949).
OPR	John Keble, *Occasional Papers and Reviews* (Oxford: James Parker and Co., 1877).
OUS	John Henry Newman, *Fifteen Sermons Preached before the University of Oxford*, in the uniform edition.
PPS	John Henry Newman, *Parochial and Plain Sermons*, eight volumes, in the uniform edition.
Przywara	Eric Przywara, "St. Augustine and the Modern World," trans. E. I. Watkin, in *Saint Augustine* (Cleveland and New York: World Publishing Co., Meridian Books, 1964).
Sartor	Thomas Carlyle, *Sartor Resartus*, ed. Charles Frederick Harrold (New York: The Odyssey Press, 1937).

Sillem	*The Philosophical Notebook of John Henry Newman*, ed. Edward Sillem (Louvain: Nauwelaerts Publishing House, 1969–1970), two volumes.
Song of Songs	Origen, *The Song of Songs, Commentary and Homilies*, trans. R. P. Lawson (London: Longmans, Green & Co., 1957).
ST	St. Thomas Aquinas, *Summa Theologica*, trans. by the Fathers of the English Dominican Province (London: Burns Oates and Washbourne Ltd., 1920–1925), twenty-two volumes.
Taylor	*The Whole Works of Jeremy Taylor* (London: William Ball, 1837), three volumes.
Traherne	Thomas Traherne, *Poems, Centuries, and Three Thanksgivings*, ed. Anne Ridler (London: Oxford University Press, 1966).
Trevor-Roper	H. R. Trevor-Roper, *Archbishop Laud, 1573–1645* (London: Macmillan and Co., 1940).
Vargish	Thomas Vargish, *Newman, The Contemplation of Mind* (Oxford: The Clarendon Press, 1970).
Via Media	John Henry Newman, *The Via Media of the Anglican Church*, two volumes, in the uniform edition.
Ward	Wilfred Ward, *The Life of John Henry Cardinal Newman* (London: Longmans, Green & Co., 1912), 2 volumes.
White	Helen C. White, *The Metaphysical Poets, A Study in Religious Experience* (New York: The Macmillan Co., Collier Books, 1962).

Introduction

ANY valid estimate of the work of John Henry Cardinal Newman (1801–1890) must take into account his place in English theology and literature, with particular reference to what we
now generally consider as "modern thought." There can be little
question that he is the most important English theologian of the
last two centuries, and it is in these two centuries that what is
called the "modern world"—the post-medieval and, some say, the
post-Christian world—has come into being. The medieval edifice
was collapsing in England during those very years in which Newman's own thought was taking its characteristic shape, namely,
in the eighteen-twenties and thirties. Moreover, during the later
decades of the nineteenth century, while Newman was developing
his own distinctive theories of dogma and belief, the subjectivism,
individualism, and relativism which constitute the lineaments of
modern thought were also defining themselves and gaining the
political, philosophical, and theological ascendancy which they
still occupy. In working out his religious position, Newman was
obliged to take the new world view into account. He was, in
fact, faced with an important choice in regard to it; he had to decide whether to make terms with it or to oppose it, and he chose
to make terms. It seems no exaggeration to say that in doing so he
prepared for the revolution in Catholic teaching, in both the
Roman and Anglican communions, which is so prominent a
factor in the theology and literature of the twentieth century and
which promises to be a prominent factor for a great many years
to come.[1] It is that choice, Newman's decision to accept the

1. Newman's influence on the Second Vatican Council is generally acknowledged; for a brief summary and bibliography on the major issues see
Charles S. Dessain, "Cardinal Newman as Prophet," *Prophets in the Church,*

philosophical premises of modern thought as his own and to treat them as though they were capable of synthesis with Catholic dogma, with which the following chapters deal.

The choice is implicit in all Newman's work; however, it is stated explicitly on only one or two occasions. One of those is the familiar "Prospects of the Anglican Church," published in 1839 at the height of the Oxford Movement's influence.[2] The essay serves as a sort of *credo* by which Newman defines his place in the movement, and we shall deal with it in due course. Another explicit statement, and Newman's fullest, comes in his *Letter Addressed to the Duke of Norfolk* in 1875, in the chapters dealing with the *Syllabus of Errors*.[3] Here we may begin our consideration of the matter, for here Newman surveys the whole question of Catholicism and modern thought from the point of view of his own maturity. That survey leaves no doubt where the mature Newman stood.

The *Syllabus of Errors* (1864) was a defense of the old world; the medieval idea of a Christian society is implicit in all its propositions. As an obedient Catholic and also as a man who felt a great deal of nostalgia for that old order of Christian life, Newman is willing to defend the *Syllabus*, but only with qualifications which ultimately negate its effect.

He begins by pointing out that Englishmen have no reason to be shocked at the Pope's intransigence: that they are so indicates that "men of the present generation" have forgotten "the words, ways, and works of their grandfathers."[4]

Modern Rome then is not the only place where the traditions of the old Empire, its principles, provisions, and practices, have been held

ed. Roger Aubert in *Concilium: Theology in the Age of Renewal* (New York: Paulist Press, 1968), XXXVII, 79–98. See also B. C. Butler, "Newman and the Second Vatican Council," *The Rediscovery of Newman: an Oxford Symposium*, ed. John Coulson and A. M. Allchin (London: S.P.C.K., 1967), pp. 233–246.

2. *Essays Critical and Historical*, I, 263–308. Henceforth cited as "*Essays.*" Reference to Newman's works, unless otherwise indicated, are to the uniform edition (London: Longmans, Green & Co., 1874–1921), 40 volumes.

3. *Certain Difficulties Felt by Anglicans in Catholic Teaching*, II, 175–378. Hereafter cited as *Diff.*

4. *Diff.*, II, 263.

in honour; they have been retained, they have been maintained in substance, as the basis of European civilization down to this day, and notably among ourselves. In the Anglican establishment the king took the place of the Pope; but the Pope's principles kept possession.[5]

"Their action," he adds, "was restrained but they were still in force, when this century opened." "In my own lifetime has that old world been alive, and has gone its way."[6] The *Syllabus*, then, says nothing new. In issuing it, the Pope has done no more than keep faith with the "old idea of a Christian Polity,"[7] with "the tradition of fifteen hundred years." "All this," says Newman, "was called Toryism, and men gloried the name; now it is called Popery and reviled."[8]

What has replaced that "old idea of a Christian Polity"? The answer, of course, is the very relativism and subjectivism which the *Syllabus* condemned—all those philosophical assumptions about social equality and religious freedom which most men now glorify as "modern." Newman mentions in particular "the plea of conscience . . . for the toleration of every sort of fancy religion," the freedom of the press to say what it pleases against Church and crown, the right of public gatherings in the name of democracy or "republicanism," the right of "monster processions" and the placing of squares and parks "at the mercy of Sunday manifestations," the freedom of *savants* to insinuate atheism "in scientific assemblies" and of "artisans" to practice that atheism "in the centres of political action."[9] These are the fruits of the new order in England, and the *Syllabus* has done no more than register an old-fashioned disapproval, the very sort of disapproval which the Anglican grandfathers of the present generation would have registered with equal vigor had they lived to witness the new state of affairs. Could these modern practices have gone on in England even as late as the beginning of the nineteenth century? "No; law or public opinion would not suffer it; we may be wiser or better now, but we were then in the wake of the Holy Roman

5. *Diff.*, II, 262.
6. *Diff.*, II, 263.
7. *Diff.*, II, 262.
8. *Diff.*, II, 263.
9. *Diff.*, II, 263.

Church, and had been so from the time of the Reformation. We were faithful to the tradition of fifteen hundred years."[10]

What then of Newman's "modern" choice? Though he defends the *Syllabus* ostensibly and though he professes himself "to be an admirer of the principles now superseded in themselves,"[11] those ancient traditions of popery and Toryism, nevertheless he clearly regards those principles and traditions as "superseded" and the new principles as being in possession. Therefore, though he admires the *Syllabus* and the spirit which conceived it, he also regards it as futile. Essentially his attitude toward the "old idea of a Christian Polity" is a combination of regret for its loss and at the same time of resignation to its end. Emotionally he may prefer the old ways, but his reason has convinced him that the progress of thought, of knowledge, in the modern world has made the medieval idea of the Christian commonwealth an impossibility. "When the intellect is cultivated, it is as certain that it will develope into a thousand various shapes, as that infinite hues and tints and shades of colour will be reflected from the earth's surface, when the sun-light touches it."[12] As a consequence, in modern Europe there can be no longer a general consent to a common body of religious, political, and philosophical assumptions about the nature of man and of human society. England has discovered this difficulty and attempted to adjust herself to it within Newman's lifetime, and the consequence of those adjustments has been the death of an order. "During the last seventy years, first one class of the community, then another, has awakened up to thought and opinion." The result is "multiform views on sacred subjects" which "found expression in the governing order." "The State in past time had a conscience; George the Third had a conscience"; but in the new order of affairs that common conscience of the nation has been fragmented, and "this brought on a dead-lock in the time of [George's] successor." The result was the death of Toryism: "The State ought to have a conscience; but what if it happened to have half-a-dozen, or a score, or a

10. *Diff.*, II, 263.
11. *Diff.*, II, 267.
12. *Diff.*, II, 267.

hundred, in religious matters, each different from each?"[13] When such a circumstance occurs, it is evident to Newman that the only alternative is to acknowledge, however sadly, that the old principle of Christian order is no longer defensible and to seek out new philosophical foundations for civilization.

However, if such a conclusion was evident to Newman, it was clearly not evident to Pius the Ninth nor to the many Catholics who endorsed the *Syllabus* of 1864. Nor was it fully evident to many old-fashioned Tory High-Churchmen such as William Palmer,[14] for whom the defense of the Faith was inseparable from a defense of that "old idea of a Christian Polity." When we realize that such a difference of opinion existed between Newman and his Catholic contemporaries, both Roman and Anglican, we begin to see how important, historically, his "modern" choice was. He becomes the first major English theologian of a High-Church or Catholic persuasion to accept as a philosophical possibility a union between the Christian faith and modern modes of thought, between Catholic teaching and what Newman calls, rather caustically, the "New Civilization."[15] Orthodox Anglican theology from the sixteenth century until the end of the eighteenth, from Hooker to Samuel Johnson, had taken as axiomatic the union of Christianity with "the old idea of a Christian Polity" and with the medieval metaphysics and, in some cases, the medieval cosmology attendant on that polity. The poets, with a few exceptions, followed suit. It is important to recollect that traditional alignment and to remember that, though Newman was just as orthodox in matters of dogma as any of those earlier defenders of the Christianity (indeed more so than some of them), he divorced himself from their essentially conservative modes of thought and from their medieval inheritance. For Hooker, Andrewes, and Laud, for Spenser, Donne, and Herbert, for Dryden, Pope, and Johnson, what was once called "Toryism" was considerably more than a political arrangement which could be dispensed with

13. *Diff.*, II, 267.
14. For instance see Palmer's A *Narrative of Events Connected with the Publication of the "Tracts for the Times"* (1843); also his *Treatise on the Church of Christ* (1838), 2 vols.
15. *Diff.*, II, 225.

(albeit wistfully) if "the times" demanded it. Rather it was a name for a philosophically consistent vision of the world and of human society in which metaphysical, political, ethical, aesthetic, and theological beliefs coincided. In relinquishing that vision, Newman separated himself from what may be called the main line of European theological development since Augustine. As he himself acknowledged, it was "the tradition of fifteen hundred years," "the basis of European civilization down to this day, notably among ourselves."

If Augustine was the father of that tradition, Aquinas was its chief exponent; the *Summa* gave it its full articulation. It was St. Thomas (and, through him, Aristotle) who made it possible for Europeans to justify and defend the "idea of a Christian Polity." St. Thomas's realism,[16] his reliance upon sense experience as the source of knowledge, provided philosophical grounds for accepting the natural order as a reality in its own right, not merely as a symbol or metaphor for supernatural realities. At the same time, St. Thomas's principle of the analogy of being, itself inseparable from a realistic epistemology, made it possible for human reason to discover in the visible world, in the evidence of the senses and in the operation of the human reason, a way to the "things not seen." In other words, Aquinas's theology offered sound reasons for taking the present world—its manners, its arts, its politics— seriously; and yet, with no derogation from the natural, human order in its own right, to find in nature and in human society a way to the knowledge of God. Therefore, under the influence of Thomism, it became customary to regard the order of kingdoms and of families as analogous to the order which is in God Himself and which He has planted as an image of Himself in the creation. To take the order of nature and of society seriously is to come to understand the order which is in God, while to violate the bond of kind—of family or of kingdom—is almost tantamount to blasphemy against God, who is both father and king. Thus in the "old idea of a Christian Polity" it becomes virtually impossible to conceive of religious experience except in terms of the whole ordered life of the creation; for it is only in that life—in the hier-

16. Throughout this study, the term *realism* is used in opposition to idealism rather than to nominalism.

archy of plants, beasts, men, and angels—that we have access to the knowledge and love of God. In such a vision of the world, there is simply no such thing as personal or private religion in the modern sense, and the great accomplishment of English theology and poetry until the end of the eighteenth century was the fusion of the most delicate, the most sensitive, the most deeply "personal," religious experience with the experience of the society, natural and supernatural, and with the order of the cosmos. In Spenser, for instance, the New Jerusalem is compared in analogy with Cleopolis, the city of the Fairy Queen; she, of course, is Elizabeth, and Cleopolis is London. Red Cross's quest for personal holiness is inseparable from the quest for order and virtue in England, and Elizabeth is symbol of the entire experience, both personal and public, both religious and political.

What replaced that old view of man and of human society was the modern idea of the autonomy of the individual mind, which Newman understands so clearly and which, with reservations, he accepts. In that acceptance, however hesitantly, he embraces a conception of man and of religious experience which is as radically different from the old as any which we can imagine—more radically different than we usually realize. Where the old "Polity" was corporate, the modern is individualistic. Where the old was objective and public, considering all Christian experience as inseparable from the life of the body politic and of the cosmos, the new is subjective and ultimately private. Where the old was predicated on the principle of hierarchy as both an ethical and metaphysical necessity, the new is essentially egalitarian. Such differences are manifestly great; yet Newman seems to have seen no final nor absolute conflict between these modern principles and his own thoroughgoing doctrinal orthodoxy. Therefore, though he does not like the new ways, he can still afford to give them a grudging acceptance, looking forward as he does so to some eventual synthesis of Catholic teaching and the "New Civilization." "And thus, in centuries to come, there may be found out some way of uniting what is free in the new structure of society with what is authoritative in the old, without any base compromise with 'Progress' and 'Liberalism.' "[17]

17. *Diff.*, II, 268.

In light of the radical differences between the old principles and the new, it is easy to understand why Newman's more conservative contemporaries could not imagine such a union without "base compromise"—why William Palmer persisted in his Tory High-Churchmanship, why Monsignor Talbot took the view that Newman was "the most dangerous man in England," and why others thought him, very simply, a heretic. Of course there were no grounds for the latter charge. So far from Newman's being a heretic, it is the very strength of his doctrinal conservatism which makes his position so remarkable. Had he indeed been a heretic, or an apostate of the typically modern type, we should have been able to see clearly the point at which his views of Catholic teaching and of the new civilization converge. We cannot even talk, however, at least not justly, about his *"views* of Catholic teaching"; he held no private "views," but rather submitted himself to the whole body of Christian dogma, and it is for that very reason that his attempts at a reconciliation with the new philosophical modes are so important and also so nearly germane to our understanding of his thought. To deal with Newman fairly, we must keep three things in mind at once: his doctrinal orthodoxy, his philosophical "modernism," and the implications and consequences of the union of the two. To lose sight of any one of these aspects of his thought is to misrepresent him and to misunderstand his place in English theology and literature.

It seems not unfair to say that many of Newman's disciples and critics have lost sight of one or the other of these three considerations. Some of the older critics, such as Sarolea and Bremond, mistook the "modern" elements in Newman's philosophy for indications of heterodoxy in dogma. The Modernists, Loisy and his school, made the same mistake and attempted, unfairly, to claim Newman as the father of their heresy. More recent critics—in fact, the great body of Newman scholars for the past thirty or forty years—convinced of his orthodoxy and sympathetic toward it, have given him a fairer reading than he received during the years of the Modernist controversy. In doing so, however, these commentators have overlooked the fact that Newman's philosophy *does* present problems. That is not to say that they have ignored his philosophy or failed to recognize its modernity; on the contrary, the strongest emphasis in recent Newman studies is philosophical and epistemological, and the modernity of that philosophy and epistemology has been generally acknowledged. What has not been acknowledged, however, is the third consideration which I have mentioned, the implications and consequences of that modernity. These, for the most part, have been ignored or misunderstood.

One suspects that that ignorance and that misunderstanding derive from the fact that most of the scholars in question are themselves philosophical modernists—that however orthodox they may be in matters of dogma, they are so deeply immersed in the "new civilization" that they are unable to keep it in perspective. Indeed, the tendency in Newman studies since the Second Vatican Council has been not only to acknowledge but to applaud his "modernism," and such applause is largely unqualified by any respect for that "Toryism" which Newman himself respected so highly even as he relinquished it. These newest of Newman's critics write as though his yoking of the "new civilization" with orthodoxy were an unmitigated and unquestionable good— as though it were one of the great intellectual achievements in the history of theology. In all fairness, let us admit that it may indeed be. On the other hand, we must recognize that it cannot be proved to be until what we might call the "Tory objections" have been duly acknowledged and duly answered; until Newman scholars are prepared to admire, as Newman himself admired, the "tradition of fifteen hundred years"; to recognize, as Newman himself recognized, what the world was like as recently as the age of Pope and Johnson, before the French Revolution and the new spirit of the nineteenth century, when "the traditions of the old Empire, its principles, provisions, and practices" were still held in honor. Admittedly Newman relinquished those principles, provisions, and practices, but if we, as critics, are to understand that relinquishment, its implications, and its consequences, we must first understand as fully as we can the world he gave up, and why, for fifteen hundred years, its "provisions" were considered indispensable to Christianity and to civilization. To do that we must enter imaginatively into those modes of thought of which Aquinas's philosophy is the fullest manifestation; we must learn to think in the terms in which most Christians thought while Christendom was still a reality. Moreover, we must keep ourselves open to two possibilities: first, that those ancient modes of thought may be better—more harmonious with Christian dogma and with human nature—than those which have replaced them; and, second, that Newman may have made a grave mistake in relinquishing them.

This book explores those possibilities. Or, to be more precise, it argues their probability, from three points of view: first, that of Newman's departure from the old orthodoxy of England, from "the traditions of the old Empire" as they manifested themselves in the theology of Hooker and the Caroline divines and in the imagery of English Renaissance poetry; second, that of Newman's close philosophical kinship with his nineteenth-century contemporaries; third, that of the philosophical terms on which Newman accommodated his doctrinal orthodoxy to the demands of the "new civilization." In each of these relationships, Newman's philosophical modernism and its consequences for theology and literature are clearly evident.

PART ONE

Newman and the Old Orthodoxy

In the early days of the Oxford Movement, Newman thought of himself and of his fellow Tractarians as defenders of the Caroline
theological tradition. He even described the movement as a return to
the principles of seventeenth-century Anglicanism.[1] The Caroline divines, however, were committed to a defense of the "old idea of a
Christian Polity" and of the traditional Thomist views of nature and
reason, of the cosmos and of human society, which Newman's philosophical and political "modernism"[2] made impossible for him. These
differences in philosophical assumptions are both subtle and far-
reaching. Their consequence is that Newman's ostensible espousal of
seventeenth-century theology amounts, paradoxically, to a repudiation
of the basic assumptions of the traditional English school, in much
the same way that his "defense" of Pius's *Syllabus* amounts, in effect, to its rejection.

The easiest way to begin a delineation of these differences—which
in turn provide a key to Newman's entire mode of thought—is to
compare the respective positions of Newman and Hooker; for Hooker
is the intellectual and spiritual father of Caroline Anglicanism, and

1. Cf. *Apologia Pro Vita Sua*, ed. Martin J. Svaglic (Oxford: The Clarendon Press, 1967), p. 50. All subsequent references to the *Apologia* are to this
edition. Hereatfer cited as *Ap.*
2. When I use "modernism" or "modernist" in lower case and in quotation
marks, I refer to matters philosophical and political rather than doctrinal.
When I refer to the doctrinal heresy of that name, I use *Modernism* or
Modernist with an initial capital and without quotation marks.

though some of his successors differed with him on specific points of theology, all the major seventeenth-century figures accepted his philosophical premises. For Lancelot Andrewes, Jeremy Taylor, and William Laud, for Hammond, Cosin, Pearson, Bramhall, and Ken, Hooker's work was the point of departure; and though he died in 1600, before the flowering of the Caroline school, Andrewes, Laud, Taylor, and the rest have their significance in light of him. Moreover, the intellectual assumptions which he bequeathed to his successors are those very Aristotelian and Thomist principles which Newman ultimately rejected.[3] Helen Gardner, discussing Donne's debt to Hooker, says that orthodox Anglicanism as it was understood in the seventeenth century came to exist because Hooker taught men of Donne's caliber not so much "what" but "how" to think: "how to see particular controversies in the light of certain philosophic principles."[4] Newman also taught his successors "how" to think, but he approached "particular controversies" in the light of principles quite different from Hooker's. Hooker's vision is essentially medieval—corporate, hierarchical, objective; Newman's, as we have suggested, is essentially modern. Therefore, to draw out the philosophical differences between the two serves very well to illustrate Newman's departure from traditional English Christian thought.

3. Among the many critics who have dealt with the matter of Hooker's Thomism, the most lucid is A. P. d'Entreves. See his *The Medieval Contribution to Political Thought* (Oxford: Oxford University Press, 1939) and *Natural Law* (London: Hutchinson & Co., 1951). See also Peter Munz, *The Place of Hooker in the History of Thought* (London: Routledge & Kegan Paul, 1952). Munz's "Appendix A" (pp. 175–193) lists more than a hundred points of correspondence between Aquinas's work and the *Ecclesiastical Polity*. Many of these are acknowledged by Hooker himself in numerous citations of St. Thomas.

4. "Introduction," *The Divine Poems* (Oxford: The Clarendon Press, 1959), p. xxi, n. 1. Hereafter cited as *Divine Poems*.

✤

Newman and Hooker

AT the risk of banality, I begin with the simplest possible statement of the distinction between Hooker and Newman. Hooker's view of the world and of man's condition is generally bright, Newman's often very dark. The distinction between doctrine and philosophy should be emphasized here. Just as Augustine and Aquinas give different emphases and different modes of expression to the same beliefs, so too do Hooker and Newman. Of course, we should have to admit that the beliefs of the latter pair are not so nearly identical as those of the former, but, in spite of some discrepancies, Hooker and Newman are close enough to one another in doctrine that their divergence in philosophical principles is clearly evident by contrast. For instance, with reference to their respective views of man and his condition, we should remember that both of them hold the same doctrine of man—that he is a fallen creature and that nature, the world, has fallen with him. Both of them likewise believe that by the merits of Christ's passion and death man and, through man, nature has been redeemed. In fact, Hooker insists strongly on the doctrine of original sin and man's absolute dependence on God's grace, and, in their respective discussions of justification, Hooker tends to be more nearly Calvinist than Newman.[1] On the other hand, Hooker's imaginative understanding of the consequences of sin and redemption are quite different from Newman's, and here we see how identical beliefs can be subject to divergent philosophical emphases. The evidences of man's redeemed condition and of God's merciful operation among his

1. Compare, for instance, Hooker's "A Learned Discourse on Justification" (1585–86 [?]) and Newman's *Lectures on the Doctrine of Justification* (1838).

creatures is much more readily apparent to Hooker than to Newman. For the latter, the miserable darkness, contradiction, and
frustration of man's and nature's fallen state is oppressively obvious.

Hooker's purpose in the *Ecclesiastical Polity* helps explain his
position. He is immediately concerned with arguing against his
Calvinist opponents that, in spite of the fall and of the presence
of evil in the world, God is still present in nature and that man
can still apprehend and worship Him. He is writing to refute the
partially Manichaean notion that fallen nature and fallen man
are all but totally depraved and, as a consequence of that de-
pravity, are in complete alienation from God. Newman, on the
other hand, shares many of the attitudes of those Calvinists whom
Hooker was attacking, and we should not forget that the influence of Walter Mayers and of a number of Calvinist writers
whom he read in his youth had drawn him strongly in that direction.[2] As a Catholic, both Anglican and Roman, he had repudiated the Calvinist's near approach to Manichaeanism, but in
spite of his theological position, what impressed itself upon his
consciousness was not a world flooded with God's presence but
rather a creation alienated from its Creator.

We can scarcely find a page in Hooker that does not at some
point declare the harmony between God and nature, God and
man. Our guide in ecclesiastical affairs should not be Scripture
alone, as it must be for the Calvinists who distrust everything in
creation except God's precise commandment, but rather the combination of "nature, Scripture, and experience."[3] As to the matter in question, ecclesiastical polity, Hooker builds his defense of
apostolic orders in the English Church, not upon sacred power or
divine commandment alone, but upon the union of that power
and commandment with nature and human reason. "As for the
orders which are established, sith equity and reason, the law of
nature, God and man, do all favour that which is in being . . . it is
but justice to exact of you, and perverseness in you it should be to

2. Cf. *Ap.*, pp. 17ff.
3. *The Works of . . . Mr. Richard Hooker*, ed. John Keble (Oxford: The
Clarendon Press, 1888), I, 166. All subsequent references to Hooker are to
this edition.

deny, thereunto your willing obedience."[4] No man who did not believe that the laws of man and nature coincide in most cases with the law of God could argue from such a position. It is significant of Newman's darker view of the world that he rests his argument for orders and sacraments almost exclusively on the Church and its authority. Distrusting nature and reason in their fallen state, he insists on the infallibility of the Church much more strenuously than Hooker and his Caroline successors ever need to do. This is characteristic of Newman both before and after his conversion to Rome; for it is contrary to his philosophic principles to trust as Hooker does in a general harmony between God and the world.

Hooker also speaks of the expectation of joy and comfort in this world as well as in heaven. "All men desire to lead in this world a happy life." Obviously, he admits, that is not always possible. In fact St. Paul warns us that we may have to content ourselves at times with "no more than very bare food and raiment." Such deprivation is not, however, and should not be, our desire or expectation. Rather, in warning us of that dark possibility, St. Paul is actually giving us to understand that deprivation is the exception rather than the rule; "that if we should be stripped of all those things without which we might possibly be, yet these [the bare minimum of food and clothing] must be left; that destitution in these is such an impediment, as till it be removed suffereth not the mind of man to admit any other care."[5] In other words, Hooker is saying that not only is the order of earth in some sense correspondent with that of heaven, but even the bounty and pleasure of earth.

The first book of the *Laws of Ecclesiastical Polity* is the most important one for our purposes, for it is here that Hooker defines the way in which God's laws bind earth to heaven and man to God. It is worth mentioning at the outset that, as Hooker's own numerous footnotes indicate,[6] he builds his system of law directly on Aquinas's. Indeed, it is Hooker's introduction of Thomist categories at this crucial point in the *Ecclesiastical Polity* which,

4. Hooker, I, 170.
5. Hooker, I, 240.
6. See above, Part One, note 3.

more than any other single influence, serves to bind Caroline to medieval theology. To see how this is so, it is worthwhile to distinguish three propositions to which Hooker and his successors, as well as Aquinas and the Schoolmen, agree: that God establishes all things according to law, that this law is the expression of the very mind of God, and that God works in all of his creatures according to this law. Another way to state the same thing is to say that the eternal law from which all laws—natural, divine, civil, or physical—depend, is itself the image of God which He implants in his creatures and to which he subjects his own will. One point at stake for Hooker is an attack on Calvinist voluntarism. He wants to make it quite clear that God does not work capriciously and that "they err therefore who think that of the will of God to do this or that there is no reason besides his will."[7] As Hooker proceeds to develop his argument, however, it becomes clear that this distinction between the operations of reason and will speaks directly to the fact of a harmony between God and nature, God and man. Hooker can speak legitimately of the union of divine and human orders, of the goodness even of a fallen nature, and of Scripture's being matched with experience (by which we infer human or natural experience), because the laws of both heaven and earth are founded upon the same *reason*, that which literally is the mind of God. Had God worked merely by will there would be no reason to expect that the laws of earth would in any way be conformable with those of heaven or that man's own reason and experience would be able to perceive anything at all about God except through direct revelation—for the Puritans, the precise word of Scripture. For Hooker, however, as for St. Thomas, since God's reason serves both as a model for the laws of heaven and earth and for man's reason, we have the possibility of harmony. God is in all things, present in nature and man by virtue of that reason or "wisdom" which, manifested in various types of law in various provinces of creation, governs all things, which is the very mind of God and to which man, by virtue of sharing the same law, the same reason, has access.

That law eternal which God himself hath made to himself, and thereby worketh all things whereof he is the cause and author; that

7. Hooker, I, 203.

law in the admirable frame whereof shineth with most perfect beauty the countenance of that wisdom which hath testified concerning herself, "The Lord possessed me in the beginning of his way, even before his works of old I was set up"; that law, which hath been the pattern to make, and is the card to guide the world by; that law which hath been of God and with God everlastingly; that law, the author and observer whereof is one only God to be blessed for ever: how should either men or angels be able perfectly to behold?[8]

The answer, manifestly, is that neither angels nor men can behold it perfectly. It is a book which "we are neither able nor worthy to open and look into." On the other hand, "that little thereof which we darkly apprehend we admire,"[9] and that little is sufficient to fill our world with light. We are limited by our fall to a dark and partial apprehension of God's wisdom, but even that darkness is bright. The result of the fall is the loss of an even more intense brilliance and clarity; however, our present state is by no means one of complete blackness or total alienation. Even in a fallen condition we share sufficiently in God's wisdom to perceive "the countenance of the wisdom" shining in the "admirable frame" of the law; and because this vision of divine order is accessible to us in creation, "the old idea of a Christian Polity," of the unified and corporate life of the whole society of men and angels, becomes a possibility.

Newman's emphasis is quite different. Of course he does not believe, either, that man is in total darkness, but what light there is for him, in its way an intense one, lies in a single point—which is Christ—and is surrounded by darkness. Hooker conceives of the darkness of sin as the damping down of an original brilliance which shall be restored to us in heaven, but, even damped, the light and clarity of God is so intense in the "admirable frame" of His law that we may live in the world with very little sense of tragic gloom. We cannot imagine Oedipus or Orestes in Hooker's world; Spenser belongs there, as does the Dante of *Purgatory and Paradise*. There are few dark corners in it. Newman, on the other hand, conceives of the darkness of sin as a literal darkness, and his world is full of tragic possibilities. From a poet's point of view,

8. Hooker, I, 203–204.
9. Hooker, I, 204.

the two men represent antithetical sensibilities and sets of antithetical images. Yet, as we have already noted, those sensibilities and images are referred to almost identical doctrines. The differences are philosophical, epistemological, rather than doctrinal, and, as we have suggested, it is Newman's philosophy, not his theology, which is modern.

Wherever we turn in Newman's work we find propositions about the relationship between God and nature which directly contradict those fundamental philosophical tenets which Hooker adopted from Aquinas and bequeathed in an English shape to his Caroline successors. Perhaps the passage which best serves to illustrate these differences is a familiar one in the last chapter of the *Apologia*, the "Position of My Mind Since 1845." The paragraph is very important, and, in spite of its familiarity, I quote it in full:

Starting then with the being of a God, (which, as I have said, is as certain to me as the certainty of my own existence, though when I try to put the grounds of that certainty into logical shape I find a difficulty in doing so in mood and figure to my satisfaction,) I look out of myself into the world of men, and there I see a sight which fills me with unspeakable distress. The world seems simply to give the lie to that great truth, of which my whole being is so full; and the effect upon me is, in consequence, as a matter of necessity, as confusing as if it denied that I am in existence myself. If I looked into a mirror, and did not see my face, I should have the sort of feeling which actually comes upon me, when I look into this living busy world, and see no reflexion of its Creator. This is, to me, one of those great difficulties of this absolute primary truth, to which I referred just now. Were it not for this voice, speaking so clearly in my conscience and my heart, I should be an atheist, or a pantheist, or a polytheist when I looked into the world. I am speaking for myself only; and I am far from denying the real force of the arguments in proof of a God, drawn from the general facts of human society and the course of history, but these do not warm me or enlighten me; they do not take away the winter of my desolation, or make the buds unfold and the leaves grow within me, and my moral being rejoice. The sight of the world is nothing else than the prophet's scroll, full of 'lamentations, and mourning, and woe.'[10]

10. *Ap.*, pp. 216–217.

Several important points should be noted here. Whereas Hooker, like Aquinas, sees the mind of God reflected in the structure of the world, in the reason of man and in human society, Newman looks "into this living busy world, and see[s] no reflexion of its Creator." No statement could be more completely antithetical to Hooker or to the traditional Christian philosophy, both medieval and Caroline, in which he occupies so important a place. Of course, Newman is careful not to deny the real existence of such a reflection; in fact, he could not have denied it without running the risk of heretical statement. As we have already noted, however, doctrine is one thing, the philosophical emphasis which is placed upon it quite another. So far as the doctrine of God's immanence is concerned, it has little effect on Newman's epistemology. He does not deny that the creation reflects its Creator; he simply says that he cannot *see* the image. But the very fact that he cannot see it makes it impossible for him to trust in natural law, in the judgments of human reason, or in any other created thing in the confident way that Hooker can. He does not deny the validity of arguments of the Thomist sort, "drawn from the general facts of human society and the course of history,"[11] or, as Hooker would say, from "nature, Scripture, and experience"; he simply says that these traditional modes of theological inquiry have no meaning, no appeal, to him. They "do not warm me or enlighten me" or make "my moral being rejoice."

This passage from the *Apologia* provides summary statement of a theme which Newman develops, as we shall see, in great detail in other works. In fact, it may not be an oversimplification to say that the problem of God's "absence," as he calls it in the *Grammar of Assent*, is the central issue in all his theological writing and also the key to his "modernism." Wherever he discusses that issue the terms of his argument are the same; he never denies the *fact* that God is present in his works or that the world with its institutions, customs, and orders has divine significance, but he is always quick to add that that significance is by no means clearly

11. When he wrote that sentence, Newman was probably thinking of Paley and the *Evidences of Christianity* (1794); however, in his reliance on rational proofs of God, Paley is in a direct line of descent from Aquinas and Hooker.

evident to the inquiring mind. Because it is not evident, it is difficult for Newman to embrace the traditional view of Christendom, for that view depends upon the assumption—St. Thomas's and Hooker's—that God's reason and law, the very mind of God, is manifest in the order of creation, in the body politic as well as in the cosmos. In other words, Newman seems to be telling us that he believes in the abstract or theoretical proposition that God's presence and order reach to all His works, but, because he cannot bring that belief home to his heart as a practical reality, he can build neither apologetics nor polity upon it, nor embrace it imaginatively in the way that such medieval and Renaissance Christians as Dante or Spenser embraced their traditional cosmology and politics as the stuff of poetry.

The terminology of the *Grammar of Assent* may help us here, in particular the distinction between the notional and the real. As we recall, these two modes of apprehension or assent are distinguished by their subjects. "According as language expresses things external to us, or our own thoughts, so is apprehension real or notional."[12] In other words, the apprehension of things—trees, chairs, or people—is *real*; the apprehension of thoughts about those things is *notional*. One of Newman's most familiar illustrations of the distinction is that of the difference between medical terminology and the reality of disease itself. "Pathology and medicine . . . veil the shocking realities of disease and physical suffering under a notional phraseology, under the abstract terms of debility, distress, irritability, paroxysm, and a host of Greek and Latin words."[13] Our apprehension of the abstractions is notional; our apprehension of the actual suffering to which the abstractions refer is real. Newman refers to the latter as "images" or "things," to the former as "notions." An old woman dying in great agony, who is the subject of a real apprehension, is a particular image. The medical description of her condition is an abstract or general notion. When we apprehend "man" *notionally* rather than *really*, he ceases to be an image, "an individual presented to us by our senses," and becomes instead an abstraction, "man," which is an

12. *An Essay in Aid of a Grammar of Assent*, ed. Charles Frederick Harrold (London: Longmans, Green & Co., 1947), p. 17. All subsequent references to the *Grammar of Assent* are to this edition. Hereafter cited as *GA*.
13. *GA*, p. 18.

individual image, as Newman says, "attenuated into an aspect."[14]

Of course Newman argues vigorously that we may assent to a notion just as we may assent to a reality, and that assent "is in all cases absolute and unconditional."[15] Notional assent will be less intense than real, however, merely because we do not engage a notion with the same immediacy with which we grasp a thing or image. Because assent is assent, and by its very nature unconditional, no matter how weak or how strong the apprehension of its object, notional assent makes the same demands upon us as real. Thus a man may be martyred for a notional assent, though it would perhaps be "easier" for him if the assent had been real and consequently more intense and compelling.

When we apply these categories to the less precise language of *Apologia* and to Newman's failure to see the image of God in the creation, we might say that he is lamenting his failure of real apprehension but in no way denying the truth of the notion. His notional assent to the doctrine that God is reflected in his creation, in the polity and history of the world, has never been transformed into real assent. He is still agreeing to the medical terms, not to the particular image of the sick woman. Nevertheless, it is assent and consequently unconditional, and it is this qualification which distinguishes his approach toward a Manichaean or Calvinist fideism from the heresy involved in actually embracing such a view. Or, to put the matter another way, it is this qualification which distinguishes Newman's doctrine from his philosophy. He never denies the Catholic doctrine that God is present in His world; that revealed fact is the subject of an assent. It is only a notional assent, however, for Newman is unable to *imagine* or to *realize* that presence or divine order. Hooker is representative of a more nearly traditional Christian epistemology to the very extent that he was able to give a real assent to that divine presence and order in the world, to imagine it, to bring it home to his feelings and affections. It seems clear that Newman would have liked to do the same, for he insists repeatedly that real assent "is the stronger," the "more vivid and forcible"; "intellectual ideas cannot compete in effectiveness with the experience of concrete

14. GA, p. 25.
15. GA, p. 28.

facts"—" 'seeing is believing.' "[16] Unable to *see*, the "winter of my desolation" remains.

There are, in the *Grammar*, several poignant passages which lament that desolation. One, in particular, recapitulates the section which I have quoted from the *Apologia* and, like that earlier treatment of the matter, points up the principal philosophical divergence between Newman and Hooker, between the "modern world" and the medieval.

This established order of things, in which we find ourselves, if it has a Creator, must surely speak of His will in its broad outlines and its main issues. This principle being laid down as certain, when we come to apply it to things as they are, our first feeling is one of surprise and (I may say) of dismay, that His control of this living world is so indirect, and His action so obscure. . . . What strikes the mind so forcibly and so painfully is, His absence (if I may so speak) from His own world.[17]

Here again what strikes us immediately is the difference between Newman's epistemology and Hooker's. Where the latter sees God plainly, Newman finds Him absent. In fact Newman goes on to ask, "Why does not He, our Maker and Ruler, give us some immediate knowledge of Himself? Why does He not write His Moral Nature in large letters upon the face of history, and bring the blind, tumultuous rush of its events into a celestial, hierarchial order?"[18] Clearly Hooker, like his medieval predecessors and his Caroline heirs, would answer, "But He does, and, of course, it *is* a celestial, hierarchical order which we see." Because those older theologians do, in fact, *see* it, they are able to build a cosmology, a polity, and a poetry upon it. For Newman, who must go on faith rather than sight, the object of the imagination, the central poetic image, is the "night battle" in "encircling gloom." It is the latter circumstance which makes the "modern" choice a possibility and, perhaps, even a necessity; for subjectivism, relativism, and many other characteristically "modern" attitudes are the logical consequences of philosophical scepticism.

16. GA, p. 9.
17. GA, p. 301.
18. GA, p. 301.

✤

CHAPTER II

Newman and the Carolines

THE philosophical differences between Newman and Hooker are indicative of Newman's divergence from the Caroline tradition as a whole. There is a remarkable continuity of philosophical emphasis among seventeenth-century Anglican divines; for almost to a man they share with Hooker and, through him with the medieval Schoolmen, an understanding of grace as the completion rather than as the destruction of nature and reason. Like Hooker and Aquinas, they believe that God is manifest in the laws which govern the comos and human society and that by the exercise of his reason man can come to the knowledge of divine reality. Generally speaking, they accept Hooker's argument from "equity and reason, the law of nature, God and man."

Lancelot Andrewes was Hooker's contemporary and friend. He disagreed with Hooker on some important points of dogma—his understanding of the Sacrament was more nearly orthodox than Hooker's—but his "philosophic principles" are essentially the same. In his *A Pattern of Catechistical Doctrine* (1630), under the general question "whether there be a God," Andrewes argues along the same lines which Hooker follows in the *Ecclesiastical Polity*. He appeals, not to sacred authority alone or even primarily, but rather to human experience and to the laws of nature; in short, he argues from those very evidences which Newman believes in notionally but finds unconvincing in reality. Andrewes cites "the universality of the persuasion of God in all nations and all places," pointing out that "there is no history which sheweth the manners of any people, but it sheweth also their religion."[1] Like-

---

1. Lancelot Andrewes, *A Pattern of Catechistical Doctrine and Other Minor Works* (Oxford: John Henry Parker, 1846), pp. 23–24. Hereafter cited as MW.

wise, in language which is specifically reminiscent of Hooker's, he maintains that "the power and art in the creation shew plainly that it was of God. . . . And even them whom miracles would not move, have the least things of all made astonished and confounded, and forced them to confess God's power."[2] Notice that, like Hooker, Andrewes neither hesitates nor qualifies. Nature does not just manifest God to those who already believe in Him, who have assented as Newman has, against sight, to the fact that this apparently blind, tumultuous rush of things really is filled with God's presence and order. On the contrary, according to Andrewes, God is clearly visible in His works for all to see; the "power and art in the creation shew *plainly* that it was of God."[3]

Moreover, just as nature and common human experience manifest Him, so does human reason. Like Hooker and Aquinas, Andrewes believes that the human intellect is capable of demonstrating God's existence from the phenomena of His creation, and in pursuing that line of argument he appeals not only, as we might expect, to Hooker, but also to Hooker's and Aquinas's acknowledged philosophical master, Aristotle: "The reason of the philosophers is manifest to prove that there is a God, namely, that there is a first mover and a first cause of all; for if this were not so, there should be before every mover, another mover, and so *in finitum*."[4] Likewise, human reason proves the fact of God's existence both "from the spiritual nature of man" and "from the frame of the world," and "the agreement of so many divers things sheweth that of necessity there must be some modulator of such a harmony."[5] The same spectacle of creation, submitted to the same rational scrutiny, gives Newman an impression, not of modulated harmony, but of God's absence and the consequent chaos.

Andrewes's philosophical principles are perhaps seen most distinctly in his application of them to specific points of theological and ecclesiastical debate, particularly where the argument concerns Christendom's traditional polity and cosmology. In his *Dis-*

2. MW, p. 28.
3. Italics mine.
4. MW, p. 26.
5. MW, p. 26.

course of Ceremonies, again following Hooker, he undertakes to defend the outward and visible signs of religion, the established orders and customs of the English Church and nation, against Puritan attack. He admits, as matter of undeniable fact, the familiar Puritan charge that "many paynim ceremonies were retained in England after Christianity was received,"[6] but this admission, so far from weakening his position, actually provides the key to his subsequent discussion. Because a ceremony is not explicitly scriptural or ecclesiastical in its origin is no reason to assume that it is not of God or in accordance with His laws.

My conceit and purpose to shew you is, that of the ecclesiastical government and policy observed in the british and english ancient pagans, as formerly having their commonwealth in frame and beautified with our common laws, they being converted unto christianity, many of the paganish ceremonies and usages, not contrary to the scripture, were still retained in their christian policy; by means whereof tranquillity and peace was observed, and the alteration in the state less dangerous or sensible.[7]

Notice that Andrewes says the same "common laws" "beautified" both pagan and Christian commonwealths and that it is upon these that common ceremonial practices rest. Behind such a statement lies Hooker's and St. Thomas's conception of the unity of all laws in the *lex aeterna* and, through the operation of law, the presence of God in the world as well as in the Church, in pagan as well as in Christian commonwealths. As Andrewes himself expresses it, quoting, appropriately, from Arnobius, "nothing was innovated for christian religion *in rerum naturâ*,"[8] which is another way of saying what Aquinas and Hooker say repeatedly, that grace completes nature rather than acting to contradict or destroy it.

From such observations it is readily apparent that Andrewes, like Hooker, conceives of a world that is flooded with God's presence and light; in which, on the common foundation, not of Scripture alone, but of "nature, Scripture, and experience," man

6. MW, p. 365 (subtitle of essay).
7. MW, p. 365.
8. MW, p. 365.

can live in harmony with God. The supernatural grace which the Christian religion alone can give is necessary to man's salvation, but this grace is given not only to combat Satan, the world, and the flesh, but also to enhance and perfect the already existing though, on account of the fall, incomplete goodness of nature, of man, and of human society.

Just as Newman's symbolic language reflects his metaphysical assumptions, so likewise does Andrewes's; and the contrasts between their uses of metaphor give a clear indication of how their assumptions differ. Whereas for Newman the recurrent image is a journey, battle, or quest by night, Andrewes's metaphors suggest the divine significance and order of common, natural, daylight things. Like the other poets and theologians of medieval and Renaissance Christendom, Andrewes thinks of religious experience, not as an inner light amid the encircling gloom of an apparently meaningless world, but as inseparable from the objective, corporate life of human and divine society in a splendidly ordered, God-filled creation. One need only mention such famous sentences as "It was no *summer Progresse*," or "A cold comming they had of it,"[9] to see how closely linked for him the divine and the natural are. As both the sermon itself and Eliot's development of its theme and imagery in the "Magi" make clear, for Andrewes the very seasons have their metaphysical significances and participate in the economy of the Incarnation. Consider, in the same context, a passage from the *Devotions* (in Newman's translation as a matter of fact) in which, in good medieval and Renaissance fashion, Andrewes invokes God's blessing upon the entire hierarchy of being. He begins by linking together divine and human government, God and king, praying that God, the "King of nations," will "strengthen all the states of the inhabited world." That, in itself, is an altogether conventional prayer, but Andrewes adds a qualifying phrase which is characteristic of his philosophical orientation. These states which God the king is asked to strengthen are described as "being

---

9. Lancelot Andrewes, *Sermons*, ed. G. M. Story (Oxford: The Clarendon Press, 1967), p. 109.

Thy ordinance, though a creation of man."[10] The state, in other words, is the work both of God and man, of revelation and reason, of Scripture and experience. Such is the "old idea of a Christian Polity." Man may both fear God and honor the king without contradiction, for the two loyalties, though distinct according to their objects in the hierarchy of being, are none the less analogous and harmonious. God's "ordinance" and man's "creation," the city of this world and the city of God, correspond to one another.

In the same passage, Andrewes ranges through the great chain of being, celebrating on various levels the harmony which exists between "sacred power" and the goodness of nature. He prays that God, "by whom are ordained the powers that be," would grant "to the courts of law, Thy judgments" and "to the Parliament Thy holy wisdom"; that He would "give a prosperous course and strength to all the Christian army"; that He would

> Grant to farmers and graziers good seasons;
> to the fleet and fishers fair weather;
> to tradesmen, not to overreach one another;
> to mechanics, to pursue their business lawfully,
> down to the meanest workman,
> down to the poor.[11]

The entire sequence, from kingship to poverty, assumes that all created things, including both kings and paupers, are established at God's behest, that each province of creation is sustained by His blessing, that He is deeply involved with, gloriously immanent in, the lives and activities of kings, judges, parliamentarians, farmers, fishermen, merchants, mechanics, workmen, and paupers, and that He does not "innovate" *in rerum natura*. The prayer ends, appropriately, with a passage that affirms nature and which seems to say that charity, though a theological virtue, is, indeed, in the medieval and Renaissance sense, *kind*. God is described as one who "hatest the unnatural":

10. *The Private Devotions of Lancelot Andrewes*, trans. John Henry Newman (New York: Abingdon-Cokesbury Press, 1950), p. 36. Hereafter cited as *Devotions*.
11. *Devotions*, pp. 37–38.

Thou who wouldest have us provide for our own,
and hatest the unnatural,
remember, Lord, my relations according to the flesh.[12]

Another Caroline figure who deserves scrutiny is Bishop John
Cosin, particularly so because of the high esteem in which he
was held by nineteenth-century Anglo-Catholics. Like theirs, his
churchmanship was higher than Hooker's, but, unlike theirs, it
was informed by Hooker's philosophical principles. The constantly reiterated theme of all his work is "the authority of the
ancient laws, and old godly canons of the Church."[13] At first
glance, such an explicit appeal to the authority of the Church
may sound more like Newman than like Hooker and the other
Carolines. However, in making such an appeal, Cosin is not
resting his case simply on the *lex divina*, as Newman is wont to
do; rather, his emphasis is as much on "ancient" and "old" as
upon the "Church." In other words, like Hooker and Andrewes,
he is appealing to custom and tradition, conceived as venerable
and reasonable usage rather than simply as positive law. He is
less given than either Hooker or Andrewes to explicit statements
of his philosophical principles, and, as a consequence, we must
infer them from his various theological arguments. On the other
hand the inference is relatively easy. For instance, it is clear
enough that ancient laws, old customs, and common usages can
only be appealed to for authority, over against specific scriptural
or ecclesiastical decrees, when one believes that man does participate with God, to some degree, in the knowledge of truth
and error, good and bad. Thus we are not surprised to hear
Cosin use such a phrase as "The Two Precepts of Charity, or
The Lawes of Nature."[14] Like Andrewes, he obviously believes
that charity is *kind.* Moreover, given the philosophical principles
of the Caroline tradition as it derives from Hooker, the linking

12. *Devotions,* p. 38.
13. *The Works of . . . John Cosin,* ed. J. Sansom (Oxford: John Henry
Parker, 1843–1855), II, 89. Subsequent references to Cosin, unless otherwise
indicated, are to this edition. Hereafter cited as "Cosin."
14. John Cosin, *A Collection of Private Devotions,* ed. P. G. Stanwood
(Oxford: The Clarendon Press, 1967), p. 53.

of natural and supernatural virtues is in no sense a denigration of the supernatural but rather a testimony to God's presence in *all* His works.

The book of Cosin's which is most relevant to our present discussion is *The History of Popish Transubstantiation* (1675), in which he sets himself to defend the Anglican doctrine of the "real presence" against what he conceives to be Roman Catholic errors. The argument he follows is particularly interesting, for in it we see how the central thesis which we have been exploring can be applied by seventeenth-century Anglicans against Papists as well as Puritans; how, in fact, it was applied by Laud and others. Just as Hooker and Andrewes say to the Calvinists that some things are to be done because they are reasonable and traditional, even though there may be no positive law in Scripture for them, Cosin argues against the Roman Catholics that a "positive law," so to speak, of the Church cannot be allowed against the authority of reason and custom.

Cosin's appeal to custom extends both to the Fathers and to his Anglican predecessors. He cites Hooker in particular "and many others in the Church of England, who never departed from the faith and doctrine of the ancient Catholic fathers, which is by law established, and with great care and veneration received and preserved in our Church."[15] On the contrary, he sneers at "the new-devised tenets of the Council of Trent,"[16] which contradict both the reasonableness of man, the testimony of the Fathers, and the common law and usage of the Church. Such "tenets," says Cosin, attempted "to determine the manner of the presence and manducation of Christ's Body with more nicety than was fitting";[17] and the word "fitting" is perhaps the most indicative in the entire treatise. It places Cosin squarely in the Thomist and Caroline tradition, for it assumes the rightness of things, the general goodness, even godliness, of nature, and man's ability to determine, by reason and plain common sense, what is godly. In the same vein Cosin tells us that transub-

15. Cosin, IV, 160.
16. Cosin, IV, 161.
17. Cosin, IV, 170.

stantiation "would be inconsistent with the Divine benediction, which preserves things in their proper being"[18]—a statement which reminds one of Andrewes's, that God "hatest the unnatural" and that he "innovated" nothing *in rerum natura.* In the same vein, Cosin concludes his argument with an attack on the Roman teaching that " 'The common opinion is to be embraced, not because reason requires it, but because it is determined by the Bishop of Rome.' "[19] Given Cosin's basic Caroline principles, we scarcely need to say that unless the matter be reasonable and traditional—"fitting"—no amount of ecclesiastical or papal authority can make it true.

The discussion of transubstantiation is interesting for our purposes, for Cosin's typically Caroline treatment of the doctrine would seem at first glance to separate him and his theological tradition from Aquinas and the other Schoolmen for whom this doctrine was of central importance. Yet we have been maintaining all along that Hooker and his successors take an essentially medieval approach to theological questions, and the two propositions seem to be contradictory. Actually, however, they only "seem" to be; there is no final contradiction between them, though to understand that we must recur to our original distinction between philosophy and doctrine. Aquinas teaches the doctrine of transubstantiation because in his view it is in accord both with reason and tradition; he never simply appeals to positive divine authority in support of his belief. Cosin rejects the doctrine because in his view it is contrary both to reason and tradition and therefore insupportable by positive, divine commandment. Aquinas teaches it because it is "fitting"; Cosin repudiates it because, in his point of view, it is not. Philosophically the two arguments are cut from the same Aristotelian and medieval cloth; the difference between them is on a matter of fact, stemming in part, no doubt, from a confusion on Cosin's part about what the Roman Church means by "substance." When we turn to Newman's comments on transubstantiation,

18. Cosin, IV, 180.
19. Cosin, IV, 227.

however, we find ourselves in a new philosophical world. While he was an Anglican he rejected the dogma on authority—because Anglican theologians such as Hooker, Cosin, and Andrewes rejected it.[20] When he became a Roman Catholic, he accepted the dogma because the Church taught it and because "I believed that the Catholic Roman Church was the oracle of God, and that she had declared this doctrine to be part of the original revelation."[21] There is no indication that Newman ever, so to speak, "got up" Aquinas's arguments on the subject or felt himself obliged either to accept or reject the doctrine on the basis of its own inherent reasonableness. Thus while at one time or the other he accepted both the Caroline and the Roman teaching on the subject, it seems fair to say that he never accepted the common philosophic principles which underlie both the Roman and the Caroline positions.

These remarks on the distinction between reason and authority in the interpretation of dogma lead us directly to a consideration of Archbishop Laud; for on account of his reputation for authoritarianism we should not be surprised to find in him an anticipation of Newman's philosophic scepticism. Some scholars do see Laud's theology as a departure from Hooker's on exactly the point which we are presently considering. Trevor-Roper, for instance, in his life of Laud, interprets the Archbishop's whole career as an effort to set the authority of the Church and king above reason, tradition, and the law.[22] If it is true that Laud did attempt that, or, as C. J. Sisson implies, that Hooker would have been unable to accept "that development of the Reformation in England which in some ways became a counter-Reformation and found its logical outcome in the High Church of Laud,"[23] then Laud certainly cannot be classified in the same

20. See *Ap.*, p. 91.
21. *Ap.*, p. 215.
22. H. R. Trevor-Roper, *Archbishop Laud, 1573–1645* (London: Macmillan & Co., 1940). Hereafter cited as "Trevor-Roper."
23. C. J. Sisson, *The Judicious Marriage of Mr. Hooker and the Birth of "The Laws of Ecclesiastical Policy"* (Cambridge: Cambridge University Press, 1940), pp. 100–101.

category with Hooker and Andrewes. On the other hand, I can see very little in Laud's work to warrant such an interpretation of him and a great deal to contradict it. In spite of his reputation for absolutism (not altogether a just one, I think), his constantly reiterated appeal in all his controversies is not so often to divine decree as to reason, custom, and the law. Though on some matters of specific doctrine, such as the question of whether apostolic orders are to be regarded as *de jure divino*, Laud does depart from Hooker in an authoritarian (and orthodox) direction, so too do Andrewes, Cosin and a number of other Caroline theologians, whose philosophic principles are clearly derived from Hooker. In fact, the difference between Hooker and Laud on this point is much like the difference between Cosin and Aquinas on transubstantiation. That is to say, they differ less in their principles than in the application of those principles to a specific matter of fact.

Laud gives eloquent evidence of his adherence to Hooker's principles in his "Answer to Lord Say's Speech Touching the Liturgy." Those who object to the use of "forms" in public worship attack what Laud calls "the constant and continued practice of the whole Church of Christ."[24] Set forms of prayer, says Laud, are "little less than *traditio universalis,* an universal tradition of the whole Church."[25] Moreover, Laud would have agreed with Cosin that set forms of worship are to be observed because they are "fitting." For instance, against those Puritans who advocated extemporaneous prayers, Laud's answer is "let them not make public abortion in the Church."[26] Notice that in none of these arguments is there an appeal to authority for its own sake, nor any insinuation that ecclesiastical decrees are "above the law" of nature or contrary to common experience or human reason. In fact, even when Laud is arguing for the rights of bishops (and here, as we have mentioned already, he appealed more explicitly than Hooker does to divine ordinance), he is nevertheless anxious to demonstrate that the law of God accords

24. *The Works of . . . William Laud,* ed. W. Scott and J. Bliss (Oxford: John Henry Parker, 1847–1860), VI, pt. I, 107. Hereafter cited as "Laud."
25. Laud, VI, pt. I, 117.
26. Laud, VI, pt. I, 108.

with reason and tradition. The Church should have bishops, not only because God has instituted apostolic orders, but also because in her "most learned and flourishing ages"[27] the Church had them. It is therefore reasonable, "fitting," that she should have them now. Similarly, in answer to Lord Say's contention that bishops' powers have been continued merely for " 'several politic ends,' " Laud, though he insists that the apostolic orders serve "several and great religious ends too," is none the less willing to grant that even if bishops' powers "were continued for politic ends only, so the policies be good and befitting Christians, I know no reason why they may not be continued."[28] In other words, Laud is no more willing to admit a radical opposition between the divine and the secular than Hooker, Andrewes, or Cosin are; or than Aquinas was before them. He will not allow himself to be scared by the word "politic"; what is "politic" may very well be "fitting," reasonable, natural, traditional, and hence, of God. The Church has bishops not only on account of God's positive institution but because, on this matter, as Hooker would say, God and man agree.

Laud's philosophical and theological principles show themselves most distinctly in his conference with "Mr. Fisher, the Jesuit." Among other things, he is at pains, in this debate, to refute the particular view of ecclesiastical infallibility which Trevor-Roper and other scholars have attempted to thrust upon him. He begins, appropriately, by invoking Hooker to prove that the Church rests her authority on the combined testimony of Scripture and tradition, but he is quick to deny what he takes to be the Tridentine understanding of tradition; namely that

the tradition of the present Church is divine and infallible,

. . . .

which is a doctrine unknown to the primitive Church, and which frets upon the very foundation itself, by jostling with it.[29]

What Laud, in effect, is doing is maintaining the Anglican concept of tradition against the much more legalistic and au-

27. Laud, VI, pt. I, 169 (from Laud's "Answer to Lord Say's Speech against the Bishops").
28. Laud, VI, pt. I, 174.
29. Laud, II, 104–105.

thoritarian Roman one. In Laud's view, the primary difference
between the two is what he calls, in good Caroline fashion, "the
balance of reason." In the matter in question, the interpretation
of Scripture, Laud maintains that though reason has its limitations and

can give no supernatural ground into which a man may resolve his
faith, That Scripture is the word of God infallibly: yet Reason can
go so high, as it can prove that Christian religion, which rests upon
the authority of this book, stands upon surer grounds of nature, reason, common equity, and justice, than any thing in the world which
any infidel or mere naturalist hath done, doth or can adhere unto,
against it, in that which he makes, accounts, or assumes as religion to
himself.[30]

In light of the foregoing remarks, Laud's founding of ecclesiastical polity upon the "grounds of nature, reason, [and]
common equity" needs little further illustration. It may be worth
recalling, however, that during his trial Laud was called upon to
answer with his own mouth the very charge that recent scholars
have made against him—that he had set the authority of the
king and the Church and his own authority as Archbishop above
reason, tradition, and the law. In his answer he appeals directly
to Aquinas's and Hooker's conceptions of law: "For the laws
first, I think I may safely say, I have been, to my understanding,
as strict an observer of them all the days of my life, so far as
they concern me, as any man hath."[31] He proceeds to substantiate the claim with evidence drawn from his own conduct of
public affairs and then concludes, "And how such a carriage as
this through the whole course of my life, in private and public,
can stand with an intention, nay a practice to overthrow the
law, and to introduce an arbitrary government, which my soul
hath always hated, I cannot yet see."[32] He proceeds to quote
Aristotle to the effect "that it is a very dangerous thing to trust
to the will of the judge, rather than the written law," and to
this adds one more statement which is very much to the point:

30. Laud, IV, 88–89.
31. Laud, IV, 58.
32. Laud, IV, 58–59.

"Nay more, I have ever been of opinion, that human laws bind the conscience, and have accordingly made conscience of observing them."[33]

Lest we should be tempted to take these, Laud's public statements, as rhetoric designed for the occasion, it may be worth recalling that in the privacy of his own account of the trial he records "a strong temptation in me, rather to desert my defence, and put myself into the hands of God's mercy, than endure them."[34] He resists the "temptation," largely because of his respect for the godly character of human law and custom and the "natural" obligation to defend his good name. Refusal to face trial, though it might be easier for him, would involve, as Laud sees it, both an offence "against the course of justice" and against God. The two are virtually inseparable. To refuse trial would be to appeal to God against the law, to repudiate *this* world, which God has made and made good, to imply, as the Puritans do, that this world, its laws and customs, gives no reflection of its Creator. In short, such an abnegation on Laud's part would amount to his falling into the very position from which his adversaries are attacking him. Therefore, he tells us, he places his hopes, "under God," "upon the Lords,"[35] the peers of the realm who, by law and common custom, have the authority to try him.

In thus placing his hopes, Laud is clearly ratifying his belief in that "old idea of a Christian Polity," that traditional view of Christendom in which the life of the body politic in all its hierarchical, corporate splendor is inseparable from man's knowledge and love of God. Laud's "reasonable service" to God is to submit himself to the laws of the Christian commonwealth. The fact that those laws are being manipulated unjustly against him is a sin for which his persecutors must answer to God; but the abuse of a thing does not destroy its proper use. The temptation to make some kind of private appeal to God, to violate the corporate and established order of things, is exactly that, a "temptation," a desire to confound the will of God, objectively re-

33. Laud, IV, 59.
34. Laud, IV, 49.
35. Laud, IV, 49.

vealed in custom and reason, with some purely subjective notion of that will. To submit to such a temptation, or to call it something other than a temptation, is to move in the direction of all modern thought. The fruits of such a move are scepticism about the goodness of nature and the reliability of reason and a consequent turning for authority either to the "light within" or to positive divine commandment. The result of such a turning is the fragmentation of the corporate, traditional life of the body politic, for when nature and reason cease to be regarded as reliable guides to truth, the traditional community ceases to be the locus of authority. Henceforth, God is sought outside the city or beyond the veil, and the truth of Christianity is envisioned, not as the pervasive light of being which floods the whole creation and is manifest in all law, but as a single point of light in an otherwise dark world which gives "no reflexion of its Creator."

Laud, however, marks the end of an era. He resisted the temptation to turn his back upon the established order of a traditional society and to make his private peace with God; but he was almost the last major English churchman to do so. In fact, one is tempted to think of him as the last thoroughly medieval prelate in the seat of Becket, the last person of consequence in English ecclesiastical history to defend wholeheartedly, and with a whole mind, the "old idea of a Christian Polity." Of course, if Newman is correct in saying that that traditional conception of Christendom was still alive in his own boyhood, it means that the tradition survived Laud's martyrdom by a century and a half; and, as we have already suggested, the major English poets of the Restoration and eighteenth century still conceived themselves as defenders of that old view of man. On the other hand, Newman admits that by the early nineteenth century the action of those old principles had already been "restrained," and anyone who knows the work of Dryden, Pope, and Johnson knows how desperately outnumbered they felt themselves to be. One need only recall the end of the *Dunciad* to recognize that, for Pope at least, the defense of the old order had begun to appear a well-nigh hopeless task; for he, like the rest of the Tory poets, was a man who was fighting with his back to the wall, with the full realization that the philosophical, theological, and political currents of the day had set decidedly against him. By then, Whigs ruled the state and Socinians the Church, and the High-Church party was divided by the Non-jurors. Hence the defense of the "traditions of the old Empire, its principles, provisions, and practices,"[36] long before Newman's time, had fallen upon the shoulders of a handful of poets and an occasional priest or bishop here and there. After 1645, there was no one of Laud's stature who grasped the meaning of Aquinas's or Hooker's philosophy or who was in a position to defend that old vision and polity. In fact, there was no church-man of Laud's stature in England until Newman appeared, and Newman, as we are seeing, rejected the philosophical rubrics of the old way. Therefore, though it took the clock more than a century to run down, it seems safe to say that Laud was the last major churchman and statesman to wind it.

Even within his lifetime, moreover, and even within the High-Church party, there was beginning that shift in sensibility and mode of vision which altered so radically the old orthodoxy of England. Among the prominent theologians, it can be seen most clearly in the work of Jeremy Taylor. It is true that Taylor belongs by descent to the school of Hooker, Andrewes, Cosin, and Laud, and there are many passages in his work which seem to reflect their philosophy. He certainly appears to stand in the old way when he affirms "nothing but upon grounds of Scripture, or universal tradition, or right reason discernible by every disinterested person"[37] or when he maintains that "that providence which governs all the world, is nothing else but God present by his providence: and God is in our hearts by his laws."[38] Likewise, in full accord with Hooker's basic principles, he insists that "Whatsoever therefore is contrary to right reason, or to a certain truth in any faculty, cannot be a truth, for one truth is not contrary to another." Hence it is ridiculous to argue

36. Newman, Diff., II, 262.
37. *The Whole Works of . . . Jeremy Taylor* (London: William Ball, 1837), III, 50. Hereafter cited as "Taylor."
38. Taylor, III, 55.

that Scripture or the divine law contradicts our reason, for truth cannot contradict itself: "If therefore any proposition be said to be the doctrine of Scripture, and confessed to be against right reason, it is certainly not the doctrine of Scripture, because it cannot be true, and yet be against what is true."[39] Moreover, Taylor maintains that God reasons with us in matters of right and wrong according to the standards of human justice. "God is pleased to verify his own proceedings and his own propositions, by discourses merely like ours, when we speak according to right reason." He even "exposes his proceedings to be argued by the same measures and proportions by which he judges us, and we judge one another."[40] This linking of divine and human justice seems to place Taylor in the true line of descent from Aquinas, Hooker, and Laud. Moreover, we must not forget that Taylor was one of Laud's chaplains, and one is inclined to think that, like Laud, he would have been willing, if the situation had demanded it, to place his hopes "under God," "upon the Lords." After all, God "exposes his proceedings to be argued by the same measures and proportions by which he judges us, and we judge one another."

Yet, at the same time, anyone who has read Taylor carefully will have recognized what H. R. McAdoo calls the "modern note" in his theology. What McAdoo refers to is Taylor's qualified distrust of man's reason. The modernity consists in Taylor's departure from Hooker's "belief in the natural reason and his confidence in it." Taylor, "though he does not forsake the traditional view of natural law and its bearing on human acts . . . evidently regards it as inadequate and as placing the emphasis incorrectly." Therefore, McAdoo concludes, Taylor "shifts the stress, so that revelation rather than *recta ratio* predominates in his thoughts."[41] It may be that McAdoo overstates his case; at least in the passages we have just examined Taylor's treatment of reason seems to be generally in accord with Hooker's. On the other hand, the point cannot be ignored, for there are pas-

39. Taylor, III, 85.
40. Taylor, III, 85.
41. H. R. McAdoo, *The Structure of Caroline Moral Theology* (London: Longmans, Green & Co., 1949), pp. 37–38.

sages in Taylor which substantiate it and which seem quite foreign to the Caroline school, passages which Newman would have been more likely to write than Hooker. For instance, Taylor says that the reason of man is "a right judge" *only* when "she is truly informed";[42] hence the necessity for revelation, for positive divine commandment. Hooker, Andrewes, or Laud would never have denied that necessity, but they would not have emphasized it so heavily as Taylor does; moreover, they would argue that reason is truly, if incompletely, informed by its very nature and that it is therefore not wholly dependent for its rectitude on a revelation external to it. Divine revelation completes reason's natural light, but it neither supersedes that light entirely nor is it the *sine qua non* of its effect. Taylor stresses the point that there are cases in which "our understanding is to submit, and wholly to be obedient, but not to inquire further."[43] Again, the point is one which none of the Caroline theologians, in fact which no orthodox Christian, would deny. On the other hand, it is a point which Hooker or his philosophical descendents would not be likely to make in the first place, or certainly not one which they would insist upon. Newman, however, would—does—insist upon it; and herein we see the direction in which Taylor's shift in emphasis is pointing. Such statements by Taylor are still balanced by the weight of the older, contrary emphasis on the goodness of nature and reason and of the established divine and human order of the world, but their presence in his writing is a sign of things to come, a premonition of the subjectivism and philosophical scepticism which affects later English theologians, even High-Churchmen, so prominently.

Thus, from a cursory examination of the major High-Church divines of the seventeenth century, we see quite clearly that their philosophical inheritance was medieval and scholastic. Though Newman, during his Anglican years, appealed to them as his predecessors and though he learned a great deal from them in matters of doctrine, it is clear that he did not share that philo-

42. Taylor, III, 84.
43. Taylor, III, 84.

sophical inheritance. On the contrary, as we have seen, that very inheritance was what he relinquished when he chose to "make terms" with modern thought, to follow "after the newe world the space." Of course, Jeremy Taylor does appear to be an exception to these generalizations, to be a harbinger of the "modernism" which in Newman becomes an accomplished fact. On the other hand, there seems little question, so far as Caroline theology is concerned, that he is the exception that proves the rule.

✤

CHAPTER III

Newman and the Metaphysicals

NO consideration of Newman's departure from "the old orthodoxy of England" can omit reference to seventeenth-century religious poetry. That is not because Newman was much affected by that poetry, but because it gives metaphoric expression to Caroline theology, because it articulates in image that philosophical vision which Hooker inherited from Aquinas and transmitted to Andrewes, Cosin, Laud, and others—that vision which Newman relinquished. Newman himself wrote theology in the manner of a poet; his principal mode of utterance is in image. Moreover, as we have already suggested, his characteristic images, such as the "night battle" and the "encircling gloom," reflect his most profound philosophical assumptions. It is interesting, therefore, to compare Newman's images with Donne's and Herbert's, for the latter reflect the contrary assumptions, those which inform medieval and Caroline theology. Also, it is interesting to discover that the "modern note" which Jeremy Taylor sounds is echoed in Metaphysical poetry. Here, as in the theology, "modernism" is the exception that proves the traditional rule; but the new note is heard more distinctly among the poets than among the theologians, and its manifestation is of greater interest on account of the way in which it affects poetic language. Traherne, for instance, anticipates strikingly the subjectivism and philosophical scepticism of nineteenth-century poetry and theology, and his image patterns anticipate those of his successors, including Newman's. Alterations in the shape of poetic symbol are always good indications of changes in philosophical currents; and the shift in mode of vision and expression from Donne to Traherne provides us with a view in microcosmic form of the changes which separate Newman from Laud, the changes which Taylor foreshadows.

Donne belongs fully to the Hooker tradition and, beyond Hooker, to St. Thomas and the Schoolmen.[1] Helen Gardner argues convincingly that though his "debt to Hooker is not a verbal one," nevertheless, "his treatment of law, for instance, in *Pseudo-Martyr* constantly recalls Hooker. To read the *Essays in Divinity* or the Sermons, after a rereading of Hooker, is to feel at once that Donne has absorbed Hooker's conception of the *via media* so deeply that it has become the basis of his own thinking."[2] In the same deep way, I suggest, Donne also absorbed Hooker's conception of the relationship between God and nature, which, as we shall see, is closely related to his idea of the *via media*. A willingness to accept the established order of things as holy, as being of divine ordinance, underlies both.

In almost every aspect of Donne's poetry we see Hooker's "incomparable goodness of nature," his sense of God's glorious immanence both in the creation and in the order of human society. We infer it in a poem such as the "Extasie," in which Donne embraces the body as an indispensable adjunct to the soul.[3] Admittedly, there is a kind of ecstatic experience in which, in order to "unperplex" ourselves and discover "what we love," we must "forbeare" our bodies. But such an exclusively spiritual relationship cannot be considered permanent for man. To transfer Hopkins's line to Donne, "Man's spirit will be flesh-bound when found at best"; our bodies "are ours, though they're not wee,"[4] and we must accept them accordingly. "Else a great Prince in prison lies."[5]

Similarly, man must accept the world's body, for the latter is the image of God, created by Him to reflect His glory. That fact is implicit in an analogy Donne draws in the "Exstasie": the

1. H. J. C. Grierson's annotations of the poetry establish Donne's debt to Aquinas and the Schoolmen beyond any serious question. See *The Poems of John Donne*, ed. Herbert J. C. Grierson (London: Oxford University Press, 1958), II.

2. *Divine Poems*, p. xxi, n. 1.

3. All references to the "Songs and Sonnets" are to *"The Elegies" and "The Songs and Sonnets,"* ed. Helen Gardner (Oxford: The Clarendon Press, 1965).

4. L. 51.

5. L. 68.

soul's relationship to the body corresponds to the relationship between the intelligences and their spheres.[6] The analogy is admittedly a medieval and Elizabethan commonplace, but that in itself does nothing to invalidate Donne's use of it. On the contrary, the very fact that it *is* a commonplace indicates that the medieval and Caroline tradition is fully alive for Donne—that he thinks in its terms. If he had not been able to accept the medieval and Caroline idea of nature and of the relationship between human psychology and the celestial hierarchy, he would not have found the traditional imagery convenient. Helen Gardner speaks of Donne's "devotional conservatism, his retention of traditions of Christian prayer and worship which did not seem to him incompatible with the Protestant position."[7] In the same vein, we might very well speak of Donne's, or for that matter Hooker's or Andrewes's, rhetorical or poetic conservatism, their use of images and analogies which imply a conception of the relationship between God and nature which is their inheritance from the Scholastic past.

In any event, Donne pursues the analogy between human bodies and the spheres in a manner that leaves no doubt about his philosophical assumptions. True human love is between souls, not bodies, but it is our bodies that serve as vehicles to bring our souls into union. Analogically, "heavens influence" does not touch man directly but "first imprints the ayre."[8] In either case, the spiritual force employs a physical or material vehicle:

> So must pure lovers soules descend
> T'affections, and to faculties,
> That sense may reach and apprehend,
> Else a great Prince in prison lies.[9]

It is in his emphasis on the reach and apprehension of the sense that Donne reflects most directly the Carolines' "bright view" of the world. In spite of the rigorously penitential aspects of some of his work, Donne never fails to affirm the goodness of

6. Ll. 51–52.
7. *Divine Poems*, p. xxi.
8. "The Extasie," ll. 57–58.
9. Ll. 65–68.

God's "owne Lieutenant Nature."[10] Nature shrinks and cracks and the sun winks at the crucifixion, but not because nature is evil nor because her darkness is being extinguished painfully by "Light unsufferable." Rather, nature cracks because, being our Lord's "Lieutenant," she is suffering in sympathy with him. After all, the hands which are now "peirc'd with those holes" are the very hands which "span the Poles, / And tune all spheres at once."[11] Moreover, because nature is good, God's lieutenant and handmaid, it is neither inconsistent nor indecorous to speak of Him in her tongue nor to represent Him in terms of the imagery which she provides. Thus, though the sun "winks" at Christ's death, He may nevertheless be called a "Sunne, by rising set," and by that setting begetting "endlesse day."[12]

"The Extasie" and "Goodfriday, 1613. Riding Westward" are both indicative, in idea and in mode of expression, of the whole direction of Donne's poetry and of Metaphysical poetry in general. Schools of poetry come into being because a certain mode of apprehension, a certain way of understanding God, nature, and man, finds expression in a certain kind of writing—incarnates itself, we might say, in certain rhetorical and symbolic forms. In Donne's case, we see precisely that sort of phenomenon. His acceptance of nature and the flesh as goods in their own right is no abstract theory; he tests it, gives it life and body, makes it work for him in imagery. He makes poetry out of the concrete details of his experiences as a sixteenth- or seventeenth-century Englishman. No poet was ever more precise or particular about the concrete natural fact; we recall bed curtains, a flea, tapers, a bracelet of bright hair, a bone; or, for that matter, those lovers' bodies whose souls must not forbear them. These things, these creatures, are the components of nature; they are, as Andrewes would say, part of our "relations according to the flesh." Kings, farmers, merchants, fishermen, and paupers must deal with them, for they are aspects of God's creation which help to show him "plainly." Yet because these natural facts are made by God and

10. "Goodfriday, 1613. Riding Westward," l. 19. All references to the *Divine Poems* are to Helen Gardner's edition previously cited.
11. Ll. 21–22.
12. Ll. 11–12.

show his glory, Donne never treats them simply as fact and as that alone. On the contrary, he derives from them access to an intellectual vision which, at its highest, reaches to God Himself. However, because nature is real and has her own goodness, the vision of God to which she lifts us never obliterates or destroys her. The details in Donne's poetry do not become etherealized or tenuous but remain themselves—concrete bodies, constituted of earth, air, fire, and water, of steel or wood or flesh.

In other words, Donne puts the Aristotelian-Thomist-Caroline philosophy to the proof—that the creation is pregnant with manifestations of its Creator; that "that law eternal which God himself hath made to himself," is reflected in all provinces of his creation "and thereby worketh all things whereof he is the cause and author." Donne's metaphors are such that in every detail of nature, and without any tendency to make nature less concrete than she is, God and his operations are visible. There was never a world so living and busy and yet so expressive of God's presence and order than that of his poetry. Without becoming a whit less earthy than they are by nature, the things of earth become for Donne the images of heaven. For instance, in the "Hymn to God my God, in my Sicknesse," Donne makes holy symbols out of contemporary medicine, cosmography, and exploration. In one sense, there was never a poem more deeply rooted in time, place, and historical circumstance, and yet this very particularity serves as a vehicle for new heaven and new earth. In phrases like "the Pacifique Sea" and "the Easterne riches,"[13] the natural and the holy, the concrete, everyday life of the English kingdom in Elizabethan and Jacobean times and the life of the kingdom of heaven outside of time are inextricably united.

To say that Donne used conventional Elizabethan and Jacobean imagery is certainly not to say anything new, but we may not, heretofore, have said enough about the philosophic relevance of that usage. Even Doctor Johnson's definition begins to develop a certain resonance when we realize that those opposites, apparently yoked together so violently, are in fact joined together

13. Ll. 16–17.

in that comprehensive theological vision to which Donne had given his allegiance. Moreover, when T. S. Eliot applauds Metaphysical poetry for its capacity to amalgamate "disparate experience" in order to form "new wholes,"[14] one feels that there should be added some notation on the Metaphysicals' debt to the theological and philosophical wholeness of medieval and Caroline divinity. The fact that Newman owed no such debt accounts for the fact that his characteristic images of the world express fragmentation and alienation rather than wholeness and harmony.

Of all the Metaphysicals, Donne is closest in spirit to Aquinas and Hooker and to the traditional Christian vision. It is difficult to detect anywhere in his work the "modern note" which begins to sound in Taylor and which is taken up so strongly later. Rather, it is in George Herbert that we first notice the hint of change, the widening of that division between heaven and earth into which Newman was eventually to step. Of course, in his overt statements of his philosophical premises, Herbert is at one with Hooker or with Donne; one need look no further than *The Country Parson* to see that. It is in his poetry, in his attempt to unite earth and heaven in images, that the division begins to manifest itself.

He argues convincingly in prose for the goodness of nature and reason and for the godly significance of the human order; for "it is an ill Mason that refuseth any stone: and there is no knowledg, but, in a skillful hand, serves either positively as it is, or else to illustrate some other knowledge."[15] On this principle, Herbert tells us the parson must know tillage and pastorage as well as the Fathers, the Schoolmen, philosophy, and Holy Scripture. In fact, Herbert employs a characteristically Metaphysical image to make his point about the wholeness of knowledge, saying that with his accessory knowledge the parson may "plough"

14. T. S. Eliot, "The Metaphysical Poets," *Selected Essays* (New York: Harcourt, Brace and Company, 1950), p. 247.
15. "A Priest to the Temple; or, The Country Parson," *The Works of George Herbert*, ed. F. E. Hutchinson (Oxford: The Clarendon Press, 1959), p. 228. All subsequent references to Herbert are to this edition. Hereafter cited as "Herbert."

Holy Scripture.[16] The effect of the pun is to suggest that tillage and the knowledge of God, things earthly and things heavenly, are united. In a similar vein, he maintains that the parson is to keep his house according to the pattern which God has given in nature; "wherein he admires and imitates the wonderfull providence and thrift of the great householder of the world."[17] He appeals repeatedly to nature as a godly standard. For instance, in matters of fasting, though it is, generally speaking, good to fast, sick people, those who have "weak and obstructed" bodies, ought not to, "for it is as unnatural to do any thing, that leads me to a sicknesse, to which I am inclined, as not to get out of that sicknesse, when I am in it, by any diet."[18] In general, he maintains with Hooker and the rest that nature serves grace "both in comfort of diversion, and the benefit of application when need requires; as also by way of illustration, even as our Saviour made plants and seeds to teach the people." Moreover, just as nature serves grace, reason (philosophy) serves revelation. Our Lord is "the true householder, who bringeth out of his treasure things new and old; the old things of Philosophy, and the new of Grace; and maketh the one serve the other."[19] Finally, Herbert defends ceremonies of pagan origin just as Hooker, Donne, Laud, and Andrewes do, the country parson being "a Lover of old Customes."[20]

Here is the medieval and Caroline vision at its best, and admittedly there are many manifestations of the same vision in *The Temple*. In fact, *The Temple* is usually considered to be thoroughly Caroline, and before we attend to Herbert's more nearly "modern note," the strongly traditional aspects of that book ought to be acknowledged. In the "Church-Porch," for instance, Hooker, Laud, Andrewes, or Donne would have felt very much at home; access to the temple is by way of that which is "fitting." Herbert admonishes us to obey both the king and

16. Herbert, p. 229.
17. Herbert, p. 241.
18. Herbert, p. 242.
19. Herbert, p. 261.
20. Herbert, p. 283.

the King and to live by rule, since both our houses, our commonwealths, and God's universe are built and sustained by rule.[21] There is no verbal echo of Hooker here, but, if we translate *rule* as *law*, we see immediately that Herbert is here envisioning a universe very much like St. Thomas's and Hooker's, every province of which is united with every other by analogous laws. In such a universe man can "take all that is given; whether wealth, /Or love, or language"; for "A good digestion turneth all to health."[22] The phrase might well be used to sum up the entire Thomist and Caroline tradition in theology and poetry. As we have already seen, the medieval and Renaissance digestion was very good indeed, capable of turning earth as well as heaven to its good health. "To take all that is given" is simply to believe that God gives all and orders all that He gives by rule; that no stone is to be refused by a good mason because all stones were designed by God to occupy places in the temple.

"The Church-Porch" is by no means the only portion of Herbert's book which indicates his debt to the Caroline divines or to their medieval view of Christianity. In fact, Herbert's conception of the Church, which underlies the whole body of *The Temple*, bespeaks the same sort of attachment to nature and her concrete, everyday realities which we have seen in Donne. For Herbert, "The British Church" is, in the first place, a fact—an institution "by law established." (Newman, on the contrary, called it a "paper" religion, a "road over mountains and rivers, which has never been cut.")[23] Moreover, it is important for Herbert that it is *British*, something homey and domestic, not a gleam to be followed on some distant physical or metaphysical shore, but an entity as solid, concrete, and local as Donne's imagery. As Helen White aptly says, the "regulations, the forms, the accumulations and customs" of the Church of England were not to Herbert, as they were to the Puritans, something to "stifle or usurp the place of personal spiritual life, but they recharged it and nourished it"

---

21. Ll. 133–138.
22. Ll. 355–358.
23. *The Via Media of the Anglican Church*, I, 17. Hereafter cited as *Via Media*.

—"the institution and the man had grown into each other."[24] Moreover, lest we confuse Herbert's conception of the Church with Newman's, we must remember that this institution into which Herbert had grown and which had grown into him was not considered by him as a power contrary to or at war with the realm of England or with the other powers established in this world. For Herbert, as for Aquinas or Hooker, the city of this world and the city of God, though by no means of equal importance, are nevertheless to be conceived of as being in harmony with one another, not at war. Herbert, no more than his predecessors, appeals to the divine law in contradiction to the natural or the civil law, for all laws descend from the law eternal, and, though not identical with one another, they are analogous and work to the same end, which is God Himself. All created things from the planets to the Church to the commonwealth to man must live by rule, and all rules finally agree, for all are of God. Therefore, when we say with Helen White that Herbert is "basically a church man,"[25] we are in no sense saying that he appealed to the Church as Newman characteristically did, as a source of positive divine decree and infallible direction in opposition to nature or to the nation, as a single point of light in an otherwise dark creation. The "British Church" is, after all, the reasonable "mean," the natural and fitting way; Herbert's "dearest Mother," who is "neither too mean, nor yet too gay."[26]

Nor does Herbert follow the Caroline tradition in his theological and ecclesiastical poetry alone. There are many poems in *The Temple*, as in Donne's work, in which we see the theory put to the proof, the objects of nature functioning as vehicles for their metaphysical analogues, united inseparably with those analogues in the way that Donne's vehicles are. In fact, there is one sense in which that union, when Herbert's poetry is at its best, may be considered as being even tighter than Donne's; certainly there is less sense of violence in the yoking of heaven and earth. In such

24. Helen C. White, *The Metaphysical Poets, A Study in Religious Experience* (New York: The Macmillan Co., Collier Books 1962), p. 167. Hereafter cited as "White."

25. White, p. 167.

26. Ll. 25, 8.

lines as the following, we see perhaps a richer poetic product of
the Caroline vision than in anything Donne wrote—richer because it shows less sense of strain, a greater ease, a greater confidence in the harmony of "nature, Scripture, and experience."
Prayer is

> Heaven in ordinarie, man well drest,
> The milkie way, the bird of Paradise.
> Church-bels beyond the starres heard, the souls bloud,
> The land of spices; something understood.[27]

The "land of spices" may derive from Donne's "Easterne riches";
Herbert, too, was willing to accept as holy and good the stuff of
contemporary life, the explorations, and because he could see
these as being "of God," he, like Donne, could make poetry out
of them. The "Church-bels" are also reminiscent of Donne (*Devotions upon Emergent Occasions*), but, as I have suggested, in
both images there is less effort than we feel in Donne. For Herbert, the union is "something understood," something simply
and clearly seen—that there is an analogy between earthly and
heavenly riches. We see the same kind of ease, the same direct,
simple understanding in Herbert's conversations with God; his
sense of God as "the friend," which Louis Martz attributes quite
rightly to the Salesian devotional tradition but which is also
rooted in Thomist and Caroline theology. The God who calls
Herbert "my child" is the same God who, Jeremy Taylor says, "is
pleased to verify his own proceedings and his own propositions,
by discourses merely like ours." The "still, small voice" speaks
Caroline English, is as homey, domestic, and decorous as the
British Church.

Yet, in spite of all these aspects of Herbert's work in which we
see him walking directly in the way of St. Thomas, Hooker, and
Laud and giving, at times, a more nearly effortless poetic expression of that way than even Donne is capable of, the fact remains,
as I have already suggested, that Herbert's poetry also shows
symptoms of those new philosophical directions which lead to
Newman's "modernism." In trying to identify those symptoms
one is tempted to point to the abundance of penitential poetry

27. "Prayer (I)," Ll. 11–14.

in *The Temple*; to suggest that poems such as "Mortification," meditations on man's decay, on winding sheets, death knells, and coffins, indicate a lack of trust in things natural and human which contradicts the basic premises of the tradition we have been discussing. On the other hand, we must remember that there are more death's heads in Donne than in Herbert and that nowhere, even at its brightest, is Christian literature without its penitential element. In fact, it cannot be without it and still be Christian. Indeed, though we have had no cause to dwell on those aspects of Caroline theology, the works of Hooker, Andrewes, Laud, and the rest have their strongly penitential notes, nor is there any contradiction between their penitence and the bright view they take of man and nature. In fact, the two strains in their work complement one another.

The fact of the matter is that penitential activity makes no sense at all unless we assume at the outset that man and the world whose lord he was created to be are basically good and susceptible to God's government. Penitence is ultimately a matter of discipline in which man's unruly wills and affections are made subject once again to "rule," so that he may live in harmony with the whole creation, under God's laws. Unless there is a visible, godly order in creation, and unless God's laws are accessible to man through his senses and his reason, then penitence is not only nonsensical but impossible. Penitence is only possible in an order of being in which we are able to hear God call "my child" and in which we are able to answer, in good English, "my Lord." It is no accident that Puritan Protestantism, in taking a dark view of God's creation, also gave up all commerce with sackcloth and the death's head.

Therefore, we cannot point in Herbert's poetry to the penitential element as an indication of his divergence from the Caroline tradition. However, there is a strain which, though clearly distinguishable from the penitential, appears most often in connection with it and which does point in that direction. I have reference to Herbert's fear for the loss of his metaphysical vision. Though, as we have seen, in Herbert's best moments, God's presence in His creation is something surely and simply "understood," a vision without strain and full of peace, to a much greater extent than Donne or than his other theological mentors, Herbert seems to have been threatened with the loss of that vision. Notice, for instance, the poem "Decay," which is concerned explicitly with such a loss. In the old "sweet" days, says Herbert, God

> didst lodge with Lot,
> Struggle with Jacob, sit with Gideon,
> Advise with Abraham[28]

and those who sought Him might have found Him either "at some fair oak, or bush, or cave, or well," or, more likely still, on Sinai where, if you "list, ye may heare great Aarons bell."[29] But now "decay" has come upon us; "fled is the vision":

> I see the world grows old, when as the heat
> Of thy great love, once spread, as in an urn
> Doth closest up it self, and still retreat,
> Cold Sinne still forcing it, till it return,
> And calling *Justice*, all things burn.[30]

The note of penitence is certainly here, in the reference to "cold sinne," but that is not the dominant note of the poem. The sense of loss extends beyond Herbert's personal, moral responsibility, and though the central metaphor is drawn from ecclesiastical history, it seems clear enough that that history itself is not Herbert's principal concern. Rather, the subject of the poem is the withdrawal of God from his creation, from oaks, bushes, caves, and wells. In fact it is very close to the subject of those passages from Newman which we have quoted earlier, namely the "absence" of God, and it stands in sharp contrast to the subject matter of a poem such as "Prayer." It is also in sharp contrast to the subject matter of most of Donne's poetry. Donne does strike the same note very strongly in one poem, "The First Anniversary," the "Anatomie of the World," in which the death of Elizabeth Drury becomes the vehicle or metaphor for God's absenting Himself from creation, leaving it a dead corpse in His

28. Ll. 1–3.
29. Ll. 7, 10.
30. Ll. 16–20.

withdrawal. On the other hand, it is not a note which Donne ever repeated with the same intensity; indeed, even a year later, in "The Second Anniversary," the creation has come to life again, in spite of the confusion of the "new philosophy," and even death, that darkest of natural creatures, serves God as "but a Groome / Which brings a Taper to the outward roome."[31] Nor is the note repeated in the *Divine Poems* or, for that matter, at least not with any insistence, in the sermons or the other prose. All the great abundance of worms and winding sheets, of vermiculation and incineration, strike not the sceptical but the penitential note, bespeak not the absence of God from his world but rather Donne's fear for the consequences of his sin. He has a "sinne of fear" that he may not reach his east, the "Pacifique Sea," and the "Easterne riches," that "when I have spunne / My last thred, I shall perish on the shore";[32] but there is really no doubt that there are such riches, such a sea, or that they are accessible to man's rational knowledge.

In Herbert, on the contrary, the theme of "Decay" is repeated in poem after poem. We hear it very strikingly in "Home," for our home clearly is not here in this "encircling gloom." In verse after verse of that poem, in sentiments almost totally alien to the "philosophic principles" of Thomist and Caroline theology, Herbert prays for liberation from the darkness of a hostile creation, one, we infer, which shows no image of its Creator. "Why must I stay?" he asks; "what is this world to me, / This world of wo?"[33] Or, "what is this weary world; this meat and drink, / That chains us by the teeth so fast?"[34] The questions are not altogether rhetorical; their answers confirm their drift. This world is "nothing but drought and dearth, but bush and brake."[35] Some, he admits, may "dream merrily," but the implication is that merriment in this world, before the dreamers "wake, / . . . dresse themselves and come to thee," is no more than a dream.[36] In a similar vein,

---

31. Ll. 85–86.
32. "A Hymne to God the Father," ll. 13–14.
33. Ll. 31–33.
34. Ll. 36–37.
35. L. 49.
36. Ll. 51–52.

he implies that we have no good things until we transcend those things we now call good;

> We talk of harvests; there are no such things,
> But when we leave our corn and hay:
> There is no fruitfull yeare, but that which brings
> The last and lov'd, though dreadfull day.[37]

Short of that day, we can have no knowledge of spice lands, of eastern riches. The vision of the poem is clearly apocalyptic and imposes upon us the "either—or" of a far more rigid dualism than we expect to find in Caroline theology and poetry.

If Herbert is in earnest in these statements of dualism, as he seems to be, how are we to reconcile such sentiments with those thoroughly Thomist and Caroline affirmations of nature and reason which, as we have seen, also appear in his work? How are we to account for both "drought and dearth" and the "land of spices"? In the long run, there may be no complete reconciliation, and surely in such a book as *The Temple* we need not demand absolute philosophical consistency. It is perhaps sufficient for our present purposes to note that Herbert, in spite of his debt to Caroline divinity, also sounds a different and darker note. However, I am inclined to think that there is an attempt at such a reconciliation in *The Temple*, and one which both echoes Jeremy Taylor and anticipates a similar effort in Newman's work.

We have noticed that, while Hooker and Andrewes believe firmly in the Christian revelation, they also maintain, to use Andrewes's quotation from Arnobius, that nothing was "innovated" *in rerum natura* by or for that revelation. It follows that "right reason" remains a constant and that, by its exercise, man, in addition to what revelation shows him, can see God "plainly" in all His works. As we have seen, both Taylor and Newman (the latter more radically) shift the emphasis, implying that man can only see God in His works through the aid of revelation or, as Newman says, on account of the voice of God in our conscience and our heart. Thus for both of them the apprehension of God's presence demands that man achieve a certain point of view, that he gain a certain perspective, that he use a certain lens. That is

37. Ll. 55–58.

clearly what Taylor means when he says that man's reason is "a right judge" *only* when "she is truly informed."

It seems to me that in *The Temple* Herbert takes a position very close to Taylor's and in doing so foreshadows Newman's more radical subjectivism. The difference between Herbert's two visions of the world—the spice lands on one hand, the drought and dearth on the other—is the difference between vision with and without the proper lens. It is no accident that the first vision occurs in "Prayer" and that prayer, among other things, is described as "the soul in paraphrase." The soul must be in "paraphrase," in a state of understanding beyond itself, in a state which comes with faith and prayer, in order to apprehend God's presence. Once we recognize this condition of vision, we begin to see that the whole poetic movement of *The Temple* is concerned with it—with the loss and recapture of the vision. The last line of "Repentance" might almost be taken as a succinct statement of that movement; "Fractures well cur'd make us more strong." Herbert is constantly showing us his fractures and his efforts to cure them. "The Temper (I)" is a good instance; in fact, the first stanza raises Herbert's central problem, both as a Christian and as a poet:

> How should I praise thee, Lord! how should my rymes
> Gladly engrave thy love in steel,
> If what my soul doth feel sometimes,
> My soul might ever feel![38]

The point is clearly the soul's need for a state of paraphrase, Herbert's need to see God "plainly." It is also obvious that the "reason of the philosophers," the constant, rational application of man's natural faculties, does not suffice for that vision. The light that shows Herbert God and makes it possible for him as a poet to make "rymes" about God is fitful.

> Although there were some fourtie heav'ns, or more,
> Sometimes I peere above them all;
> Sometimes I hardly reach a score,
> Sometimes to hell I fall.[39]

38. Ll. 1–4.
39. Ll. 5–8.

We can surmise that it is the first state, the vision which both includes and transcends the "fourtie heav'ns," which, rising as it does from the action of prayer, produces the poem "Prayer." It is the last condition, the total failure of the subjective vision, of the paraphrase, which produces poems such as "Decay" and "Divinitie." In "The Temper (I)" Herbert resigns himself to God's will in the matter in language which is reminiscent of Taylor's similar resignation—"our understanding is to submit, and wholly to be obedient, but not to inquire further." Herbert's lines say essentially the same thing:

> Whether I flie with angels, fall with dust,
> Thy hands made both, and I am there:
> Thy power and love, my love and trust
> Make one place ev'ry where.[40]

The last line is reminiscent of Donne; it gives voice to a philosophical vision in which the finite and infinite, earth and heaven, are united in a single image. As we have seen, however, the achievement of that vision has not come easily for Herbert. It is not something which right reason sees unaided, but rather it is the fruit of despair first, then resignation. It is a fracture healed.

"The Temper (I)," then, may be considered as an expression of Herbert's quest for that point of view or that lens from or through which he may see the vision which seems to have come, as it were, "naturally," to Hooker, Donne, Andrewes, and other Caroline figures as well as to their medieval forebears. The quest is manifestly important to Herbert, both devotionally and esthetically; for except when the soul is in paraphrase he can neither love God nor sing of Him as he ought. Perhaps the best statement of the theme, both of the fracture and the cure, is in "The Flower." There is a quickening of life toward the end of *The Temple*, a cluster of poems which suggest that at last Herbert has achieved a sort of steadiness and constancy in his vision, that Aaron is dressed and that his great bell can be heard again. "The Flower" is one of these. It celebrates God's "sweet," "clean" returns, the end of "Decay," the voice of the turtle again in the land. The Lord is once more manifest in His creation, and what has recently seemed

40. Ll. 25–28.

a desert is now seen, in fact, to be a garden. Herbert insists, however, that this renewal of sweetness and harmony is altogether dependent upon God, not on himself; it is not in any degree the achievement of natural man. On the contrary, man's job is to be obedient and to recognize that "thy word is all, if we could spell."[41] The spelling image suggests the "soul in paraphrase." God's image can only be seen in faith and trust, when we spell His Word correctly. Once Herbert does that, he may both "live and write," for he is then able to see the spice lands where, in his fractured condition, there seemed to be nothing but "drought and dearth." Thus paraphrased, he can "once more smell the dew and rain, / And relish versing."[42]

Herbert's subjectivism anticipates a similar (but more radical and more pervasive) strain in Crashaw, Vaughan, and Traherne, all of whom in varying degrees move away from Hooker and Donne. Of the three, Traherne moves the farthest in the modern direction, and, in his representative work, particularly in "The Third Century," we encounter a sensibility and a mode of vision which are much closer to Newman's and those of his contemporaries than to Hooker's and his. Actually, what we find in Traherne (as we find, to a lesser degree, in Vaughan and Crashaw) is a further development of Herbert's emphasis on the need for a proper lens. In fact, in the *Centuries* the matter of perspective, the need for the soul's paraphrase, has become an issue of overwhelming philosophical and esthetic importance, and the movement of the mind in the direction of private vision has been carried so far that Traherne leaves very little of the medieval and Caroline edifice intact. He believes that God is present in the world and that the world is consequently good; but what Newman would call a "real assent" to that belief, a realization or experience of it, is only possible when man transcends his natural, rational capacities. That vision is to be apprehended *only* through the eyes of faith, and Traherne comes very close to agreeing with the Puritans that it can only be known through the Bible.

41. L. 21.
42. Ll. 38–39.

When the mind is enlightened by grace, when the soul is in paraphrase, Traherne's view of the world resembles Herbert's or Donne's at its brightest: "The WORLD is unknown, till the Value and Glory of it is seen: till the Beauty and the Serviceableness of its Parts is Considered. When you enter into it, it is an illimited feild of Varietie and Beauty: where you may lose your self in the Multitude of Wonders and Delights."[43] In this glorious creation we see God "in His Gifts, and Adore his Glory."[44] Out of context the passage sounds as though it might have been inspired directly by Hooker; we would only need to add that this vision of God's glory is plain, visible to all men by the light of nature and reason, and we should be able to place Traherne shoulder to philosophical shoulder with Hooker and Laud. Traherne, however, unlike Hooker, would not allow that addition. "The Third Century" is about a fracture and its cure, about the loss of the vision of God in his works and about how that vision has been regained; about "imagination and taste, how impaired and how restored." The allusion to Wordsworth is not capricious, for "The Third Century" is, as many critics have observed, a "spiritual autobiography" very much like those which we associate with Romantic and Victorian literature. Just as Wordsworth must restore *in himself* the capacity to see the "splendour in the grass," the "glory in the flower," Traherne, having lost by apostasy "those things" which he once knew "by Intuition," he must "collect" them again "by the Highest Reason,"[45] in "years that bring the philosophic mind." Wordsworth's experience is largely a secular version of Traherne's, and we shall see in Newman's pilgrimage something resembling a fusion of the two.

What is common to all three is the subjective element which we have already mentioned—the dependence upon a proper state of soul, a proper spiritual point of view. Traherne states the matter very clearly: "I saw moreover that it did not so much concern us what Objects were before us, as with what Eys we beheld them;

43. Thomas Traherne, *Poems, Centuries and Three Thanksgivings*, ed. Anne Ridler (London: Oxford University Press, 1966), p. 173. All references to Traherne are to this edition. Hereafter cited as "Traherne."

44. Traherne, p. 172.

45. Traherne, p. 263.

with what Affections we esteemed them, and what Apprehensions we had about them."[46] The world may appear to be paradise or the wasteland, charged with the grandeur of God or totally devoid thereof and, consequently, meaningless. For Traherne, the capacity to see the world as a paradise depends explicitly on Christian revelation. In that respect, he is at one with Newman and, of course, quite distinct from Wordsworth. He differs from Newman, however, in his almost exclusive insistence upon Scripture as the vehicle for that revelation. (It is probably no mere coincidence that he attended Brasenose, that "most puritan" of Oxford Colleges.)[47] "Among other things," he tells us, "there befel me a most infinit Desire of a Book from Heaven";[48] and that book, of course, is discovered to be the Bible. The Bible taught him that to see the world as paradise, to see God in His creation, he must simply, as Herbert says, learn to "spell." "This taught me that those Fashions and Tinsild vanities, which you and I despised ere while, fetching a litle Cours about, became ours. And that the Wisdom of God in them also was very Conspicuous."[49] The Bible taught him how to fetch this "litle Cours about." It taught him that all along there had been "nothing wanting to my Felicity but mine own Perfection."[50] When one's spiritual condition is rectified, when one's soul is enlightened or placed "in paraphrase," he may see the image of God in the world.

It should be fairly clear that the strongly subjective element in Traherne, which we see anticipated in Herbert, stands in direct correlation to these poets' varying degrees of scepticism about the evidence of God in His works. There is no need for a straight or narrow way (epistemologically), no need for a particular vision or special condition of the soul if nature and reason show God *plainly*. If the creation is literally full to overflowing with His glory, the mind can range freely through the whole of it, through the estates of the realm and through all nine concentric, harmonious spheres, with no fear of losing sight of Him. As I said earlier,

46. Traherne, p. 298.
47. White, p. 291.
48. Traherne, p. 278.
49. Traherne, p. 280.
50. Traherne, p. 280.

there are no dark corners in Aquinas's or Hooker's world; consequently, there is no need to search for some single point of light in which man may see. That the later Metaphysicals felt such a need is an indication that as the seventeenth century progressed the "modern note" which Taylor and Herbert sounded was becoming the dominant one. Andrew Marvell could never be said to have belonged to the old tradition, but his sense of the change which was taking place was more accurate, perhaps, than that of any other seventeenth-century poet. The deepening scepticism about the goodness of nature and about the sweetness of man's present life, finds its archetypal statement in "To His Coy Mistress." The poem recapitulates the experience of the century and thus gains its greatness:

> But at my back I always hear
> Time's wingéd chariot hurrying near;
> And yonder all before us lie
> Deserts of vast eternity.

The deserts appear as the division widens between earth and heaven. In them we find the philosophical assumptions of modern philosophy and literature, of the world in which Newman wrote, of the chaos which replaced the "old idea of a Christian Polity."

Between the two epic poems of the English Renaissance, Spenser's and Milton's, we see a contrast which defines exactly the alteration in sensibility and in philosophical attitude which was taking place. Spenser's "Mutability Cantos" were probably written at the same time Hooker was writing the *Laws of Ecclesiastical Polity*, and in them Spenser treats nature in a fashion of which Hooker and his Caroline descendents, as well as his medieval forebears, would have approved. Dame Nature is a being almost divine. She is "far greater and more tall of stature / Than any of the gods or powers on hie."[51] She is clearly not God, but she speaks for Him; in fact Spenser's imagery insists that she be considered as a type of the Incarnation:

> Her garment was so bright and wondrous sheene,
> That my fraile wit cannot devize to what
> It to compare, nor finde like stuffe to that:

51. VII, vii, 5.

> As those three sacred saints, though else most wise
> Yet on Mount Thabor quite their wits forgat,
> When they their glorious Lord in strange disguise
> Transfigur'd sawe; his garments so did daze their eyes.[52]

Moreover, Dame Nature's doctrine is essentially the optimistic one to which the major Caroline theologians subscribed; namely, that even in its mutability, mortality, and constant change, the creation manifests God's glory. In the first place, mutability leads not to our decay but to the dilation or magnification of our being. In the second place, and more important, the natural processes, so far from being meaningless, are so designed by God to lead us to that time when "all shall changed bee,"

> And from thenceforth, none no more change shall see.[53]

The date of *Paradise Lost* links it with the spiritual atmosphere in which the later Metaphysicals wrote, well after Milton's party martyred Archbishop Laud; the contrast with Spenser is striking. Now God no longer speaks in the voice of Dame Nature on Arlo Hill (and notice that Spenser has Donne's and Herbert's sense of the local and domestic), but instead He withdraws His divine influence from the world. The dragon has come, the stars are "blasted" and look "wan," and henceforth instead of holy angels ascending and descending upon the sons of men, Sin and Death will "dominion exercise" on earth and in the air. The natural, external paradise is lost; nature and reason are now so darkened that without the divine help of revelation man can see no reflection of God in His works. Adam and Eve, like Traherne and like Newman, must seek some point of light in the encircling gloom, "a Paradise within thee."[54]

52. VII, vii, 7.
53. VII, vii, 59.
54. Milton's phrase in this context suggests Professor Louis Martz's treatment of the same tendency toward subjectivity in seventeenth-century religious poetry. See *The Poetry of Meditation* (New Haven: Yale University Press, 1954) and *The Paradise Within* (New Haven: Yale University Press, 1964).

PART TWO

The Spirit Afloat

THE quest for a "paradise within," which begins in English literature in the seventeenth century, becomes, by 1798, the dominant impulse in poetry, philosophy, and theology. In fact, it would be no exaggeration to say that the principal effort both of Romantic and Victorian writers (there is no clear philosophical distinction between the two schools) is to work out a new symbolic model of the world,[1] a new mythology for civilization, which will replace the presumably outmoded medieval model and which will be based on what Hegel called "pure interiority." That interiority informs nineteenth-century literature in two distinct ways: first, as we might expect, in a renaissance of Platonist or, more generally, idealist metaphysics and epistemology, and, second, in a conception of history according to which the old forms of religion and society are periodically destroyed and replaced by revolutions in the realm of pure idea. Moreover, there is no great difficulty in discerning the relationship between these two aspects of the new mythology; for if the locus of truth is the mind, nothing external to the mind can be regarded as finally fixed or necessary. Therefore, the constant transmutation of all forms in the flux of history is justified by the demands of temporal circumstance. Thus we see that philosophical scepticism—doubt about the goodness and intelligibility of creation, doubt about the capacity of reason to proceed from things visible to things invisible—breeds idealism, and

1. I am indebted to C. S. Lewis for the idea of "models" in general and of the medieval model and its demise in particular. See *The Discarded Image* (Cambridge: Cambridge University Press, 1964). Hereafter cited as *DI*.

idealism, in turn, brings forth historical relativism and a mythology of revolution.

Newman, in spite of his Catholic orthodoxy, was a man of his times. Though he was, in Dean Inge's words, a "stiff conservative" in matters of dogma, he may legitimately be described as an idealist and a relativist in his philosophy. Inge says that Newman introduced "into the Roman Church a very dangerous and essentially alien habit of thought, which has since developed into Modernism," a habit of thought which "when logically drawn out, must lead away from Catholicism in the direction of an individualistic religion of experience, and a substitution of history for dogma which makes all truth relative and all values fluid."[2] That Newman intended no such "substitution" requires no argument; that he was careful to guard his philosophical position against any such consequences in the realm of dogma we shall demonstrate subsequently;[3] that the tendency of his thought is toward subjectivism and relativism is, however, undeniable. It is that tendency which led him in 1875 to say farewell to "the old idea of a Christian Polity," but it was not a tendency new to his later years. Rather, it lurks just beneath the undeniably conservative surface of the Oxford Movement, and even in those years when Newman was deploring Whiggery and revolution in all its forms, its presence shows him to be a man of his Whiggish and revolutionary times.

Indeed, he was never unaware of his temporal identity. In 1839, in his well-known essay "The Prospects of the Anglican Church," he espouses both the new modes of idealist and relativist thought and the new poetry in which the quest for an inner paradise, the scepticism about nature and reason, was finding its characteristically Romantic expression. The essay deserves attention, for it gives clear in-

---

2. William Ralph Inge, "Cardinal Newman," in *Outspoken Essays* (London: Longmans, Green & Co., 1923), pp. 201–202. Newman was attacked on the same grounds in his lifetime, most notably by A. M. Fairbairn and by Orestes Brownson. Cf. A. M. Fairbairn, "Catholicism and Religious Thought," in *The Contemporary Review*, XLVII (May 1885), 652–674. Newman responded with "The Development of Religious Error," in *The Contemporary Review*, XLVIII (October 1885), 457–469. For an account of the controversy between Brownson and Newman see Daniel R. Barnes, "Brownson and Newman: the Controversy Re-examined," in *Emerson Society Quarterly*, L, supplement (1968), 9–19.

3. Cf. Part Three of this study.

dication that, from several years before he undertook his major theological work, his character of mind was firmly set in the modern
mold. The central argument of the essay is that the "spirit" which
is at work in the *Tracts for the Times* is the matter of great importance; the forms of its expression are of secondary concern. Since the
habitation of "spirit" is mind, heart, or conscience, we are not surprised to hear Newman make a distinction between "spirit" and
"form"—to hear him argue that the liturgical and doctrinal forms
which the Tractarians are defending or instituting are justified, not
primarily by their inherent truth and permanence, not primarily because they are of worth in themselves as forms, but because they do
serve as adequate expressions of religious truth in terms of the times.
Tractarianism is only a manifestation, a form of utterance, and as
such it must be identified historically, in terms of "a when, and a
where, and a by whom, and a how"; but that state of mind which
is the subject of the manifestation, that "spirit" which is antecedent
to and independent of all forms and in relation to which all forms
are mutable and relative, "is in a manner quite independent of things
visible and historical." "It is not here or there; really it has no progress, no causes, no fortunes; it is not a movement, it is a spirit, it is a
spirit afloat, neither 'in the secret chambers' nor 'in the desert,' but
everywhere."[4] It is a spirit which is within us, "rising up in the heart
where it was least expected." It is a state of mind independent of all
external manifestations but capable of expressing itself in a variety of
ways; "it is an adversary in the air, a something one and entire, a
whole wherever it is, unapproachable and incapable of being grasped,
as being the result of causes far deeper than political or other visible
agencies—the spiritual awakening of spiritual wants."[5]

Because the spirit is "afloat," because it dwells in the mind rather
than in forms or institutions, the *Tracts* which attempt to give it a
timely mode of utterance neither counsel a return to the seventeenth
century, to the Middle Ages, nor to Antiquity. Rather, they seek to
embody it in forms of thought and expression appropriate to the
nineteenth century. Therefore Newman claims literary kinship, not
with the orthodox poets of the Middle Ages and the Renaissance, but
with the Romantics. He even goes so far as to maintain that, before
the Oxford Movement began, the "spirit afloat" had found its clearest expression in the work of Scott, Coleridge, Southey, and Words-

4. *Essays*, I, 272.
5. *Essays*, I, 272.

worth.[6] The mission of the *Tracts* is to give that spirit a more complete but no less modern expression than the secular novelists and poets had been capable of. The Tractarians are not "antiquarian fanatics [that is, believers in fixed, traditional forms], urging the ancient doctrine and discipline upon the present age in any other except essential points, and not allowing fully that many things are unessential, even if abstractedly desirable."[7] Among those "unessential things" we may legitimately infer that Newman would include Thomist and Caroline metaphysics and epistemology, the traditional language of English Christian poetry, and many other constituents of the "tradition of fifteen hundred years." With regard to such things, "Let the age acknowledge and submit itself to them in proportion as it can enter into them with heart and reality."[8] In other words, let the "spirit" be the measure of our religion and our poetry, not the inherited forms in which that spirit has expressed itself in the past;

6. The question of Newman's debt to the Romantics is often mentioned, but the treatment of the subject remains largely superficial. However, a few of the more important discussions of the relationship ought to be mentioned. Basil Willey, for instance, compares the *Apologia* to *The Prelude* in his "Introduction" to the World Classics edition of the *Apologia* (London: Oxford University Press, 1964), p. xi; and in his "Newman and the Oxford Movement" [*Nineteenth Century Studies* (New York: Columbia University Press, 1949), pp. 73–101] he discusses Newman's relations to Coleridge at some length and suggests that the Oxford Movement was one manifestation of Romanticism. Graham Hough also explores the connections between Newman and Coleridge ["Coleridge and the Victorians," *The English Mind*, ed. Hugh Sykes Davies and George Watson (Cambridge: Cambridge University Press, 1964), pp. 175–192]. In the same collection of Essays John Beer discusses the question of "Newman and the Romantic Sensibility" (pp. 193–218). Owen Chadwick sees as a common term between Tractarianism and Romanticism the revolt against the age of reason ["Introduction," *The Mind of the Oxford Movement* (London: A. and C. Black, Ltd., 1960), pp. 11–64]. Dwight Culler refers at several points to similarities between Coleridge's thought and Newman's [*The Imperial Intellect* (New Haven: Yale University Press, 1955), pp. 112, 181, 206, 218, 308.], and Wilfred Ward [*The Life of John Henry Cardinal Newman* (London: Longmans, Green & Co., two volumes, 1912); hereafter cited as "Ward"] discusses Newman's literary relations with the Romantics. Perhaps the fullest discussion of the subject is Charles Frederick Harrold's "Newman the Romantic" in chapter X of his *John Henry Newman* (Hamden, Conn.: Archon Books, 1966), pp. 246ff.; hereafter cited as "Harrold."

7. *Essays*, I. 285.

8. *Essays*, I, 285–286.

the idiosyncrasies of theology and worship in each age are the products of the times which produced them, "theological differences of rite, usage, opinion, and argument, which fairly admit of a mutual toleration."[9] The truth is constant, and its dwelling place is the conscience and the heart; the forms of its manifestation change with the changes of the "living busy world."

Such is Newman's statement of his "modernism" in 1839. It binds him to the idealism and relativism characteristic of the secular thought of his day. We should not overlook the fact that he qualified that statement considerably in his work on doctrinal development and religious assent, for he evidently came to see the danger for Catholicism in taking theories of subjectivism and relativism to their logical conclusions. In fact, in a footnote to the 1839 essay in the uniform edition, he confesses that he had taken the principle of mutability too far and "given utterance to a theory, not mine, of a certain *metamorphosis* and recasting of doctrines into new shapes— '*in nova mutatas corpora formas*'—those old and new shapes being foreign to each other, and connected only as symbolizing or realizing certain immutable but nebulous *principles*."[10] Newman would prefer to distinguish between "nebulous *principles*" and "*dogmatic truths*," and with this distinction, as we shall see, he safeguards his relativism and subjectivism against heretical conclusions.[11] It seems safe to say, however, that the distinction, though a valid one, rests more on an arbitrary limitation of a common intellectual principle than on genuine philosophic differences. So far as I can see, it leaves Newman's original distinction between "spirit" and "form" just where it was in 1839; and though he may have accepted the consequences of that distinction in a more gingerly way in later works, there seems little question that he still did accept them.

Therefore, it is incumbent upon us to examine Newman's idealism and relativism more thoroughly than we have thus far and also to show how his thought resembles that of his contemporaries—in particular that of those Romantic poets in whom he found anticipations of Tractarianism.

9. *Essays*, I, 286.
10. *Essays*, I, 288 n. See also "Note on Essay VII," p. 308. It is also worth mentioning that the essentially relativist views in the 1839 essay are also stated in "How to Accomplish It" (1836), in *Discussions and Arguments on Various Subjects*, pp. 1–43; hereafter cited as DA.
11. See below, Chapter X.

❖

CHAPTER IV

Newman's Idealism

W E have hitherto used the term *idealism* loosely. It now be-hooves us to define it more precisely; however, we must recognize from the outset that, in reference to Newman, complete precision is impossible. In fact, it is impossible to give an exact definition to any of Newman's philosophical positions, for he was not a pure philosopher and never wrote with a pure philosopher's consistency; his mind moves more as a poet's or a critic's. For all his training in logic, he was never a systematic logician, and he never worked out a fully consistent system of ideas. In fact, as everyone knows, he distrusted systems. He preferred to think in images rather than in concepts, in terms of the factual rather than the theoretical, the historical rather than the metaphysical. These are truisms among Newman scholars, but they bear repeating as a preface to consideration of his philosophy, lest we should be tempted to look for a greater consistency than we can find. Bergson seems to be quite right when he says that Newman's thought does not achieve full philosophic clarity;[1] and to talk about his "idealism" as though that were, for him, a system-atically developed epistemological category would be to misrepre-sent him.

On the other hand, if we may draw some broad distinctions, it does appear that both Newman's metaphysical and epistemo-logical tendencies are in the idealist rather than the realist

1. Quoted by Maurice Nédoncelle in his *La Philosophie Religieuse de John Henry Newman* (Strasbourg: Société Strasbourgeoise de Librairie, 1946), p. 24. Hereafter cited as "Nédoncelle." Bergson's statement is: "Or une pensée, même géniale comme celle du Cardinal Newman, n'arrive à la pleine clarté philosophique que si elle se situe elle-même par rapport à des doctrines con-nues."

direction. Most of his major commentators agree on this matter, and Newman's own comments on the subject seem to leave little doubt of the fact. Very early in the *Apologia* he speaks of certain "childish imaginations" which had the effect of isolating him "from the objects which surrounded me" and of "confirming me in my mistrust of the reality of material phenomena, and making me rest in the thought of two and two only absolute and luminously self-evident beings, myself and my Creator."[2] A little further on, in commenting on what he had learned from Butler's *Analogy* and from Keble's poetry, he says he embraced "the doctrine that material phenomena are both the types and the instruments of real things unseen."[3] In the same connection, he mentions the similarity between such a view and "what is sometimes called 'Berkeleyism,' "[4] and, though he disclaims Berkeley as an influence on his thought, he does not disclaim the similarity.

As to Berkeley, I do not know enough to talk, but it seems to me, while a man holds the moral governance of God as *existing in and through his conscience*, it matters not whether he believes his senses or not. For, at least, he will hold the external world as a *divine* intimation, a scene of trial whether a reality or not—just as a child's game may be a trial.[5]

He goes on to remark that

to what extent Berkeley denied the existence of the external world I am not aware; nor do I mean to go so far myself (far from it) as to deny the existence of matter, though I should deny that *what we saw* was more than accidents of it, and say that space perhaps is but a condition of the objects of sense, not a reality.[6]

In such remarks, the lack of philosophical consistency is obvious; but equally obvious is the idealist tendency of the thought

2. *Ap.*, p. 18.
3. *Ap.*, p. 29.
4. *Ap.*, p. 29.
5. From a letter to his sister, May 18, 1834; in *Letters and Correspondence of John Henry Newman During His Life in the English Church*, ed. Ann Mozley (London: Longmans, Green & Co., 1911), II, 36. Hereafter cited as "Mozley."
6. Mozley, II, 36.

on the whole. We might say that "for all *practical* purposes" Newman was an idealist; for where the question is of a mode of vision, of philosophic presuppositions which may be only half-conscious, it does not matter a great deal whether one denies the existence of matter, *per se*, or simply that *"what we saw* was more than accidents of it." In either case, the mind rather than the external reality becomes the primary source of knowledge. Berkeley's idealism, in fact any pure idealism, would have been impossible for Newman; no orthodox Christian can deny the existence of matter. On the other hand, there is an idealist tradition in orthodox Christian thought, and Newman, unquestionably, belongs in it. Its most illustrious early proponents were those very Alexandrian theologians who exercised such a great influence on his intellectual youth. In its subsequent developments, it becomes the Augustinian tradition in which matter and the evidence of the senses is never denied but in which the mind itself in its internal perceptions is regarded as the ultimate source of all knowledge. For Augustine, learning is finally remembering, discovering what already exists within the mysterious recesses of the intellect; and in the act of perception it is the mind that directs the senses to their object rather than the object, the external reality, which compels the senses and through them the mind.[7]

The opposing tradition (St. Thomas's) reverses Augustine's teaching and rests cognition on sense perception. The central proposition in Thomist epistemology is that the senses are the source of all our knowledge. It is this tradition in which the major Caroline theologians stand, and we are now in a position to see that Newman's departure from them is, among other things, a repudiation of a realist in favor of an idealist epistemology. The latter is more "convenient" in a sceptical age, for if the "living

7. See, for instance, Book X of the *Confessions;* see also *De Magistro.* For an exhaustive discussion of Augustine's theory of knowledge see Etienne Gilson, *The Christian Philosophy of St. Augustine,* trans. L. E. M. Lynch (New York: Random House and Alfred A. Knopf, Vintage Books, 1967). It is interesting in this regard that Eric Przywara finds in Newman a modern reincarnation of the true Augustinian spirit. Cf. his "St. Augustine and the Modern World," trans. E. I. Watkin, in *Saint Augustine* (Cleveland and New York: World Publishing Co., Meridian Books, 1964), pp. 249–286. Hereafter cited as "Przywara."

busy world" with its external and sensible realities is no longer believed to show God plainly, where will one go in search for Him if not deep into the mysteries of his own mind? There he may be able to find in the world of pure intellect that most Holy Trinity, one God, whom he has been unable to discern amid physical things.

We can define *idealism* in several different senses. The term may refer to an epistemology like that of Plato's, in which man is conceived of as possessing innate ideas or *a priori* knowledge. Or it may be used to define a philosophy like Berkeley's which is much less precise than Plato's with regard to the doctrine of ideas as such but which, in common with Platonic thought, stresses the dichotomy between the intelligible and the sensible. In fact, we might say that the distinguishing characteristic of Berkleyism is that it makes reality dependent upon the mind and reduces what we normally call the real world to illusion. Still again, we may use *idealism* to refer to philosophies of Hegel's, Kant's, and Bradley's sort, which think not so much in terms of Plato's "ideas" as of "the Absolute" but which, like all idealisms, stress the distinction between appearance and reality—the latter, of course, being the character of "the Absolute." Though Newman could not be said to fit any one of these categories exactly, he has certain affinities with all three. As we shall see, he denies the existence of innate ideas;[8] however, as we shall also see, the practical tendency of his philosophy is virtually the same as that which stems from belief in *a priori* knowledge. Unlike Berkeley, he does not deny the reality of the visible world,[9] but he does insist that what is of final epistemological importance is not the external reality in itself but the mind's apprehension of it. Finally, though the Hegelian doctrine of the Absolute forms no part of his philosophy, he does have certain affinities with Bradley, particularly in his acute awareness of the epistemological distinction between reality and appearance.[10]

8. See below, p. 77.
9. See above, notes 5 and 6.
10. Nédoncelle points to similarities between Newman and Bradley: "Pour une âme éprise d'absolu, le monde s'écroule. Inversement, le moi qui accepte

These essentially idealist characteristics of Newman's thought show themselves in all his major theological works, most notably in the *Grammar of Assent*. However, our clearest view of them and of Newman's thought simply as thought, before its theological applications, is in the *Philosophical Notebook*, particularly in the chapter called "Proof of Theism." This essay is dated November 7, 1859, and it belongs to a series of notes, all of which were written between 1859 and 1864. The dating is important, for it indicates, among other things, that these are Newman's mature reflections. Moreover, coming as they do in the dark and relatively silent years between the end of his Irish campaign and the publication of the *Apologia*, they serve both to sum up his prior philosophical development and to prepare the way for his later and more complex treatment of the same issues in the *Grammar*.[11] Therefore, we may feel quite certain that what Newman says in the *Notebook* about matters of philosophy reflects his profound and enduring convictions on the various subjects. In fact, he says of his argument from conscience that "it has been my own chosen proof of that fundamental doctrine [of God's existence] for thirty years past,"[12] and the statement could probably be applied with some reservations to most of the contents of the *Notebook*. For "thirty years past" and more Newman had distrusted the visible phenomena of a busy world and rested instead upon the thought of "two and two only

---

sa prison mondaine et s'y complaît, fait surgir en lui un ensemble d'apparences illusoires dont il est dupe. Bradley fera écho de nos jours à cette doctrine. Certes, le style des anglo-hegeliens n'est pas celui des théologiens d'Oxford. Mais à la *pars destruens* d'*Appearance and Reality* correspond par avance la critique éparse des *Parochial and Plain Sermons*. Après avoir taillé, Bradley est bien obligé de recoudre et rétablir des degrés de réalité. De même, Newman atténue son mouvement premier et destructeur; dans la fantasmagorie, il sait bien qu'il y a l'ébauche d'une solidité. Si parfois il semble prêt à nier l'objectivité du monde, il finit toujours par en reconnaître la valeur de réalité initiale et de stimulation, tout en la déclarant insuffisante et dangereuse pour notre pensée et notre action éprises d'infini." (pp. 33–34).

11. *The Philosophical Notebook of John Henry Newman*, ed. Edward Sillem (Louvain: Nauwelaerts Publishing House, 1969–70), I ("General Introduction to the Study of Newman's Philosophy"), 248–249. Hereafter cited as "Sillem."

12. Sillem, II, 67.

absolute and luminously self-evident beings, myself and my Creator." The contents of the *Philosophical Notebook* serve simply to give a technical shape to that lifelong conviction.

The "Proof of Theism" begins with an exploration of how we know ourselves and how we know God. The arguments are, by now, familiar to all students of Newman's thought, but they are worth recapitulating on account of their epistemological implications. Newman begins by arguing that our consciousness of certain faculties is as intimate and indisputable as our consciousness of our existence. "I am conscious of my own existence. That I am involves a great deal more than itself. I am a unit made up of various faculties, which seem to me parts of my being and to be as much facts as that being itself."[13] Consequently, Newman cannot say, as Ward does, that he has "faith in" these various faculties, such as reason, feeling, or memory, for knowledge precludes faith. He can no more "believe in" reason than he can "believe in" his own existence, for he has a direct and intuitive knowledge of both.

Not only then is it as improper to say I have faith in consciousness, sensation, memory, thought, reason, as to say I have faith in my existence, but of all these improprieties, none is so great as to say I have faith in consciousness, and in reason or reasoning, for reasoning is the very breath of my existence, for by it I know that I exist.[14]

Among those faculties, such as reason, which are bound up with our very being and which are like "the very breath of my existence," Newman includes the *conscience*. He calls it one "of those primary conditions of the mind which are involved in the fact of existence"[15] and which can, therefore, be taken as needing neither faith nor proof to establish its existence. From that point, Newman's familiar "proof from conscience" follows quite simply. " 'Conscience is the essential principle & sanction of Religion in the mind. Conscience implies a relation between the soul & a something exterior, & that, moreover, superior to itself; a relation to an excellence which it does not possess, & to a

13. Sillem, II, 31.
14. Sillem, II, 37.
15. Sillem, II, 43.

tribunal over which it has no power.' "[16] The latter, of course, is God; and the effect of Newman's argument is to prove God's existence from the fact of our own existence and from a faculty which is inseparable from that existence.

Newman's comments on the nature of this "proof" are interesting, for they all suggest what I have been calling the idealist nature of his thought. Its advantage, in Newman's view, is that it depends on nothing external to ourselves; the mind arrives at it without having to rely on syllogisms or on any of the questionable phenomena of the visible world. Such independence is a great advantage to a man who distrusts nature and reason and for whom the world gives "no reflexion of its Creator." The traditional proofs, those which belong to the "Aristotelic-scholastic philosophy," rely without hesitation on the phenomena of the physical creation and on the capacity of the mind to abstract universal truths from those phenomena. Since such methods would never suffice for Newman, he develops instead a mode of proof in which the knowledge of God is given to us immediately and, if you will, "internally"; as inseparable from our knowledge of ourselves. He "would draw a broad line between what is within us and without us."[17] That which is "without" is subject to "the principle of scepticism" and can only be held on faith. That which is within can never be doubted because such things are "prior to faith." We know them rather by something like a "complex act of intuition"[18] in which we grasp our existence, the existence of our faculties and, through one of those, the existence of God. Therefore, we can see why, in the *Apologia*, Newman says that he can no more doubt the existence of God than he can doubt his own being; for the two are apprehended simultaneously in the same subjective or intuitive act of cognition.

Thus Newman praises the "proof" from conscience for being one "common to all, to high and low, from earliest infancy." Moreover, being independent of the visible world, it is likewise

16. Sillem, II, 49–51. Newman quotes here from "*Univ. Serm.* II, 19" (Newman's citation).
17. Sillem, II, 71
18. Sillem, II, 71.

unrestricted by any external circumstances; it can be "carried about in a compact form in every soul."[19] Therefore, such a mode of proof is independent of traditional views and teachings. "The being of a God being once brought home to me [by the proof from conscience]," can then be "illuminated . . . in its various aspects by reflection, tradition, &c."[20] Such "illumination," however, is secondary; our original knowledge of God, the foundation of our religion, does not depend upon tradition. As we have already suggested, one reason why Newman was willing to relinquish the "old idea of a Christian Polity" was because, for him, the knowledge of God and the Christian faith is independent of such a polity. Here, then, is the philosophical explanation of that independence—what we might call the positive side of Newman's "modernism." It is by virtue of the conscience that the knowledge of God can be "carried about in a compact form in every soul." Thus he provides the means of what we might call a "portable" Christianity, admirably adapted to modern man in his temporal and spiritual deracination. If Christians must adapt themselves to modern life, such portability may be an advantage. On the other hand, we cannot fail to see that Newman's proof encourages that very deracination for which in some sense it is designed to compensate; for it eliminates the metaphysical necessities which keep men rooted in a traditional social and spiritual order. It provides for a degree of spiritual independence and, one might almost say, of "individualism," which would be simply impossible for a Thomist, or for Hooker or Laud. Newman declares the mind's independence from "the mere tradition of schools or the superstitions of the nursery";[21] whereas it is in these very sources of traditional wisdom that his medieval and Caroline predecessors, rooted as they were in time and place and in the apprehensions of the senses, sought the knowledge of God.

We are now in a position to say in what sense Newman can legitimately be called an idealist. As to the three categories I suggested above, it should be clear in what way and to what

19. Sillem, II, 67.
20. Sillem, II, 63.
21. From Newman's "Elements of Thought," Sillem, II, 25.

extent the proof from conscience fulfills each. It is obvious that, for Newman, as for Berkeley, reality is dependent on the mind. Newman does not deny that the external, visible world exists; but he does consider its existence as being subject to the principle of scepticism and therefore an object of faith, rather than of knowledge. On the other hand, the mind's knowledge of itself and of its faculties, and through them the knowledge of God, is immediate and intuitive. It should be clear, by the same tokens, that Newman resembles Hegel and Bradley in his careful distinction between appearance and reality; the senses provide the former, the conscience provides the latter, and it is the conscience on which Newman depends. Finally, as to the matter of innate ideas, we are now in a position to see that the practical tendency of Newman's theory is virtually the same as that which issues from genuine Platonism; that similarity, however, demands further comment.

Edward Sillem, in his commentary on the *Philosophical Notebook*, says that Newman "developed a philosophy of mind conceived not as the faculty of pure ideas, nor of ideas abstracted from sense data, but of mind as the power of knowing existent beings."[22] "The faculty of pure ideas" is the Platonic doctrine of knowledge; "ideas abstracted from sense data" provides a description of the Aristotelian-Thomist epistemology. It is obvious that Newman did not accept the latter view, and Sillem is correct in maintaining that he abjured the former as well. In fact, Newman lumps together "innate ideas" with the "tradition of the schools" and the "superstitions of the nursery" and rejects all three as essentially unsatisfactory explanations of cognition.[23] In other words, Newman's concept of ideas, strictly speaking, is neither Platonic nor Aristotelian; but its effect, its tendency, is closer to the former than the latter. The reason is that, though Newman denies an idea of God planted, *a priori*, in the soul, to which we recur in recollection or contemplation, in withdrawal from the world and from the experience of the senses, nevertheless, what Sillem calls a philosophy of "mind as the power of knowing existent beings" places its emphasis on the power of

22. Sillem, I, 75.
23. Sillem, II, 25.

the knowing mind, rather than on the existent beings which are the objects of its knowledge. In other words, the difference between Newman's view and that of a pure Platonism is not in where we seek God, but how He got there. Both philosophies look into the mind, and both find God there. Hence, both scorn, in varying degrees, the knowledge of the senses. The believers in innate ideas, however, say that we find Him without recourse to sense impressions because He planted an idea of Himself in the innermost recesses of the intellect and that the discovery of that idea requires a withdrawal from sense activity. Newman, on the other hand, says we find Him without recourse to sense impressions because the conscience which apprehends Him works independently, both of the senses and of the material world which they apprehend. From one point of view, the difference is of considerable importance, but the two philosophies are alike in this respect—that in both it is the subjective apprehension of God which serves as the foundation of our religious experience, and in neither is the knowledge gained from sense experience of the living, busy world of any final importance. Therefore, it seems to me reasonable, as I suggested above, to say that Newman is "for all *practical* purposes" an idealist; for the issues of his philosophy are very nearly identical with the issues of traditional idealism.

It should now be clear in what respect Newman's reliance upon the conscience as the foundation of his epistemology unites him with his nineteenth-century contemporaries. On account of it, he shares with them a highly subjective mode of vision, and when we use that phrase we imply that, for the person in question, reality and meaning are finally states of mind, conditions of the subject, rather than of the external object. It is interesting in this regard that medieval usage generally reversed our current meanings of the terms *subjective* and *objective*. If we were speaking as the Schoolmen spoke, we should use the adjective *subjective* to refer to those qualities or attributes which a thing possesses in itself, those qualities which are inherent in the subject and which have their being independently of the mind's apprehension of that subject. Thus the greenness of a tree is subjective, a quality or property belonging to the tree, to the subject as it exists in itself. On the contrary, according to medieval usage, those properties or attributes of a thing are objective when they belong to a thing only as that thing is presented as an object to the mind. By way of illustration the *Oxford English Dictionary* gives Occam's argument that *"Universale non est aliquid reale habens esse subiectivum nec in anima nec extra animam, sed tantum habet esse obiectivum in anima et est quoddam fictum habens esse tale in esse obiectivo, quale habet res extra in esse subiectivo."*[24] The modern reversal of the terminology is interesting, for it suggests that the mind has come to be thought of as pre-eminently the subject of all experience and that all external realities have been reduced to mere objects.[25] In other words, the bias of the modern connotation is idealist, at least in the general sense in which we have been applying the term to Newman, and Occam's denial of the subjective reality (in the old sense) of universals is an important step in the modern direction.

Newman's use of the terms is consistently the new one and is one link, though he was probably not conscious of it, between his theology and modern thought. In another passage from the *Philosophical Notebook,* Newman says that the "Objects of Consciousness," are "my impressions, sensations, judgments, affections, imaginations &c."[26] In other words, our consciousness is not primarily an experience of things external to us, either physical or spiritual things, but rather of those faculties such as the conscience whose apprehension is inseparable from the apprehension of our existence. The mind is conceived as living, so to speak, on its own terms, as being fed, not by things, objects (subjects) external to itself, but upon the judgments, affections

24. Sent. I, Dict. 2, qu. 8E.
25. See, for instance, Jacques Maritain, *The Degrees of Knowledge,* trans. Gerald B. Phelan (New York: Charles Scribner's Sons, 4th ed., 1959), p. 91, n. 1: "In this case [reference to his own proper Thomist usage of 'object'], the word 'object' is taken in the strictest scholastic sense (formal object). It is superfluous to point out that in current modern language it has received a very different meaning inasmuch as the opposition of *objective* to *subjective* has finally made the values proper to 'thing' or the 'real' pass on to the object."
26. From Newman's "On the subject-matter [objects] of Consciousness," in Sillem, II, 79.

and sensations by which it reacts to those objects but which are still the products of its own activity. Such a conception does not deny the existence of the external reality, but it does suggest that its importance lies not in itself but in the mind's apprehension of it, that it is the mind which bestows subjectivity upon it. Thus, as Newman says, "I am not conscious of the object[ive] reality, but of the subjective sensation or impression."[27]

The last statement, taken out of context, does not *demand* an idealist epistemology, but in Newman's case the emphasis is in that direction. At first glance, Aquinas himself seems to be saying nearly the same thing in his doctrine of "intelligible species"—those images which exist altogether on the intellectual level and by which "the intellect comes to be in act."[28] These seem to be *subjective* in the modern sense and would appear to correspond to Newman's "subjective sensation or impression." Aquinas insists repeatedly, however, as Newman does not, that the subjective image, the "intelligible species," depends directly for its existence on the "sense image" which produces it, and that human intellection is impossible without the apprehension of "things" in the external creation which the senses give us. "In the present state of life in which the soul is united to a passible body, it is impossible for our intellect to understand anything actually, except by turning to the phantasms [or sense impressions]."[29] Moreover, where Newman seeks a direct subjective awareness of God which is independent of the visible world, "two and two only absolute and luminously self-evident beings, myself and my Creator," Aquinas maintains that it is only by knowing the "natures of visible things" that the intellect "rises to a certain knowledge of things invisible."[30] Hence the "sense images" drawn from a real, objective, physical creation are the only foundation for our understanding of God. Newman's po-

27. Sillem, II, 79–81.
28. *Summa Contra Gentiles*, I, 53. All citations of the *Summa Contra Gentiles* are to the Image Books edition (New York: Doubleday & Company, Image Books, 1955–1957). Hereafter cited as *CG* and by book and chapter.
29. *Summa Theologica*, I, 84, 7. Hereafter cited as *ST*. All references to the *Summa* are to the translation by the Fathers of the English Dominican Province (London: Burns, Oates & Washbourne, 1920–1925), except where citations are made of the Latin text.
30. *ST*. I, 84, 7.

sition is very much like what St. Thomas calls Plato's error; namely "considering only the immateriality of the human intellect, and not its being in a way united to the body." Plato "held that the objects of the intellect are separate Ideas; and that we understand not by abstraction, but by participating things abstract."[31] Though Newman does not admit a doctrine of "separate" or immaterial Ideas, his theory of knowledge and his proof from conscience amount virtually to "considering only the immateriality of the human intellect, and not its being in a way united to the body." Newman, in effect, ignores the mediation of the senses and the foundation of metaphysical knowledge in "things." In Thomism, on the other hand, the "intelligible species" or the "subjective sensation or impression," though a fact and a real stage in the process of understanding, is never separable from the objective world and never in itself or in isolation the foundation of our knowledge of invisible realities. It would be interesting to see how Newman would have commented on these passages in Aquinas. Since he did not,[32] we can only speculate that, without repudiating them (which was not his way, especially with the saints), he might well have "platonized" them as he did Aristotle's *Poetics*.

The matter could be pursued at length. Suffice it, for the present, to repeat that, without committing himself to a systematic development of idealist thought, Newman moved generally in that direction. That he did so explains why the subjective tendencies of a purely idealist epistemology find their way into his work, even though he did not accept a conventional doctrine of innate ideas. It also explains why Newman found it relatively easy to make terms with modern thought; for a "compact" knowledge of God, independent of time and place, or of "angels and men in a wonderful order," a knowledge "carried about" in each individual soul, is the same in the nineteenth century as in the thirteenth or seventeenth. Whether men write *Summas* and build gothic cathedrals or whether they pursue industrial and technological power in an ugly, democratic, secular world makes no ultimate difference to such knowledge. Therefore, Christians

31. *ST.* I, 85, 1.
32. For further consideration of the relations between Newman and Aquinas, see below, Chapter VIII, n. 93.

are free to make their peace with the times in which they live, nor is there any "base compromise" in doing so; for whatever those times may be like, they can neither damage nor enhance the individual's subjective, intuitive knowledge of God.

From such considerations, we begin to see why Newman was so quick to acknowledge the Romantic poets and novelists as predecessors of the Tractarians; for, as I shall now attempt to show, they anticipate his epistemology and likewise his distinction between "spirit" and "form," between truth subjectively apprehended and its modes of objective utterance in the living, busy world.[33] Before we can understand those similarities fully, however, we must first examine another set of relationships: Newman's debt to the Christian schools of ancient Alexandria, in particular to the theology of Clement and Origen. There are two reasons for this detour: in the first place, Newman learned his philosophy initially from the Alexandrians, rather than from the Romantics; and in the second place, even after he had recognized the similarities between his own philosophy and that of his contemporaries, he continued to interpret his own idealism and that of his age primarily in terms of those Alexandrian categories. Our necessary first step, therefore, is to acquaint ourselves with those categories.[34]

33. There are also striking similarities in epistemology between Newman and his Victorian contemporaries. See, for instance, Jefferson B. Fletcher, "Newman and Carlyle: an Unrecognized Affinity," *Atlantic Monthly* XCV (1905), 669–679; Henry Tristram, "Two Leaders—Newman and Carlyle," *The Cornhill Magazine*, LXV, series 3 (1928), 367–382; Walter J. Ong, "Newman's Essay on Development in its Intellectual Milieu," *Theological Studies*, VII (1946), 3–45; Edward F. Jost, "Newman and Liberalism: the Later Phase," VNL, No. 24 (Fall 1963), 1–6; David J. DeLaura, "Matthew Arnold and John Henry Newman: the 'Oxford Sentiment' and the Religion of the Future," *Texas Studies in Literature and Language* VI (1965), 573–702; and David J. DeLaura, *Hebrew and Hellene in Victorian England: Newman, Arnold, and Pater* (Austin and London: University of Texas Press, 1969).

34. At least two of Newman's commentators allude to the same set of relationships—between the idealist bias of his thought, the influence of the Alexandrians, and his affinity with the Romantic poets. See Louis Bouyer, "Newman et le Platonisme de l'ame Anglaise." *Revue de Philosophie*, VI new series (1936), 285–305, and Thomas Vargish, *Newman, the Contemplation of Mind* (Oxford: The Clarendon Press, 1970), pp. 17 and 100ff. Hereafter cited as "Vargish."

✤

CHAPTER V

Newman and the
Alexandrian Fathers

NEWMAN'S first serious examination of the relationship between subjective and objective realities, between ideas and things, begins in 1825 with his studies of the Church Fathers. The first fruit of that study is the *Essay on the Miracles of Scripture* written during 1825 and 1826. Central to the book is the "idealist" distinction between the sensible and the intelligible, with a strong insistence upon the primacy of the latter. Newman speaks of the two modes of existence as "two systems, the Physical and the Moral, [which] sometimes act in union, and sometimes in opposition to each other."[1] In the latter circumstance, when the moral system intrudes upon the physical, the intelligible upon the sensible, the consequence is what we call a miracle.

We should note from the first that though Newman grants that these two systems "sometimes act in union," the weight of his emphasis is placed on those circumstances in which they interrupt each other or conflict with one another. Moreover, he thinks always in terms of the relative obscurity of the moral system to the physical eye; indeed, the quality of wonder which attaches to miracles lies partially in the fact that "while writers expatiate so largely on the laws of nature, they altogether forget the existence of a moral system." Actually, says Newman, the latter, could we recognize it, "is as intelligible in its laws and provisions as the material world."[2] However, because we are blinded by things sensible and material—because we rely upon our senses rather than upon our consciences and upon the other faculties of

---

1. *Two Essays on Biblical and on Ecclesiastical Miracles*, p. 17. Hereafter cited as *Miracles*.
2. *Miracles*, p. 16.

our souls—we find it difficult to understand or even believe in moral and spiritual realities. Therefore we must learn to recognize that sensible and material objects are symbols of moral and spiritual truths, forms which represent or embody those truths, but which are clearly distinct from the truths themselves.

However, if the physical creation is a symbol, it is by no means a clear or obvious one. The creation may show God but never *plainly*. We must apprehend Him, and the whole "moral system," subjectively, in our consciences, before we can recognize Him and the moral order in the visible world. In the *Apologia* Newman characterizes the "broad philosophy" of Clement and Origen as being "based on the mystical or sacramental principle." They "spoke of the various Economies or Dispensations of the Eternal. I understood these passages to mean that the exterior world, physical and historical, was but the manifestation to our senses of realities greater than itself."[3] The key word here is *economy*; it suggests both showing and hiding at once. In talking about the relationship between the physical and the moral systems and the ultimate subordination of the former to the latter, Newman speaks of the "economy of nature" in which "a Miracle is a deviation from the subordinate for the sake of the superior system."[4] In *The Arians of the Fourth Century* he goes into considerable detail in his discussion of the economy, and he uses the word in two senses. When it is applied strictly to the interpretation of Scripture, economy is the principle of "accommodation to the feelings and prejudices of the hearer, in leading him to the reception of a novel or unacceptable doctrine."[5] In this sense, the principle applies primarily as an exegetical technique, nor does this sense of the term concern us except in so far as it is related to another and broader sense in which the terms *economy* and *symbol* become virtually interchangeable. Used in this latter and broader sense, the principle of the economy is manifest in the dealings of God with man. Just as Christians, in teaching scriptural truths to the heathen, temper the wind, economically, to the shorn lamb, so God does in showing Himself to men. Thus

3. *Ap.*, p. 36.
4. *Miracles*, pp. 17–18.
5. *The Arians of the Fourth Century*, pp. 71–72. Hereafter cited as *Arians*.

nature and history come to be considered less as physical realities in their own right than as symbols for the spiritual truths which they at one and the same time reveal and veil. Nature and history, the whole "physical system," are to be considered as "Economies or dispensations, which display His character in action, [and] are but condescensions to the infirmity and peculiarity of our minds, shadowy representations of realities which are incomprehensible to creatures such as ourselves."[6]

From these metaphysical premises, certain epistemological conclusions follow, and all of them are in accord with the idealist tendencies of Newman's thought. In a realist epistemology of Aquinas's sort, there is no difficulty in regarding the senses as the source of all knowledge, for the objects of sensible experience are real and contain in their actuality traces of the Holy Trinity. The intellect, itself an image of that Trinity, may then, in its normal processes of abstraction, recognize those traces and move from them to a knowledge of God Himself. In such a process no special or arcane gift is necessary. However, when "the phenomena of the external world" cease to be thought of as realities in their own right and become merely "a divine mode of conveying to the mind the realities of existence, individuality, and the influence of being on being,"[7] then the role of the intellect increases in importance. It must no longer simply respond, according to its nature, to what is given; it must, in some sense, do the giving. Nature remains a veil unless the intellect brings with it its prior knowledge of God; only then can it recognize God within and beyond that veil. If nature and history are parables, as Newman says, they demand interpretation and explanation. In fulfilling that demand, the intellect bears very nearly the whole responsibility for the vision of God in creation. For "most men," who fail to exercise that special capacity of intellect, the "physical system" beguiles them "with a harmless but unfounded belief in matter as distinct from the impressions on their senses."[8] To escape that beguilement, to read correctly an economical manifestation of spiritual reality, we must be

6. *Arians*, p. 75.
7. *Arians*, p. 75.
8. *Arians*, p. 75.

prepared to recognize that our subjective understanding rather than the objective fact is the ultimate source of the truth.

In a pure idealist or "innatist" philosophy such as Plato's, it is the knowledge of the Ideas which equips the mind to interpret the parable. For Clement and Origen, though the Ideas form part of their system, the key for interpreting the sensible world is the revelation of God in the Incarnation. Charles Bigg makes this point quite clear from very early in his lectures on the Alexandrians: that "all knowledge must rest ultimately on the same small group of Axioms, which cannot be proved, as the Greek understood proof."[9] These axioms are the exclusive property of Christian revelation, and it is only in the light which they shed that God can be seen in His works. Their effect upon the mind which receives them in faith is to render it capable of moral and spiritual perception. Such an intellect might be said to possess Christ and therefore to be in a position to perceive Him economically in the physical creation. On the other hand, to the uninstructed mind, to the intellect in which the knowledge of Christ has not been formed by faith in revealed truth, the interpretation of the economy is impossible, and the creation which manifests God so gloriously to the enlightened remains opaque. Bigg, therefore, concludes that in Alexandrian idealism "there is . . . no third term between a self-communication of the Divine and absolute scepticism";[10] for it is the "self-communication" and only that which can make "natural theology," the knowledge of God drawn from nature and reason, a possibility.

These alternatives need to be emphasized, for it is common to think of the "broad philosophy" of the Alexandrians as a great deal broader than it really is. The consequence for Newman studies has been to lead unwary readers (I speak from experience) into the notion that, on account of his devotion to Clement and Origen, Newman took a brighter view of nature and the secular world than he actually did. Thomas Merton's com-

9. Charles Bigg, *The Christian Platonists of Alexandria, The 1886 Bampton Lectures* (Oxford: The Clarendon Press, 1968), p. 87. Hereafter cited as "Bigg."

10. Bigg, p. 87.

ment on the school of Alexandria is a typical one, namely, that Clement understands the Resurrection triumph as a victory which leads to "a true, pure, serene love, filled with compassion, able to discover and to 'save' for Christ all that is good and noble in man, in society, in philosophy and in humanistic culture. This is the greatness and genius of Clement, who was no Desert Father";[11] as if to say that he was, instead, the father of Christian humanism. That, at least, is the fashion in which both Clement and Origen have often been read, and no doubt, in one sense, they were humanists. If so, however, they were humanists of quite another sort from either St. Thomas Aquinas and the Scholastic philosophers or from Hooker and the Caroline divines.[12] The medieval synthesis, to which Hooker's Anglicanism belongs, embraced the "human," not in an economy, but directly; not with a doctrine of strenuous division, but with a firm belief in the manifest harmony of all creatures. If Thomas Merton emphasizes more heavily than he should the humanist character of Alexandrian teaching, at the same time, in another passage, he comes to terms with the very factor which distinguishes Alexandrian theology from that of the medieval and Renaissance schools. For Clement, Merton says, "without the light of Christ man is little more than a 'fowl fattened in the dark for the butcher's knife' and his life is practically without significance. But 'in Christ,' on the contrary, everything is significant, everything comes to life, even the most simple and ordinary task acquires a spiritual and supernatural dimension."[13] In other words, nature, which Christ made and sustains by laws of his own institution, appears in herself of little or no worth. She comes to have worth, or to be seen as having worth, only when the mind of the Christian is flooded by the light of revelation.

The obvious difference between such a position and that of Aquinas, Hooker, Andrewes, or Laud is that for the latter, though

11. Thomas Merton, "Clement of Alexandria," in Clement of Alexandria, *Selections from "The Protreptikos,"* ed. Thomas Merton (New York: New Directions, 1962), p. 2. Hereafter cited as "Merton."

12. G. K. Chesterton makes a strong case for Aquinas's "humanism" in his *St. Thomas Aquinas* (London: Hodder & Stoughton, 1956).

13. Merton, pp. 7–8.

of course it is still true that without Christ there is no salvation, the "light of Christ" is never conceived in a subjective or idealist fashion as it is by the Alexandrians. It is not simply the light of the mind but rather a metaphysical light which suffuses the visible creation, whereby God is manifested, objectively and externally, in His works. Thus these later Christian humanists are in a position to embrace nature and reason, history and secular learning, as those realities are in themselves, not simply as they are refined and interpreted by the initiated intellect. For St. Clement, secular learning and the goods of nature are of value, but only to the "gnostic," the man who possesses the true Christian gnosis, which is the knowledge of God in Christian revelation. He alone possesses the capacity to see beyond the veil of visible things to things which are intelligible.

For instance, in his *Exhortation to the Greeks,* Clement might be said in one sense to be embracing pagan learning and to be saving for Christ the goods of the natural order. On the other hand, the presupposition of the whole book is that the pagan inheritance is not good as it is in itself, but only in so far as the gnostic is able to perceive the good in it. It is "the light of truth, the Word," which will "break the mystic silence of the dark prophetic sayings, by becoming good tidings."[14] Christ is "the door," in the sense that He is our way into understanding. "And I know well that He who opens this door, hitherto shut, afterwards unveils what is within, and shows what could not have been discerned before, except we had entered through Christ, through whom alone comes the vision of God."[15] Without the gnostic vision man invariably falls into superstition, for the visible things of the world, though they are indeed signs or images of God, do not give up their truth save to the enlightened eye. "Trusting solely to sight, [the heathen] gazed at the movements of the heavenly bodies, and in wonder deified them, giving them the name of gods from their running motion."[16]

---

14. *Exhortation to the Greeks,* trans. G. W. Butterworth, in *The Loeb Classical Library* (Cambridge: Harvard University Press, 1960), p. 25. Hereafter cited as *Exhortation.*

15. *Exhortation,* p. 27.

16. *Exhortation,* p. 53.

The consequence of such blindness is what Clement calls "the stupidity of custom."[17] He attacks the traditionalists who maintain "it is not reasonable to overthrow a way of life handed down to us from our forefathers." Such conservatism Clement thinks absurd: "Why then do we not continue to use our first food, milk, to which, as you will admit, our nurses accustomed us from birth?"

Again, in voyages by sea, deviations from the usual course may bring loss and danger, but yet they are attended by a certain charm. So, in life itself, shall we not abandon the old way, which is wicked, full of passion, and without God? And shall we not, even at the risk of dis pleasing our fathers, bend our course towards the truth and seek after Him who is our real Father, thrusting away custom as some deadly drug?[18]

From a Thomist or Caroline point of view, such a statement begs one major question. It assumes, without proving it, that "the old way" is necessarily "without God" and that the interests of "our fathers" and of "our real Father" are at odds with one another. From St. Clement's point of view, Lancelot Andrewes would no doubt seem to be begging another question in his argument against the Puritans in behalf of English Christmas customs; for Bishop Andrewes makes the contrary assumption, that God is clearly manifest in the natural order and in all its fruits, including the inherited customs of civilization, pagan as well as Christian. Between these two unvoiced assumptions lies a philosophical distance which is so great that it might almost be said to define the outer limits of Christian thought with regard to the *visibilia*. It is the difference between Aristotelian conservatism and Platonic radicalism, between the acceptance at its face value of what is and is visible as good and the imposition on creation by the mind of what either is not present in or is invisible in the world of matter. The former view accepts all things which are, for *being* is God's signature; the latter would annihilate "all that's made, / To a green thought in a green shade."

The process of annihilation, the abjuring of custom, is ele-

17. *Exhortation*, p. 9.
18. *Exhortation*, p. 197.

mental to the gnostic vision as Clement conceives it. The point is made again and again in the *Stromateis*. As we have seen, the truth is hidden in visible things by economy or in a "mystery." The gnostic's role, as we have also seen, is to perceive, "invent" (in the old sense) or interpret that truth, but this he does, neither by embracing the sensible objects in which the truth is immured nor by exercising the senses of his body in apprehending those objects, but rather by "unswerving abstraction from the body and its passions." "And is not, on this account, philosophy rightly called by Socrates the practice of Death?"[19] Not by living in the "world's body" according to sensible and visible things (and all "custom" exists in the sensible, visible and concrete) but by "abstracting all that belongs to bodies and things called incorporeal [such as physical light], we cast ourselves into the greatness of Christ, and thence advance into immensity by holiness."[20] The consequence of this abstraction, this "practice of Death," is Clement's renowned *eclecticism*. He is willing to accept his inheritance of pagan custom only on the condition that he, as the Christian gnostic, can pick and choose, that he can pluck out the kernel of truth from the husks of those sensible and corporeal entanglements which hide it save to the enlightened mind. "Philosophy, then, consists of such dogmas found in each sect (I mean those of philosophy) as cannot be impugned, with a corresponding life, collected into one selection."[21] Only on such terms is he prepared to defend philosophy against the charges of those who said that it was of the devil, or to argue that God gave philosophy to the Greeks as a special covenant with them.[22] Therefore, when all has been said that may

19. *The Miscellanies* (or *Stromateis*), trans. William Wilson in *The Writings of Clement of Alexandria* (Edinburgh: T. & T. Clark, 1869), II, 261. Hereafter cited as "Clement."

20. Clement, II, 264. It is worth mentioning that when Aquinas speaks of *abstraction*, he means something quite different from what Clement means by the word. In Thomist philosophy it is necessary to abstract "intelligible species" from sensible objects, but the process does not entail, as it does for Clement, a denial of the validity of sense impressions. In fact, as we have already seen (*ST*, I, 84, 7 and 85, 1), exactly the contrary is true.

21. Clement, II, 335–336.

22. Clement, II, 342.

legitimately be said in behalf of Clement as the "serene" lover
of nature and human learning—Clement, an Alexandrian, "not a
Desert Father"—the fact remains that the way to God, for him,
is a subjective, internal way, a practice of death and of the death
of custom, a way of breaking and exile. "For thoroughly a
stranger and sojourner in the whole of life is every such one,
who, inhabiting the city, despises the things in the city which
are admired by others, and lives in the city as in a desert."[23]

On all these matters Origen echoes Clement directly. In fact,
Bigg conceives of Origen as being more strenuously consistent in
his idealism than Clement was. Whereas Clement embraced an
allegorical or economical reading of Scripture, in part, at least,
because it was the tradition of the Apostles and the earlier Fathers,
Origen's reason "never rests till it has brought the particular
affirmation under the scope of some all-embracing law."

To him Allegorism is only one manifestation of the sacramental mystery of Nature. There are two heavens, two earths—the visible is but
a blurred copy of the invisible. The divine wisdom and goodness,
which are the cause of both, are in this world of ours distorted by
refraction arising from the density of the medium. Yet they may be
discerned by those that have eyes to see.[24]

When Bigg uses the word *sacramental* in reference to nature he
follows the Alexandrian practice. Newman uses the term in the
same sense, and we should remember that in that sense it is
virtually interchangeable with *economical* or *symbolic*.[25] The
relations between Origen's two heavens and two earths, the visible
and the invisible, are sacramental in that the visible realm of
being manifests, though only darkly and partially, the invisible.
We see how close Origen's concept is to Newman's idea of two
systems, one physical, one moral, and we may also see that Newman conceives of miracles as being sacramental or economical in
precisely the sense in question. It follows that the seven sacra-

23. Clement, II, 462.
24. Bigg, pp. 172–173.
25. For instance, see *Ap.*, pp. 36–37.

ments of the Church are really just special cases of a general rule, a point to which Newman alludes in the *Apologia* when he speaks of "Holy Church in her sacraments" being "after all but a symbol of those heavenly facts which fill eternity."[26] It should also, now, be clear that Newman, Clement, and Origen agree as to the obscurity of those symbols. The gnostic may discern them, but only he; only "those who have eyes to see."

We should never mistake such a phrase in Origen as "two heavens, two earths," for a mere figure of speech. He taught such a doctrine in a literal way, and one can easily understand that the passages in which he describes the "supercelestial sphere," the "good land," would have come like "music to [the] inward ear"[27] of a young man who had already learned to distrust the present world. Origen denies "certain imaginary forms which the Greeks call 'ideas.' For it is certainly foreign to our mode of reasoning to speak of an incorporeal world that exists solely in the mind's fancy or the unsubstantial region of thought." Though it does not exist simply as idea, however, it does exist invisibly and is known by the mind rather than by the senses; "there is no doubt, however, that the Saviour alludes to something more glorious and splendid than this present world, and invites and exhorts all who believe in him to direct their course towards it." That world may be widely "separate from this [one] in space," or it may in some way be "contained within the limits of this world" and be distinguished from it, not spatially, but by excelling this one "in quality and glory." These matters are uncertain, but there seems no uncertainty about the existence of that other world. Origen thinks it is to this which Clement refers "when he says 'The ocean, which is impassable to men, and the worlds beyond it.' "[28] Nor is Origen disposed to doubt what "some" maintain: that beyond the sphere of the fixed stars "there is another; and that, just as in our system the heaven contains all things that are under it, so this sphere, with its immense size and indescribable span, encloses the vast extent of all the other spheres

26. *Ap.*, p. 37.
27. *Ap.*, p. 36.
28. Origen, *On First Principles*, trans. G. W. Butterworth (New York: Harper Torchbooks, 1966), p. 90. Hereafter cited as *First Principles*.

in its yet more magnificent circuit, so that all things are within it as this earth of ours is under the heaven."[29]

Thus we see that we have literally "two heavens, two earths," and "just as there is a heavenly Jerusalem and Judaea, and no doubt a people dwelling therein who are called Israel, so it is possible that near to these there exist certain other places, which apparently are called Egypt, or Babylon, or Tyre or Sidon."[30] Thus whatever we read in Scripture must be understood as referring not only to this world but to the supercelestial one as well; in fact, more fully and truly to the latter than to the former. For the "present visible world" was not instituted as a good thing in its own right but, as St. Paul says, " 'the creation was subjected to vanity, not willingly, but by reason of him who subjected the same in hope.' " To Origen, St. Paul's statement means that the visible world, the "natural system," was instituted as a place of purgatorial cleansing "for those souls which on account of their excessive spiritual defects required these grosser and more solid bodies and also for the sake of those others for whom this arrangement was necessary that the present visible world was instituted."[31] It is upon this theory of two worlds that Origen's heretical doctrine of the pre-existence of souls and his very strange and equally false idea of the Incarnation is based. Needless to say, Newman shunned Origen's heretical conclusions; in fact he has very little to say about them. It is quite clear, however, that Origen's philosophic speculations contributed, if not in detail, at least in ethos or quality to Newman's concept of the visible world as being important primarily as a symbol or economy of the *invisibilia*. Both shared the same intense belief in the primacy of the latter.

The fullest exposition of Origen's system is in his *Commentary on the Song of Songs*. Here we see the sacramental or economical principle applied to the interpretation of literary symbol, and the consequence of the application is that we discover within the images what is not visible at all to the uninitiate or to the unpracticed eye. We discover, not this world of visible things, but

29. *First Principles*, p. 91.
30. *First Principles*, p. 303.
31. *First Principles*, p. 241.

that other heaven and earth, that other Jerusalem which, if we know how to see subjectively, shows itself economically through the forms of this one.

Paul the apostle teaches us that the invisible things of God are understood by means of things that are visible, and that the things that are not seen are beheld through their relationship and likeness to things seen. He thus shows that this visible world teaches us about that which is invisible, and that this earthly scene contains certain patterns of things heavenly.[32]

As we have shown, the Scholastics and the Carolines all quote the same Scripture to generally the same effect, but in the last analysis the mode of showing which either Hooker or Aquinas conceives is quite different from that which Origen proceeds to describe. For Aquinas, the visible things have concrete reality and are important in themselves. They show God *plainly*, not in an economy, but on the principle of the analogy of being. For Origen, the thing or subject, in itself, is relatively unimportant and shows God as through a glass darkly. We are concerned with the *visibilia* primarily because they are steps from which we "mount up from things below to things above, and . . . perceive and understand from the things we see on earth the things that belong to heaven."[33]

On the other hand, this perceiving and understanding, this mounting up, is not an easy matter open to all who read or see. In fact, Origen considers it dangerous for those who lack the requisite capacity for sacramental or mystical vision to read the *Song of Songs* lest they be misled by a natural or corporeal interpretation and fall into lust. "But it behoves us primarily to understand that, just as in childhood we are not affected by the passion of love, so also to those who are at the stage of infancy and childhood in their interior life . . . it is not given to grasp the meaning of these sayings."[34] We are led into a grasp thereof by divine Wisdom itself, and we should not forget that Origen

32. Origen, *The Song of Songs, Comentary and Homilies*, trans. R. P. Lawson (London: Longmans, Green & Co., 1957), p. 218. Hereafter cited as *Song of Songs*.

33. *Song of Songs*, p. 218.

34. *Song of Songs*, p. 22.

is thoroughly orthodox in understanding scriptural allusions to Wisdom as referring to God the Son or to the Word of the Father. That Word by whom all things are made, when He informs our minds and souls, opens the eyes of our understanding to grasp the sacramental or economical meaning of all those things which are made. Origen's position on this aspect of the matter is virtually identical with St. Clement's. It is a high doctrine of the "soul in paraphrase"; it is by the Wisdom of God, who is God Himself, that we are enabled to mount up to a vision of "the good land." Hence, he relies heavily on passages from the Wisdom literature in developing and explaining his concept of images: "and this, perhaps, is what the writer of the divine Wisdom means by saying: *For He hath given me the true knowledge of the things that are . . . and all such things as are hid and manifest have I learned*"; "and he doubtless shows by this that each of the manifest things is to be related to one of those that are hidden; that is to say, all things visible have some invisible likeness and pattern,"[35] which Wisdom reveals to the gnostic. Even "the creation of the world itself, fashioned in this wise as it is [i.e. economically], can be understood through the divine wisdom, which from actual things and copies teaches us things unseen by means of those that are seen, and carries us over from earthly things to heavenly."[36]

It would be easy to cite numerous other examples of the same basic ideas in Origen, but the matter of central importance is sufficiently illustrated from those passages which we have already examined; namely, that Newman clearly found in him an idea of the relationship between the physical and moral systems, the visible and invisible worlds, which appealed to him strongly. Of course, if we are to speak technically, as pure philosophers, we must admit that Newman's theories of knowledge and belief differ from the Alexandrians' at several points. Neither Clement nor Origen offers a "Proof of Theism" from the intuitive grasp of our mental faculties, and Newman never expounded the doctrine of two heavens and two earths in Origen's exhaustive fashion. Moreover, St. Clement's "gnosticism" is more strictly

35. *Song of Songs*, p. 220.
36. *Song of Songs*, p. 223.

intellectual, less involved with feeling, less "intuitive," than New-man's concept of mind. These things, however, they do hold in common: the reality of an invisible world and the fact that that reality, in one way or another, is grasped subjectively. For all three, the believer surveys the living, busy world, not as one sub-missive to the perceptions of the senses, but as one who brings to the visible creation his prior, intelligible, or ideal knowledge of the Creator, one who can thereby understand the economical or sacramental function of nature.

Because of these similarities, Newman's study of Clement and Origen strengthened in him the conviction held from earliest childhood; that there is a

really perfect knowledge which is beyond this world, which is engaged in intellectual objects, and upon those more spiritual, which eye hath not seen, nor ear heard, nor the heart of man conceived, before they were made clear to us by our Great Teacher, who reveals the holy of holies, and still holier truths in an ascending scale, to those who are genuine heirs of the Lord's adoption.[37]

Such a vision seems also to have been evident to Newman in Romantic fiction and poetry, for like many of his contemporaries he seems to have discerned in the new literature a "deeper philosophy," a more profound sensibility, than that which had informed the realist and rationalist character of eighteenth-century philosophy and poetry. Moreover, if the mysticism and idealism of Romantic thought was new from one point of view, it was also, from another, very old; if radical, also reactionary. It had characterized the most ancient schools of Christian phi-losophy; now, after centuries of "realism" and "rationalism," it was reasserting itself. A "majestic river," dammed "till it has become a flood," was being freed.[38] The theology of the Fathers belonged to the torrent. The Tractarians, as Newman conceived them, were moving on the crest of the released tide, but Scott, Coleridge, Wordsworth, and Southey had anticipated and con-tributed to its liberation.

37. *Arians*, p. 89.
38. *Essays*, I, 272.

✤

CHAPTER VI

Newman and Coleridge:
The Whole Man Reasons

TO turn directly from Clement and Origen to Coleridge and Wordsworth is to see why Newman recognized an affinity between the Patristic theology and modern poetry and why his early love of Antiquity prepared him to accept the subjectivism and relativism of "modern thought." I cite Wordsworth and Coleridge in particular, for of the four poets whom Newman mentions in the 1839 essay only these two give serious attention to epistemological and metaphysical questions. Newman evidently recognized that fact. Scott, he says, set before men "visions, which, when once seen, are not easily forgotten," and he stimulated "their mental thirst";[1] but it is to Coleridge, in spite of his indulgence in "a liberty of speculation which no Christian can tolerate," that Newman ascribes "a philosophical basis" for Catholic principles. Similarly, Newman distinguishes between Southey and Wordsworth as between a master of "fantastic fiction" and a poet characterized by "philosophical meditation." It is to that "philosophical basis" and that "philosophical meditation" that I now turn—first to Coleridge and then to Wordsworth.[2]

Newman read Coleridge for the first time in 1835. By then he had been acquainted with the Fathers for a decade and had given several years to the serious study of them which issued in the *Arians of the Fourth Century*. From them he had worked out his own characteristic approach to theology, and it is interesting that

1. *Essays*, I, 268.
2. *Essays*, I, 269.

when he read Coleridge against such a background he was surprised that so "much I thought mine" was to be found there.[3] Newman's familiar comment is usually glossed, and appropriately so, with notices of similarities between his and Coleridge's views on inference and assent. What is not generally mentioned is how much of what Newman found in Clement and Origen is also to be found in Coleridge; how much there is in common between the "idealism" of the ancient Alexandrian school and that which Coleridge preached at Highgate. So far from recognizing the similarities, at least one of Newman's most distinguished commentators sees a distinct antithesis between the Patristic and the Romantic influences on his thought. C. F. Harrold says that what Newman learned from the Church Fathers saved him from the sort of vague "nature-mysticism" which was being taught by Wordsworth and Coleridge. Whereas the Fathers place their emphasis upon the vast gulf which separates man and nature from God, the visible world from the invisible, according to Harrold, the romantic poets muddle the two and become very nearly Pelagian in the process. "Newman is thus an un-Romantic insofar as he fought the implicit or explicit Pelagianism of his day."[4]

There can be no doubt that there is, in a loose sense of the term, a Pelagian strain in both Coleridge and Wordsworth. It seems to me, however, that Harrold has overemphasized it and in doing so has missed the striking similarities between Coleridgean, Wordsworthian, and Patristic philosophy. Certainly in the prose work of the mature Coleridge one encounters the same distrust of the visible and natural world and of the evidence of the senses, the same heavy reliance upon the supernatural, invisible, and intelligible, and consequently the same basis for a doctrine of economies or sacraments which Newman found so compelling in the school of Alexandria. In fact, so striking are these similarities that one is led to conclude that it is this idealist strain in Coleridge, more perhaps than similar views on assent,[5]

3. Mozley, II, 35, n. 1.
4. Harrold, p. 253. See also Harrold's essay, "Newman and the Alexandrian Platonists," *Modern Philology* XXXVII (1939–1940), 279–291.
5. Of course the two are closely related.

that led Newman to associate him with the "spirit afloat," of which Catholic doctrine was allegedly a "just expression."

Nor are we left altogether to speculation on this matter. If we return to the 1839 essay, we find, embedded in Newman's discussion of the age's "new character of mind," the well-known comment that "Poetry then is our mysticism." The remark rises from Newman's view that mysticism and poetry both have the capacity "to draw men away from the material to the invisible world."[6] Had Newman said no more than that on the subject, his context would have made the meaning obvious; for it is the context which defines what he means by "mystical." In speaking of the Alexandrians, Newman uses the adjective "mystical" almost interchangeably with "economical" and "sacramental"; all three describe the drawing away "from the material to the invisible world." The "mysticism" of the early ages of the Church, manifested in such treatises as Origen's on the *Song of Songs*, has been replaced in our "practical" times by poetry which tends to move men's minds in the same, ideal, supernatural, or mystical direction. And who are these poets? Obviously, among others, Wordsworth and Coleridge.[7] Therefore, we conclude that the statement, "Poetry then is our mysticism," considered in context, amounts to a fairly clear identification in Newman's thought between the philosophical presuppositions of certain modern poets and those of the Church Fathers.

Newman went further than that, however; he made the identification explicit. When he makes the statement in question, he has just been explaining and illustrating the principle of the economy, the "calculus," as he calls it here, whereby things invisible and eternal are translated into visible, temporal, and hence perceivable terms. The genius of the early Church is expressed above all else in its employment of this principle, in its embodiment of eternal truths in economical symbols.[8] In fact, the whole passage in the essay is a résumé of what he has said on the subject in the *Arians*. He then proceeds to a view of his own times, and

6. *Essays*, I, 291.
7. As we would expect, Newman's primary example is Keble, in the *Christian Year*. See *Essays*, I, 291.
8. *Essays*, I, 288–290.

he says that the weakness of Christianity "in our age" derives, at least in part, from the forfeiting of the economical or mystical principle in the name of practicality. Where the Church in its early centuries "adopted a mystical religion," in the nineteenth century it has embraced a "literal" one. "How, then, in our age are those wants and feelings of our common nature satisfied, which were formerly supplied by symbols, now that symbolical language and symbolical rites have almost perished?" The answer, of course, is that "poetry . . . is *our* mysticism" and that poetry "has in modern times . . . taken the place of the deep contemplative spirit of the early Church."[9]

In light of such a comparison, it is interesting to note, though Newman does not, that the common presence of an idealist or mystical strain in Alexandrian philosophy and Romantic poetry is by no means simply an accident. There is a demonstrable link in the history of ideas between the English lakes and Alexandria; Plotinus and the other principal neo-Platonists are the common term. The latter were, themselves, the secular progeny of the Alexandrian Church, and we know that, both directly and through the translations of Thomas Taylor, such important poets as Blake, Wordsworth, Coleridge, and Shelley were influenced by them— by Plotinus, Porphyry, and others.[10] As I say, Newman makes no allusion to this historical connection, nor is there any positive indication that he was aware of it. So far as I know, he was neither familiar with Thomas Taylor nor with Wordsworth's and Coleridge's indirect debt to Clement and Origen. However, it is interesting to consider the possibility that he may have associated these modern poets with Tractarian Catholicism because of an instinctive recognition that they did, in fact, owe a great deal to the same philosophical tradition on which he and the other tract writers were nourished. Or, to take a slightly different view of the matter, we might suggest that similar philosophical and religious pressures in early nineteenth-century England

---

9. *Essays*, I, 290–291. Italics mine.

10. For a good discussion of this matter and, in particular, of the role of Thomas Taylor see Kathleen Raine's "Thomas Taylor in England," in *Thomas Taylor the Platonist*, ed. Kathleen Raine and George Mills Harper (Princeton: Princeton University Press, 1969), pp. 3–48.

pushed Newman, Coleridge, and Wordsworth in parallel directions. Both the new Catholics and the new poets were re-
acting against what they considered to be a desiccated and
secularized realist philosophy; in the Church against what Newman calls "cold Arminianism" and Latitudinarianism; in society
as a whole, against Benthamism and political economy. Both
turned to forms of idealism, of Platonism in a broad sense, and
both, in one form or the other, embraced the mystical or sacramental principle as a mode of vision. The great difference between them lies in the fact that Newman turned to a Christian-
ized Platonism, which nourished his belief in the autonomy of
conscience, while Wordsworth and Coleridge accepted a secularization of that same, earlier Christianization, a system of thought
which placed less emphasis upon ethical imperatives and upon the
knowledge of God.

In spite of these distinctions in theological emphasis, however,
the philosophical similarities among the three schools—the
Alexandrian, the Newmanian, and the Coleridgean—are more
striking than their differences; and, in particular, Coleridge's neo-
Platonist idealism is remarkably like Newman's Christian idealism
or subjectivism. Both men distrust the senses and what the senses
reveal. Both believe very strongly in a sharp division between the
visible and invisible worlds, between what Newman in the
"Essay on Scripture Miracles" calls the physical and moral systems. Both would agree that a theology such as Paley's, which depends on evidences drawn from the lower system, will be thwarted
in its ultimate purpose and aim. That purpose, the end of any
theology, is to pierce the veil of nature and to apprehend that
within which eye hath not seen nor ear heard. Coleridge's
idealism, as we would expect, is more radical than Newman's, but
the basic direction is the same. In fact, when Newman speaks of
a "harmless but unfounded belief in matter as distinct from the
impressions on [men's] senses,"[11] and when he courts Berkeleyism
with the statement that "space perhaps is but a condition of the
objects of sense, not a reality,"[12] he is not far from Coleridge's
statement that "the highest perfection of natural philosophy

11. *Arians*, p. 75.
12. Mozley, II, 36.

would consist in the perfect spiritualization of all the laws of nature into laws of intuition and intellect."[13] The "*husk*," says Coleridge, must drop off, and "the phaenomena themselves become more spiritual and at length cease altogether in our consciousness."[14]

Also, Coleridge maintains a theory of symbolism which resembles the economy very closely. In both systems, the visible, sensible realities are to be regarded as symbolic representations of the invisible or intelligible world, and, in both cases, the translation of the symbol, the transcending symbol to reality symbolized, is reserved for the man who possesses the requisite capacity for spiritual vision. Newman might possibly have had the following passage from Coleridge in mind when, in 1839, he drew the analogy between the principle of the economy and that of mathematical calculus: "the optical phaenomena are but a geometry, the lines of which are drawn by light, and [with reference to recent scientific theories] the materiality of this light itself has already become matter of doubt."[15] As geometric shapes represent invisible truths, so in analogous fashion do all visible phenomena. In other words, the physical creation is related to the invisible world in a "mystical," "economical," or "sacramental" fashion. Where Newman drew his terminology from Clement and Origen, Coleridge derived his from Plotinus, but on the matter of symbolism or the economy the effect is very nearly the same. According to Plotinus, as Coleridge interprets him, "the highest and intuitive knowledge as distinguished from the discursive" allows men "within themselves" to "interpret and understand the symbol."[16] There is a world of sense; there is also a world of spirit. (One is reminded, immediately, of Origen's two heavens and two earths, of Newman's moral and physical systems.) Our "organs of sense are framed for a corresponding world of sense; and we have it." Similarly we have "organs of spirit" which "are framed for a correspondent world of spirit."

13. *Biographia Literaria*, ed. J. Shawcross (London: Oxford University Press, 1958), I, 175. Hereafter cited as *BL*.
14. *BL*, I, 176.
15. *BL*, I, 176.
16. *BL*, I, 166–167.

Those organs of spirit Coleridge calls collectively "the philosophic imagination." When a man puts that faculty to its proper use, he enables himself to "interpret and understand the symbol."[17]

On the other hand, when the "philosophic imagination" lies in abeyance, the symbol loses its power to symbolize. Coleridge seems to imply that it still conveys invisible reality, but, lacking the capacity to interpret its meaning, man loses any benefit he might otherwise gain from it. Under those circumstances, the "noblest treasures" of a man's being "are reported only through the imperfect translation of lifeless and sightless *notions*."[18] Such a man is in the condition which Origen fears: that of the person who, resting in the economical representation rather than in the invisible reality, in the parable itself rather than in its meaning, reads Scripture with only this heaven, this earth, this flesh in view. Such a man may be drawn into lust by the *Song of Songs*. Moreover, these "lifeless and sightless *notions*" immediately call to mind Newman's distinction between the *notional* and the *real*, whether in apprehension or assent. As we have seen, it is in reference to the *Grammar of Assent* that Newman and Coleridge have been compared most frequently, but it should now be clear that those similarities in theories of belief rest on prior similarities between theories of cognition. For both men, notions are the fruit of syllogistic abstraction and are not to be compared in their effectiveness with the reality of direct apprehension. Newman considers some notions to be abstractions from invisible or intelligible truths; thus the doctrine of the Trinity is a notional derivation from what the Scriptures reveal about the Father, the Son, and the Holy Ghost. For the most part, however, he speaks of the notional as an abstraction from the visible or sensible, from the physical as opposed to the moral system. Thus the man who rests in a mere notion of God which is drawn from "evidence" has failed to make the ascent from the economy to the reality. The latter seems unquestionably to be Coleridge's sense. The presence of "lifeless and sightless *notions*" is an indication of spiritual blindness, the failure of the "philosophic imagination."

17. *BL*, I, 167.
18. *BL*, I, 168.

He contrasts "sightless notions" to "the IMMEDIATE"; "shadowy abstraction" to the "living and actual truth."[19] We must remember, however, that the *immediate* and the *real* are not visibly and physically but invisibly and spiritually so.

In connection with these distinctions between the real and the notional, we must consider Newman's and Coleridge's similar views of reason. Coleridge distinguishes between *reason* and *understanding*, and he considers the distinction rudimentary to all sound philosophy.[20] He does so, however, in such a fashion as to reverse the traditional Scholastic usage. For the Schoolmen it is the intellect or understanding (*intellectus*) which is the higher faculty of the rational soul and which serves to grasp those metaphysical first principles which lie beyond the range of mere reason (the ratio). The latter is the syllogistic process which depends upon the understanding for its antecedents. For Coleridge, it is exactly the other way around: reason (*ratio*) is the higher faculty, understanding (*intellectus*) the lower. Nor do the differences end there. Reason for Coleridge is more nearly a faculty of mystical apprehension than is the Scholastic *intellectus*. If we are justified, as I believe we are, in using "reason" and "the philosophic imagination" interchangeably, it appears that reason, for Coleridge, is inseparably connected with the Platonist and idealist presuppositions of his metaphysics. Hence, "reason" provides a quasi-mystical or, perhaps, idealist transcendence of the sensible. Its consequences are a real or immediate rather than notional apprehension. For the Schoolmen, on the contrary, the mind always works by a process of abstraction, and though in one sense it may be said to transcend the evidences of the senses, we must remember that it is always rooted in "sense images." Even in its grasp of "first principles," the Thomist *intellectus* can scarcely be regarded as a faculty capable of mystical apprehension; for those principles which it grasps serve less as sources of knowledge in themselves than as the foundation for subsequent abstractions from sense images. Thus, for Aquinas, the senses retain their supreme importance as the foundation for spiritual knowledge, and that is because in Thomist realism the visible or sensible

19. *BL*, I, 168.
20. *BL*, I, 109–110.

world manifests the invisible, not economically, but in the reality of its own contingent being: *"Philosophus probat, quod principium nostrae cognitionis est a sensu."*[21] Coleridge's periodic use of Thomist terms is likely to blind us to the radical differences between the former's idealism and the latter's realism.

Newman seems never to have embraced the scholastic terminology at all. However, his distinction between *implicit* and *explicit* reasoning is analogous to Coleridge's between *reason* and *understanding* and St. Thomas's between *intellectus* and *ratio*.[22] All three men agree upon the functions and the limitations of the secondary power: Newman's *explicit reason*, Coleridge's *understanding*, and St. Thomas's *ratio* all signify the logical or syllogistic activity of the soul. When we consider, however, the "higher" activity—*implicit reason, reason,* or *intellectus*— Coleridge and Newman both offer an idealist or neo-Platonic interpretation which contradicts St. Thomas's meaning. In Thomist thought, as we have just mentioned, the work of the intellect in apprehending first principles complements rather than supersedes the work of the reason in the process of abstraction. For Newman, on the other hand, the implicit reason is the activity of supreme importance, for which the explicit reason serves primarily as a mode of expression. The implicit reason moves mysteriously and deep within the invisible recesses of our psyche, like a "clamberer on a steep cliff," who proceeds by guess and intuition rather than by rule and who cannot, subsequently, map his progress.[23] The explicit reason has little or no autonomy but serves primarily for that mapping—to record, economically, what the superior activity has apprehended. For Coleridge, the reason's operation is equally mysterious; for reason, "contemplated distinctively in reference to *formal* (or abstract) truth," is that *"spirit* of the regenerated man, whereby the person is capable of a quickening inter-communion with the Divine

---

21. *ST*, I, 84, 6. For Latin citations of the *Summa* I have relied on the Blackfriars' edition, ed. Thomas Gilby *et al.* (London: Eyre & Spottiswoode, 1964–).

22. Cf. "Implicit and Explicit Reason," *Fifteen Sermons Preached Before the University of Oxford*, pp. 251–277. Hereafter cited as OUS.

23. *OUS*, p. 257.

Spirit."[24] Reason, thus considered, is "pre-eminently spiritual, and a spirit, even *our* spirit, through an effluence of the same grace by which we are privileged to say Our Father!"[25]

Likewise, in its end or purpose, Newman's implicit reason, like Coleridge's reason or philosophical imagination, is conceived as a mystical or intuitive power. The end of Coleridge's reason is the immediate apprehension of the invisible truth within the visible symbol or economy; that of Newman's implicit reason is *assent* or *certitude*. I take it that the two ends are analogous. In any event, they have this much in common: that both are states of mind which are ultimately independent of external reality or of abstractions from sense images. The Coleridgean reason, the "highest and intuitive knowledge as distinguished from the discursive," allows men, *"within themselves"* to "interpret and understand the symbol."[26] Similarly, certitude, as Newman defines it, is something "within themselves." In that respect, it is distinct from *certainty* which depends on sensible or syllogistic evidences. "Certitude was a state of mind, certainty the quality of a proposition." The implicit reason ranges mysteriously over "convergent probabilities" in order to arrive at certitude, but certitude, once gained, is independent of the probabilities which contributed to it. It exists as a "state of mind" independent of external reality and of sense images, as a subjective or idealist, as opposed to an objective or realist, state of knowledge.[27] In other words, the process of believing is analogous

24. *Aids to Reflection* (London: George Bell and Sons, 1904), p. 143. Hereafter cited as AR.

25. AR, p. 144.

26. BL, I, 166–167; italics mine.

27. See canceled passage from original manuscript of the *Apologia*, printed by Svaglic; *Ap.*, p. 498. Newman makes the same distinction, though not so fully, in the portion of the text from which the passage was canceled: "I considered that Mr. Keble met this difficulty by ascribing the firmness of asent which we give to religious doctrine, not to the probabilities which introduced it, but to the living power of faith and love which accepted it" (p. 30). See also the full treatment of this matter in the *Grammar*, pp. 262–263, and see below, chap. IX. The matter is also treated extensively in the correspondence, both in the letters to William Froude [*Cardinal Newman and William Froude, A Correspondence* (Baltimore: The Johns Hopkins Press, 1933)] and in many other letters as well. One particularly good statement of Newman's position is to be found in a letter to Frank Scott

to that of knowing. In either activity, the movement of the "highest and intuitive" faculty is from the symbol or economy (the evidences or probabilities) to the reality which lies within or beyond the symbol, to the intuitive knowledge or certitude of which the probabilities are a kind of economical or symbolic manifestation or preparation. Certitude, like the knowledge of ideal truth, is the kernel within the nut, that which is left when Coleridge's reason or Newman's implicit reason has stripped off the husks.

We have been considering thus far the link between Newman and Coleridge almost exclusively in terms of their common inheritance from the schools of Alexandria and of the probable consequence of that inheritance, their common idealism and subjectivity. However, the foregoing remarks on the nature of reason suggest, at least implicitly, another similarity or philosophical bond between them: a modification or development of the traditional neo-Platonism that they inherited. Our key to understanding this modification is Newman's substitution of conscience for St. Clement's "gnosis." The effect of that substitution is to shift the emphasis from the mind as such, the faculty which apprehends pure ideas, to the whole composite of faculties—"consciousness, sensation, memory, thought, reason"[28]—which constitutes a man's existence as man. Thus Newman teaches that we apprehend God not through the exercise of pure mind in grasping the idea of Him but by a "complex act of intuition"[29] whereby we seize upon Him in the very act by which we apprehend our own existence. Both modes of cognition, the Platonic and the Newmanian, are equally subjective; therefore, both stand at the opposite epistemological pole from Thomist realism. Newman differs from the Platonists, however, in thinking of the apprehending subject as being emotional and imaginative as well as simply intellectual.

Thus he argues that the "whole man reasons." And the corol-

Haydon (April 1858) in *The Letters and Diaries of John Henry Newman*, ed. C. S. Dessain (London: Thomas Nelson and Sons, 1968), XVIII, 333–336. Hereafter cited as *Letters and Diaries*.
28. Sillem, II, p. 37.
29. Sillem, II, p. 71.

lary of that familiar dictum is that no man reasons quite like any other man, simply because no man *is* quite like any other man. On the intellectual level, as pure minds, we are presumably all alike. Our sensations, consciousnesses, and memories, however, distinguish us from one another, and once these faculties are admitted to function in the act of knowing God, their diversity prevents any one man's apprehension of God from being exactly like that of any other. Thus Newman argues that according to God's providence, each human being takes his own way to certitude, "a way which cannot be analyzed or generalized by science" and "that neither the means nor the measure of truth which fitted one man fitted another."[30] From these corollary propositions proceed two principles which we might label the principles of *totality* and of *individuality*, that of the wholeness and that of the distinctiveness of each human being in his subjective apprehension of divine truth. Neither principle, so far as I can see, forms a part of traditional idealist thought, but both are characteristics of the ethos of the early nineteenth century.

Both principles arise from the introduction of feelings and sensations into traditional idealist epistemology, that of "totality" most obviously so. As we have just said, when the "whole man reasons," the heart—the passions, sensations, the conscience—as well as the mind is involved. It is interesting in this regard that neither Newman nor Coleridge pay much attention to the traditional hierarchical division of the soul according to its faculties, and, for both, the higher faculties of the mind gain their power not so much by liberating themselves from the bondage of those lower faculties as by deliberately recognizing and employing them. This is particularly true of the conscience, which, for Coleridge as well as Newman, is deeply involved with the feelings of the heart. The conscience gives warm, passionate convictions about right and wrong, not cold, intellectual certainties. In this emphasis upon the passions, both Newman and Coleridge reverse not only the Scholastic but the older neo-Platonist epistemology. It seems no exaggeration to say that the common European assumption about intellection from Plato and Aristotle

30. *Ap.*, p. 498.

until almost Newman's day, whether in idealist or realist thought, was that the capacity of the mind to apprehend metaphysical truths grows in direct proportion to the mortification of the passions. Certainly for Clement and Origen, contemplation is a pure activity of the mind, whereas for Newman and Coleridge it is as much involved with feeling as with thought. Thus Coleridge is at one with the Tractarians in disliking mere "rational systems." He would agree not only with Newman but also with Keble, Pusey, and Froude that the Church must recapture an understanding of "the *heart,* the *moral* nature" of man and recognize that these are "the beginning and the end." "Speculative systems" blind us to our intuitive or mystical perceptions, to that subjective knowledge which is the end or purpose of the reason or philosophic imagination. "This was the true and first apostasy—when in council and synod the Divine Humanities of the Gospel gave way to speculative Systems, and Religion became a Science of Shadows under the name of Theology, or at best a bare Skeleton of Truth, without life or interest, alike inaccessible and unintelligible to the majority of Christians."[31]

This "affective" modification of traditional, neo-Platonic idealism is interesting, for it suggests one reason why both Newman and Coleridge found the principal theologians of their day, both High-Churchmen and Latitudinarians, so very "dry" and "cold." Not only are these "Arminians"—both orthodox and heretical—epistemological realists; they are also in bondage to what Newman calls the "rationalistic temper."[32] Not only do they rest their theology on the outer "husks" of things rather than on the mysterious, inward, and invisible realities; they also deny the heart. Clement, Origen, or even Plotinus might have objected to Paley or Whately (or to Aquinas or Hooker for that matter) on the former ground, but certainly not on the latter. The involvement of the "whole man" in the act of cognition, the identification of heightened sensation with mystical intuition, of the *imagination,* in the new Coleridgean sense, with the philosophic activity of the mind—these are signs of Coleridge's and Newman's

31. AR, p. 126, from "Aphorism IV" on "Spiritual Religion."
32. For instance, see "On the Introduction of Rationalistic Principles into Revealed Religion," in *Essays,* I, 30–99.

times and would have appeared strange indeed to those very
Platonist forebears upon whom in other respects they relied so
heavily.

It is interesting to consider the intellectual origins of the theory
of the "whole man." Professor Claude Finney, who knows as
much as any modern scholar about the neo-Platonic tradition in
English poetry, says that Coleridge and Wordsworth grafted traditional neo-Platonism on to Hartley's theory of sensation and
association. The "negative side" of traditional neo-Platonism is
its denial of the passions and of sense experience.[33] The
"positive side" is its "spiritual affirmation."[34] Professor Finney
cites Prospero's "insubstantial pageant faded" as a good example
of the former, Spenser's *Four Hymns* as instances of the latter.
Clement or Origen might well have interpreted the poetry in
question in a similar fashion. When we turn to Wordsworth and
Coleridge, however, we find that the relationship between the
negative and positive aspects of the experience has undergone an
alteration; for Wordsworth "reared a structure of mysticism upon a
foundation of empiricism."[35]

The consequence of that "rearing" is that where "the older
mystics, both Platonic and Christian, attained unto a state of
ecstasy or spiritual vision by a discipline of fasting and contemplation" Wordsworth and his contemporaries attempted to do so
"by means of physical sensations."[36] Thus "sensations of beauty
. . . stimulating his emotions, would lead him into a state of
spiritual vision."[37] One might say that the "whole man," "the
heart, the *moral* nature" moves us into "that serene and blessed
mood," in which "we are laid asleep / In body, and become a
living soul." This moment might be regarded as analogous to the
moment of real assent, in which the "living intellect," involving
the heart with all its affections and passions, comes to rest in
certitude. It is certainly analogous to that moment in Coleridge

33. Claude Lee Finney, *The Evolution of Keats's Poetry* (Cambridge:
Harvard University Press, 1936), I, 293. Hereafter cited as "Finney."
34. Finney, I, 294.
35. Finney, I, 295.
36. Finney, I, 295.
37. Finney, I, 296.

when the "speculative system" is transcended by a true theology of the heart. The *Biographia Literaria* seems to bear out Professor Finney's thesis, for the first several chapters describe a deliberate effort to fuse Hartleyism and idealism. If Newman was not a disciple of Hartley, the fact remains that he would probably have recognized there, as he did in Coleridge, much which he had thought his own. (In fact, it would be interesting to interpret the movement of Newman's mind in the *Apologia* in Hartleyan terms.)[38] Moreover, though Newman fasted and prayed as conscientiously as any of the "older mystics," the ascetic disciplines were not factors in his epistemology.

Thus we see how the fusion of sensationalism and idealism, whatever its merits from the standpoint of pure philosophy, sheds light on the principle of totality in Newman's "proof" from conscience and in his theory of assent. It should be clear also how it is related to the principle of individuality; for, as we have pointed out, no "whole man" is quite like any other "whole man." In a system such as Aquinas's it is possible to lay down universal principles of epistemology, for the intellect is the form of man, matter the principle of individuation. Thus, on the level of the intellect, what applies to one man applies to all. But if the "heart" is involved, if the senses and the imagination function in an inseparable union with the intellect, if, in fact, intellect might be said not to exist at all except perhaps nominally, merely as a way of labeling the whole man in the process of intellection, then general rules cease to apply. The truth, which is the object of intellection, is fixed and constant; metaphysically, of course, Newman was an absolutist. On the other hand, God, "in His superintending providence, took man by man, each in his own way, a way which cannot be analyzed or generalized by science, and supplied the means of certitude suitable to each."[39] It appears to follow from such a position that to know the truth *really* rather than *notionally*, we must not only shun the Thomistic abstractions from sense images, we must also concentrate upon the character, personality, and history of the knower. In

38. Edward Sillem has suggested that Newman learned a theory of "Associationist Psychology" from Abraham Tucker; cf. Sillem, I, 122ff.

39. *Ap.*, p. 498.

other words, we must be not only subjective but also individual- '
istic. Thus from the principles of totality and of individuality
proceeds the necessity for biography or autobiography; for we
can only apprehend that "serene and blessed mood" in which
the husks of things drop away and the economy is transcended,
when we approach it in the subjective experience of a mind for
whom that condition has become a reality. On this matter, also,
Coleridge and Newman agree, and so, needless to say, does
Wordsworth.

✤

CHAPTER VII

Newman and Wordsworth:
The Growth of a Poet's Mind

IN no aspect of his character of mind is Newman so distinctly a man of his times as in his emphasis upon autobiography. Though he did not say with Carlyle, at least not in so many words, that history is biography, he does come very close to insisting that metaphysics and even dogmatic theology are biography. The truth is to be apprehended subjectively; its locus is the mind of man, or to be more exact, the unity of experience which constitutes each person as an individual human being. Therefore, to talk about the truth one must have recourse, not to the systematic exploration of ideas, but to the story of a soul's life and its progress toward the truth. "I gain more," he says, "from the life of our Lord in the Gospels than from a treatise de Deo."[1] In the same vein, he confesses that one reason for his particular devotion to the "Ancient Saints" is that they "have left behind them just that kind of literature which more than any other represents the abundance of the heart, which more than any other approaches to conversation; I mean correspondence."[2] And correspondence, of course, is a form of autobiography. Those "Ancient Saints" "mix up their own persons, natural and supernatural, with the didactic or polemical works which engaged them." They avoid the coldness of "speculative systems." "Dogma and proof are in them at the same time hagiography. They do not write a *summa theologiae,* or draw out a *catena,* or pursue a single thesis through the stages of a scholastic disputation. They

1. *Historical Sketches,* II, 217. Hereafter cited as *HS.*
2. *HS,* II, 221–223.

wrote for the occasion, and seldom on a carefully-digested plan."[3]

The opposing terms here are the "abundance of the heart" and "scholastic disputation." It is the former which is the signature of the whole and unique man in his progress to truth and hence of the truth itself. In light of such assumptions it is not surprising that Newman's apologia should also be his autobiography. In an epistemology such as his, this mixing of the polemical and the personal is inescapable. Walter Houghton has examined that relationship in the *Apologia* in some detail, but not in terms of the philosophical background which we now have before us.[4] Consequently, it seems to me that he has failed to recognize what we might call the philosophical *necessity* of Newman's rhetorical mode; that the technique of autobiography is fully as necessary to Newman's epistemological premises as the technique of the *Summa* is to Aquinas's. In both cases, the reigning philosophical disciplines find themselves a form. Moreover, it seems unlikely, had any ingredient in Newman's thought been removed, that the form would have remained the same. Had Newman's idealism been the traditional Platonist idealism of Alexandria, unmodified by "modern" theories of association and sensation, the concept that "the whole man reasons" would never have developed, and the history of the whole man's implicit reason would never have been considered necessary.

Nor does that necessity extend merely to the fact of autobiography, but also to its particular shape. The *way* in which the whole man moves toward the truth appears to be just as germane to apprehending that truth as the fact that he moves at all, and it is at this point in the discussion that purely literary considerations obtrude themselves. That is because the movement of the mind is voiced in the symbolic structure of the language which recounts that movement. Thus we see that the symbolic structure of nineteenth-century poetry, both Romantic and Victorian, is radically different from that of any English poetry which had preceded it, because a new movement of the mind

3. HS, II, 223.
4. Cf. Walter E. Houghton, *The Art of Newman's "Apologia"* (New Haven: Yale University Press, 1945). Hereafter cited as "Houghton."

demanded new symbols for its expression. Newman thinks and writes in those new symbols because they express for him, as they do for Coleridge and Wordsworth, the necessities of his philosophical existence. "Newmanism" is not only the name of a new sensibility in English theology: it is also the name of a new mode of expression. In the very shape of his symbols, in the autobiographical structure of his compositions, in the patterns of his rhetoric, his break with the medieval past and his essential subjectivism and relativism are manifest. Thus we are not surprised to find in the *Apologia* all the earmarks of nineteenth-century spiritual autobiography. Its shape is determined by two movements: that of loss and that of gain, of exile and homecoming, of sickness and return to health, of destruction and reconstruction. In short, the *Apologia* is the account of Newman's "imagination and taste, how impaired and how restored."[5] An idealist epistemology, modified by a sensationalist psychology, finds expression in the two movements and consequently in the rhetorical and symbolic structure which is their product.

To understand how this is so, we must recognize that belief in an invisible reality which is to be apprehended subjectively always leads to breaking and destruction in the process of that apprehension. The veil must be torn back so that the invisible world behind it may be seen; the nut must be cracked, the husks pulled off, to get at the kernel. Of course, the veil or shell of sensible and visible things, of laws, customs, reasons, and ecclesiastical establishments, may also serve as an economical or symbolic representation of the realities which lie within or behind it, but, as we have seen, no economy suffices to represent the invisible world in its fullness. Even Holy Church in her sacraments and hierarchical appointments still leaves creation without its final interpretation, and all nature and history are parables whose meaning is not yet fully manifest. Consequently, all symbols or economies, except the sacraments and orders officially instituted by the Church and secured by her infallible authority, are subject

5. Basil Willey has suggested the similarity between the *Apologia* and *The Prelude* but without elaborating on the comparison. Cf. his "Introduction" to the World Classics edition of the *Apologia Pro Vita Sua* (London: Oxford University Press, 1964), p. xi.

to constant revision, and in the progress of an individual soul (as in the "march of civilization")[6] many of these economies may have to be discarded and replaced periodically by different, if not necessarily better, ones.

This principle of what we might call a "progressive iconoclasm" informs all nineteenth-century autobiography. As in the history of society, so in the individual life, the "spirit afloat" must periodically seek to embody itself in new "forms." Therefore the "whole man" in his progress toward the truth moves through a series of painful leave-takings, from the innocence of childhood to the "years that bring the philosophic mind." It should be clear, moreover, that this autobiographical pattern is closely related to the nineteenth-century fusion of traditional idealism with sensationalist psychology. Each break or departure moves one further from the senses and deeper into the idea; memory is the bond between the two. The innocence of childhood, whether in the English lakes, Christ Hospital, or at Ham, is supremely a life of sensations. On the other hand, in the years of the "philosophic mind," a man is primarily aware of that moment in which "the light of sense / Goes out, but with a flash that has revealed / The invisible world."[7] Thus the operations of the senses bring man to the perception of spiritual realities beyond sense. The "flash that has revealed / The invisible world" always comes at the moment of breaking and deracination which precedes reconstruction and return.

The Prelude is the archetypal nineteenth-century spiritual autobiography, and the similarities between it and the *Apologia* demand serious consideration. I begin with "Book Six" of the former, which might be regarded as a miniature of the whole poem and, for that matter, of the entire autobiographical pattern with which we are concerned. In "Book Six" Wordsworth moves from the experiences of sense to those of mind, from rest and joy in visible things, through the moment of their denial and the extinction of the light of sense, into the higher, intelligible

6. "Prospects of the Anglican Church," *Essays*, I, 287.
7. William Wordsworth, *The Prelude*, VI, 600–602.

vision. In France, at first, he moves "unhoused beneath the evening star," enjoying "dances of liberty."[8] He moves as natural forces and sensations move him, gliding "forward with the flowing stream."[9] This condition of sensuous oneness with nature accords beautifully with the ethos of the French revolution; Wordsworth moves not only with the stream but "with a merry crowd / Of those emancipated."[10] As we can easily see, the mood of these lines recapitulates the first two books of *The Prelude*; the making one long bathing of a summer's day or the sporting like a naked savage in a thunderstorm. It is also the mood of remembered youth in "Tintern Abbey":

> . . . when like a roe
> I bounded o'er the mountains, by the sides
> Of the deep rivers, and the lonely streams
> Wherever nature led.[11]

It is not a mood to be deplored, for to live in an immediate sensuous communion with these *visibilia* produces "aching joys" and "dizzy raptures." On the other hand, the characteristic movement in Wordsworth's various autobiographies, a necessary step in the "growth of a poet's mind," is to pass from a life of sensations into "that blessed mood,"

> In which the burthen of the mystery,
> In which the heavy and the weary weight
> Of all this unintelligible world,
> Is lightened. . . .[12]

Then "we are laid asleep / In body, and become a living soul."[13] For the latter to take place, the pleasures of "unhoused" liberty need not be denied as an older and purer Platonism would demand, but they must be transcended.

That transcendence involves the breaking and the flash to which we have already alluded. The crisis does not take place in

8. VI, 370–371.
9. VI, 377.
10. VI, 386–387.
11. Ll. 67–70.
12. Ll. 38–41.
13. Ll. 45–46.

"Book Six" of *The Prelude,* but it is prepared for there by the discussion of the imagination in the "Simplon Pass" passage. First comes the realization *"that we had crossed the Alps."*[14] The phrase needs very little comment; it suggests a turning and a downward movement, a receding from "dizzy raptures." Then follows the description of the imagination, an "awful Power," which is intellectual rather than sensual, which rises "from the mind's abyss," and which, like a vapor, "enwraps, / At once, some lonely traveller."[15] The intellectual power apparently puts out the light of sense, and the consequence for the man who has been led hitherto by that lower light in that he is for the moment blinded and lost, "halted without an effort to break through."[16] Wordsworth calls that action of the mind upon the senses a "usurpation,"[17] as though it were a violent and undue infringement upon, a revolutionary destruction of, established order. As it will appear in the event, however, that usurpation is just as necessary to the completion of the individual as is the breaking of traditional forms to newer and fuller expressions of the "spirit afloat."

In "Book Ten" of *The Prelude* the expectations provoked by that metaphor are realized. There Wordsworth speaks of "change and subversion"[18] and of deracination and exile. Hitherto he has been thoroughly at home, like "a pliant harebell, swinging in the breeze / On some grey rock—its birth-place." He has been "rooted on the ancient tower / Of my beloved country."[19] The image suggests, implicitly, the life of sensations. The stationary plant and the moving river have in common their harmony with natural forces; and while man remains innocent of those awful usurping powers in the mind's abyss, he lives in happy union with such forces. When one has crossed the Alps, however, when he has been "from that pleasant station torn / And tossed about

14. VI, 591.
15. VI, 594–596.
16. VI, 597.
17. VI, 600.
18. X, 268.
19. X, 277–280.

in whirlwind,"[20] it is that higher power which alone can give him aid and lead him home.

That rapture, however, does not involve a complete repudiation of what has gone before. In fact, the paradox seems to be that the only way to preserve the life of sensations is to deny it, that the authority of the senses is usurped only to be re-established—and on new and better terms. The child remains the father of the man, although at first glance the birth pangs appear to have destroyed the parent. One really can go home again, provided he has been thoroughly exiled and uprooted to begin with; for, it is only when he is cast out that he discovers where and what home is. We should not forget that Wordsworth went back to the English lakes and became a civil servant.

These paradoxes all appear to derive from the sensationalist modification of traditional idealism. The pure idealist position involves no such notion. St. Clement admonishes the Greeks to abandon their sensual past, the customs of their pagan fathers, and never to look further on those corporeal things. Origen would have us deny, permanently, all sensuous pleasure which the *Song of Songs* may give us and to attend exclusively to the ideas for which those pleasures are the vehicles. For Wordsworth, however, the life of nature and the senses is too deeply involved in the subjective mode of cognition to be repudiated finally and completely. How, then, to reconcile the traditional hostility between the life of sensations and the life of the mind? According to the latter, it is only when the power of the former is broken or usurped that the intellect can be set free from its bondage and enabled to "see into the life of things." But suppose that seeing still involves an economy; and suppose those symbols of the invisible world which are drawn from sensible experience can be put to use by the intellect once it has broken and conquered them. The Greeks and Romans made good use, as slaves, of the savage peoples they conquered, but only after they usurped their power. By the same analogy, the spirited horse must be broken before he can be put to proper service. By a similar

20. X, 282–283.

process, Wordsworth appears to have envisioned the "saving" of the senses by subjecting them to the authority of the idea, and in this process the memory occupies an extremely important place. "Emotion recollected in tranquillity" is emotion internalized, spiritualized, made subject to the mind.

There is no proof that Newman ever read *The Prelude*, but we do know that he admired the "Intimations Ode" and thematically the two are very similar.[21] We do not know precisely what he liked about that poem, but it may not be hard to guess. For one thing, certainly, he must have found in it a great deal which would have appealed to the idealist tendencies of his thought. In fact, the hints about the pre-existence of the soul and the corollary distrust of matter, the Platonic implications of such a phrase as "shades of the prison house" used as a metaphor for the "living busy world"—all these must have reminded him of Alexandrian philosophy and in particular of Origen. In addition to these elements, however, there is in the poem the pattern of destruction and reconstruction which we have been discussing. In the past lies that state of indirect, sensuous communion between man and nature, that condition of being at home in the natural world in which there is no sense of hostility or discord between the life of the mind and the life of the body:

> . . . a time when meadow, grove, and stream,
> The earth, and every common sight,
> 　　To me did seem
> 　Apparelled in celestial light,
> The glory and the freshness of a dream.[22]

Meanwhile, however, change, subversion, usurpation, and deracination have occurred (we are not told how) and now "nothing can bring back the hour / Of splendour in the grass, of glory in the flower."[23] The Alps have been crossed. On the other hand, that very loss, even the agony of that loss, the exquisite pain of nostalgia, provides the ground of a new experience which both transcends and conserves the old one. By losing the "delight and

21. See Ward, II, 336, 354. Also see Vargish, pp. 100–101.
22. Wordsworth, "Ode: Intimations of Immortality," ll. 1–5.
23. Ll. 177–178.

liberty, the simple creed / Of childhood,"[24] the poet has discovered what real delight and liberty are. The way to that discovery involves

> . . . obstinate questionings
> Of sense and outward things,
> Fallings from us, vanishings;
> Blank misgivings of a Creature
> Moving about in worlds not realized.[25]

These are the experiences of destruction and exile, but the reconstruction and homecoming ensue and give us back what was taken away. The beauty of sensible objects remains, and the poet still possesses that beauty, but now as a symbol or economy of the intelligible world. He is no longer "rooted" in nature nor subject to it; the sensations, by a process of breaking, have been idealized and nature, spiritualized.

> And O, ye Fountains, Meadows, Hills and Groves,
> Forebode not any severing of our loves!
> Yet in my heart of hearts I feel your might;
> I only have relinquished one delight
> To live beneath your more habitual sway.
> I love the Brooks which down their channels fret,
> Even more than when I tripped lightly as they.[26]

In all Newman's autobiographical writing the critical experience is that of the "fallings from us, vanishings; / Blank misgivings of a Creature / Moving about in worlds not realized." These worlds are sometimes psychological; more often theological. In either case, he must give up the beauty of the past in order to regain that beauty; he must leave home in order to be at home; he must go through disease to be healthy. The paradoxical experience is constantly being repeated, sometimes on a grand scale, as in the *Apologia*, sometimes in miniature, as in a letter to his sister Jemima in May of 1828. The latter provides a good point of departure because it deals with one of the major crises in Newman's development; his sister Mary's death. In the letter

24. Ll. 136–137.
25. Ll. 141–145.
26. Ll. 187–193.

he describes a horseback ride "over to Cuddesdon." He comments first on the great beauty of the country, "the fresh leaves,
the scents, the varied landscape." This sensible beauty is viewed
here, however, through the eyes of a man who has already crossed
the Alps, for whom the light of sense has been eclipsed by
bereavement the previous January. The beauty of the earth in
spring does not move him immediately or sensibly but intellectu-
ally. It makes him feel "intensely the transitory nature of this
world." He proceeds to quote two lines from Keble with the following preface: "And in riding out to-day I have been impressed
more powerfully than before I had an idea was possible with the
two lines:

> Chanting with a *solemn* voice
> Minds us of our *better choice*."[27]

The couplet is from the poem for the first Sunday after
Epiphany in *The Christian Year*. Keble's point is the same as
Newman's: that the beauty of creation exists primarily to be
usurped upon or transcended. The "lessons sweet of spring re-
turning" are not taught to the senses—no sporting naked in the
thunderstorm, nor moving unhoused or emancipated with the
wind or rivers—nor, for that matter, are they taught to pure
mind, as Origen would conceive that they should be. Rather
they are taught to "the thoughtful heart," and the phrase cap-
tures very accurately the fusion of idealism and sensationalist
psychology which we have been discussing. The role of the
senses is not denied, but the heart, as the locus of sensation, is
conceived as inseparable from the intellect. Likewise, the beauty
of the physical world is embraced, but only as a symbol or
economy of the invisible. Thus,

> Every leaf in every nook,
> Every wave in every brook,
> Chanting with a *solemn* voice
> Minds us of our *better choice*.

"Our *better choice*" is clearly the choice of God who made the
waves and leaves and of those invisible realities of the kingdom

27. Mozley, I, 161.

of heaven of which the waves and leaves are the economical representations. Thus the beauty of the world leads to *contemptus mundi*, and our true hearing is through the "inward ear."

Again, however, we have a situation in which the external reality, once forfeited, transcended and made subject to the subjective intuition, is then given back. No sooner has Newman quoted the two lines from Keble and, in effect, repudiated the light of sense, than he proceeds to say that "Dear Mary seems embodied in every tree and hid behind every hill. What a veil and curtain this world of sense is! beautiful, but still a veil."[28] A veil hides what lies behind it; to get at those invisible things it must be torn aside, no matter how beautiful it may be. So much for the purely idealist and negative quality of the experience which bereavement and Keble's poetry have combined to accomplish. But notice that the positive side is also here. Nature not only hides Mary (who is now among the invisible creatures, whom the subjective experience alone can grasp); it also reveals her: she is "embodied in every tree." The latter statement would be impossible for either the pure sensationalist or the pure idealist. The two modes fuse to produce it, and, as we have seen, such crises as bereavement are germane to the point of fusion and of vision.

From that same point of fusion all religious experience seems to derive; the *Parochial and Plain Sermons* instance many such moments. "To a child this world is everything: he seems to himself a part of this world,—a part of this world, in the same sense in which a branch is part of a tree; he has little notion of his own separate and independent existence: that is, he has no just idea he has a soul."[29] Such a concept of the child is thoroughly Wordsworthian; he moves, unhoused, with wind or river, without any *conscious* awareness of an invisible world but with an inarticulated sense of God's presence in all created things. However "shades of the prison-house begin to close / Upon the growing Boy"; our "instinctive sense of right and wrong" gives

28. Mozley, I, 161. Cf. Bouyer's discussion of this passage in his *Newman, His Life and Spirituality* (New York: P. J. Kenedy & Sons, 1958), pp. 110ff.

29. *Parochial and Plain Sermons*, I, 18. Hereafter cited as *PPS*.

place to "our weak and conceited reason."[30] Then, unless we learn to think *consciously* of God and to regard that outward world as a veil, as an economy which hides more than it reveals, "to feel our separation from things visible, our independence of them,"[31] we shall have nothing left for us "but to 'grope and stumble in the desolate places,' by the dim, uncertain light of reason."[32]

That is the process of change and subversion by which the child is rooted out of his native place, cut loose from the tree where he grew as a branch. We are driven into the wilderness, to a time of temptation and choice. God visits us with bereavement or with some other form of suffering, and "the unprofitableness and feebleness of the things of this world are forced upon our minds; they promise but cannot perform, they disappoint us."[33] Mary's death was just such a "disappointment"—a proof that the "things of this world," her blood and flesh, cannot perform what they promise. So, for Wordsworth, the French Revolution's betrayal of its own ideals was a similar disappointment. So, later, for Newman, the English Church's failure to live by her own creed precipitated another crisis of bereavement. In each case, the pain of loss cuts away the *visibilia* and leaves man face to face with God, but Newman does not deny the pain: "no one can have his heart cut away from the natural objects of its love, without pain during the process and throbbings afterwards."[34]

Newman's illness in Sicily was another such cutting. He regarded it in retrospect as a part of his spiritual preparation for the Oxford Movement, as God's way of teaching him to mortify his self-will and to be passive before the demands of grace. At the height of the fever he recalls that "the very day before I left Oxford, I had preached a (University) Sermon against Wilfulness, so that I seemed to be predicting my own condemnation."[35] He considers that it was a willful act to come to Sicily

30. *PPS*, I, 219.
31. *PPS*, I, 19.
32. *PPS*, I, 221.
33. *PPS*, I, 19–20.
34. *PPS*, I, 24.
35. *Autobiographical Writings*, ed. Henry Tristram (London: Sheed and Ward, 1956), p. 118. Hereafter cited as AW.

alone, against the Froudes' advice, and that the illness is both God's punishment and His warning against future presumption. Thus we see that "Lead Kindly Light" is a proper conclusion for the whole experience.

So much for the strictly moral aspects of the Sicilian adventure; however, there is more to be said on the subject. In the accounts Newman wrote of that illness, the by now familiar pattern of loss and gain emerges very clearly. In the first place, we should remember that he was drawn to Sicily by its natural beauty and by its classical or pagan associations. He tells us in retrospect that he went "for the gratification of an imagination, for the idea of a warm fancy, drawn by a strange love of Sicily to gaze upon its cities and mountains."[36] Everything he says about the country suggests the relish of purely sensible experience which characterizes Wordsworth's youth in *The Prelude*, "Tintern Abbey" and the "Intimations Ode." In fact, visiting the classical lands was for Newman a kind of return to childhood. He had read Homer and Virgil first when he was a child; therefore, when he sees the lands they describe he is brought back to his own youth by vivid memories. When he looks at Ithaca for the first time, he does not think of Homer or the *Odyssey*; instead "I thought of Ham, and of all the various glimpses which memory barely retains, and which fly from me when I pursue them, of that earliest time of life when one seems almost to realise the remnants of a pre-existing state."[37] One suspects that these Mediterranean scenes, like Windermere and Hawkshead in Wordsworth's experience, are suffused with those clouds of glory which the child comes trailing. Before change and subversion and the crises of bereavement a child "seems to himself a part of this world—a part of this world, in the same sense in which a branch is part of a tree." As a consequence of that relationship, there is no division for him between the external and the internal, between the invisible and the visible, between the subjective intuition of God "in my conscience and my heart" and the bodily sensation of physical beauty. The world does not yet seem to be a living busy system which shows no reflection of its Creator. On the contrary, the light of glory suffuses and unites all experience into a whole;

36. AW, p. 111.
37. Mozley, I, 279–280.

hence, in Ithaca or in Sicily, which exist for Newman primarily in memories of childhood, there must be splendor in the grass, glory in the flower. Therefore Newman longs to touch Ithaca, "to satisfy myself that it was not a mere vision that I saw before me!"[38]

One suspects that the same type of longing drew him to Sicily —strangely enough, the longing to go home again. For almost all of us there is some place we long to go back to, some place we experienced when we were still innocent of change and subversion, when we were still completely at home in the world, still united to outward, visible, sensible reality as a branch is united to a tree. In our memory that place will always be a symbol of wholeness and beauty, a kind of Eden for each of us; for Newman Ham was such a place, and, by extension, through associations with what he read there, these lands which he met in classical poetry. In that sense we might say that Newman's longing to return to Sicily was like Vaughan's desire to travel back to that "shady city of palm trees." It is similar to the longing of so many exiles in modern literature who, above all else, wish to go home. It is no accident, I think, that he describes Sicily as being "like the Garden of Eden."[39]

However, the experience of the modern exile is that he cannot go home, and Wordsworth, as we have seen, knew that he could not recapture, at least not in its original terms, the splendor in the grass. When we try to go back to those places which are suffused with celestial light, we inevitably find them disappointing and commonplace. By 1833 Ham had been sold, Newman's father was dead, and the old home with its associations was long since broken up. Newman was not able to touch Ithaca, but he did reach Sicily only to learn again the same lesson that Mary's death had already taught him: that the beauty and joy of this world are too fragile to last and, if rested in as ends, become veils to separate us from invisible reality; that the only way to get home is to leave. Thus he has no sooner compared Sicily with Eden than he is reminded of Eden's loss; looking at the beauty

38. Mozley, I, 280.
39. AW, p. 123.

of the land he "fell to tears thinking of dear Mary as I looked at the beautiful prospect."[40] It is also highly appropriate to the whole symbolic quality of the episode that Castro Giovanni, where Newman almost died, is in fact, the ancient Enna where Proserpine was gathered by gloomy Dis.[41] The metaphor of the fall is subtle and exact. Whatever vestiges of Eden may remain there, the Sicily Newman encounters is a post-lapsarian world and far different from the "classical lands" he remembers from Ham. All the beauty is mixed with pain and disappointment, and he must endure "sadness, loneliness, weariness" in order to see it. He even goes so far as to say that "I never thought this expedition was to be one of pleasure only, for I wished to see what it was to be a solitary and wanderer."[42]

Memory is the compensating factor. As we have already seen, memory is the power by which the innocent past life of sensations is salvaged from wreckage and made subject to the idea or the subjective intuition of spiritual realities. Once the Alps have been crossed, sensible experience, if it is put to any good use, must be recollected in tranquillity. Only thus can paradise be regained, for only in such recollections can the natural and visible things be understood as economies or symbols. Newman touches on the subject of memory repeatedly in his letters from the Mediterranean, particularly in those from Sicily. In the first of these, from Catania on April 25, he told his sister that he "was setting out on an expedition which would be pleasant in memory rather than in performance."[43] In another, from Syracuse on April 27, after describing at some length the "excessive" discomfort which he had been suffering on account of fleas, poor lodging, and bad weather, he goes on to say that though he is "really roughing it," he is "not unwilling to do so; for I shall gain a lesson, so God does but sustain me. In retrospect all bodily pain vanishes, and mental impressions (which have been chiefly pleasant) endure."[44]

40. AW, p. 123.
41. AW, p. 117.
42. Mozley, I, 349.
43. Mozley, I, 348.
44. Mozley, I, 353.

Those "mental impressions" belong to the world of ideal or subjective experience. They embody an awareness of what is immutable behind the veil of sense, even though their apprehension springs from suffering and the usurpation of the light of sense. From such impressions Newman comes to understand the providential aspects of his adventure, and in memory the whole journey takes on a familiar symbolic shape. Looking back on the Sicilian experience he is like a traveler surveying a tract of land from some distance above it; he is then able to see in memory a pattern or direction in what happened to him, which was not clear to him while the experience was going on. Thus the account that he writes takes its place in the larger pattern of Newman's whole life; this crisis, like that of Mary's death and like his subsequent conversion to the Church of Rome, is one in which exile must precede homecoming and sickness must precede health.

These same metaphors, exile and sickness, are germane to the *Apologia*. They are introduced first by Newman's allusions to his Sicilian experience and are continued throughout the narrative. The search for home takes him first to the Church of England, then to the Church of Rome. When the movement is at its height, he tell us, "It was, in a human point of view, the happiest time of my life. I was truly at home. I had in one of my volumes appropriated to myself the words of Bramhall, 'Bees, by the instinct of nature, do love their hives, and birds their nests.' "[45] It is that very "instinct of nature," however, the whole natural order of things, which must be broken and spiritualized; and Newman passes from home, health, and sunshine to sickness and exile. By 1841 he was "on my deathbed, as regards my membership with the Anglican Church,"[46] and in 1846, when he sets out to cross the Alps, he tells us that " ' "Obliviscere populum tuum et domum patris tui," has been in my ears for the last twelve hours. I realize more that we are leaving Littlemore, and it is like going on the open sea.' "[47] The actual departure is presented in a metaphor of deracination. He recalls "much snap-dragon growing on

45. *Ap.*, pp. 76–77.
46. *Ap.*, p. 137.
47. *Ap.*, p. 212.

the walls opposite my freshman's rooms there [at Trinity], and I had for years taken it as the emblem of my own perpetual residence even unto death in my University."[48] One thinks of Wordsworth's "pliant harebell," and Newman, too, is "from that pleasant station torn / And tossed about in whirlwind." In sharp juxtaposition with the rooted, homely snap-dragon, with all its associations of those times which "in a human point of view" were the happiest of Newman's life, he presents that persistent nineteenth-century symbol of change, the railroad; "I have never seen Oxford since, excepting its spires, as they are seen from the railway."[49]

Again, however, what is lost is given back; reconstruction follows on destruction. If leaving Littlemore is like going on the open sea, entering the Church of Rome "was like coming into port after a rough sea; and my happiness on that score remains to this day without interruption."[50] Moreover, Newman gives us at least one prior hint of how the pattern will work out, that loss will be followed by gain. It comes, rather obliquely, in an allusion to the *Aeneid* at the beginning of chapter three. The passage begins with the statement that "I am about to trace, as far as I can, the course of that great revolution of mind, which led me to leave my own home, to which I was bound by so many strong and tender ties."[51] He proceeds to mention the pain and difficulty which retracing of the past demands, "for who can know himself, and the multitude of subtle influences which act upon him?" Moreover, to recall such a painful episode is to practice on oneself "a cruel operation, the ripping up of old griefs, and the venturing again upon the 'infandum dolorem' of years, in which the stars of this lower heaven were one by one going out."[52] The "infandum dolorem" sustains the earlier phrase, "that great revolution of mind"; it gives the word *revolution* its concrete symbolic quality. These are of course the words Aeneas uses to Dido as a preface to his retelling the fall of Troy:

48. *Ap.*, p. 213.
49. *Ap.*, p. 213.
50. *Ap.*, p. 214.
51. *Ap.*, p. 90.
52. *Ap.*, p. 90.

Infandum, regina, jubes renovare dolorem,
Trojanas ut opes et lamentabile regnum
eruerint Danai, quaeque ipse miserrima vidi
et quorum pars magna fui.[53]

Professor Houghton comments on the allusion as an example of Newman's symbolic usage in the *Apologia*, but he does not pursue the matter or suggest the possible ramifications of the symbol.[54] In the context of Virgil's whole passage, however, it is obvious how close a parallel may be drawn between Newman's experience and Aeneas's. For both, the beginning of exile is consequent upon the end of an order; the Latitudinarians and the Protestants have as surely betrayed and conquered the *regnum* of Oxford as ever the Greeks did that of Troy, and like Aeneas, Newman has been "pars magna" of the fruitless defense.

The parallels extend even further, however, and hint, as I have suggested, at the homecoming and reconstruction which ensues upon Newman's defeat and exile. We must not forget, surely Newman had not forgotten, that Aeneas's mission was ultimately a spiritual one, and that both the fall of Troy and the exile of her defender were ordained by the gods for ends transcending human sight. Troy must fall that Rome may be established; for Rome will be a greater Troy. Here then is the coming into port after a stormy sea, the giving back of what was taken away, the salvaging in a spiritual order of what is necessarily sacrificed in the physical or sensible order. Hector's advice, in vision, to Aeneas is implicit in Newman's cryptic "infandum dolorem":

Hostis habet muros; ruit alto a culmine Troja.
sat patriae Priamoque datum: si Pergama dextra
defendi possent, etiam hac defensa fuissent.
Sacra suosque tibi commendat Troja penatis:
hos cape fatorum comites, his moenia quare
magna pererrato statues quae denique ponto.[55]

"You have done enough for king and country. It is now your duty to salvage our nation's holy things, and this can only be done by seeking for them another, mighty city." The "stars of this

53. *Aeneid*, II, 3–6.
54. Houghton, p. 54, n. 33.
55. *Aeneid*, II, 290–295.

lower heaven" are going out; the nest and the hive are being pillaged and the only way now to save your home, that "old idea of a Christian Polity," that "tradition of fifteen hundred years," is to leave it. If Troy falls, where should one go if not to Rome? And if there is any question about the ultimate giving back, the final salvation of the *penatis*, one need only consider, as Newman had considered it, the subsequent history of Rome, both pagan and Christian.

In another autobiographical document, pagan Rome serves a slightly different symbolic purpose. I refer to *Callista*, and there seems to me no question that the novel contains many autobiographical elements. Sicca, the city in Proconsular Africa where Agellius lives, is described as resembling "Castro Giovanni, the ancient Enna, in the heart of Sicily,"[56] and what Agellius experiences there is another version of the familiar pattern of losing and regaining paradise. Agellius also suffers from a fever which renews him. It convinces him of his guilt before God and at the same time restores his trust; his words on the occasion include only a slight modification of a line from "Lead Kindly Light": "I deserve the worst, but somehow I have thought that God would lead me on."[57] As he begins to recover, Agellius suffers the same aftereffects that Newman mentions in his own case; his skin peels, his hair falls out and he draws, from the Psalms, the moral which is implicit in Newman's account of his Sicilian illness: "Renovabitur, ut aquila, juventus mea."[58]

I said that Rome here serves a different symbolic purpose from that suggested by the Virgilian allusions in the *Apologia*. It might be more exact to say that it serves exactly the opposite purpose, for Rome, in *Callista*, is the home which must be left behind, the natural human order of things which must be broken in order that a new, spiritual *regnum* may rise from the ruins. In fact, Rome in this book reminds one a great deal of nineteenth-century England, and one suspects that Agellius's jolly, pagan uncle, Jucundus, is no other than John Bull himself. He is the spokesman for the establishment. He is not disposed "to be pleased unreservedly with those who satirized anything whatever

56. *Callista, A Tale of the Third Century*, p. 5. Hereafter cited as *Callista*.
57. *Callista*, p. 155.
58. *Callista*, p. 157.

that was established, or was appointed by government, even affectation and pretence. He said something about the wisdom of ages, the reverence due to authority, the institutions of Rome, and the magistrates of Sicca."[59] His advice to Arnobius is " 'Do not go after novelties.' " He is a conservative; what Froude playfully called a *z*. He is one of the two-bottle orthodox, the high-and-dry. He is good humoured and invariably merry, and his board reminds us of Chaucer's Franklin. He belongs to the "tradition of fifteen hundred years." It is clearly a beautiful tradition and Jucundus is a likable, even admirable character; but the deficiencies of each are manifest.

These consist primarily in lack of spiritual discernment. Merry England, as Newman conceived it, in spite of all its goodness, cannot grasp the implications of an invisible world nor can Jucundus comprehend Agellius's stubborn persistence in the Faith nor Callista's conversion and martyrdom. For all the goodness of his heart, he is ultimately of the flesh rather than the spirit. In fact, he is still very much in the condition of the child who is a part of this world in the same way the limb is part of a tree; he is unaware of any distinction between things visible and invisible and has no awareness of his own soul. His are the "stars of this lower heaven," nor is he aware that they are going out. Newman leaves us in doubt of that fact. Rome has just celebrated the completion of her first millennium, but all the talk is of the end of empire. The Goths are on the Danube, the old religion is failing and mobs are in the streets; Rome "ruit alto a culmine," and if the *penatis* are to be saved it must be in spiritual rather than in temporal or political terms. Jucundus, the Tory, cannot comprehend that fact, but that is precisely what St. Cyprian teaches Agellius as his youth is renewed.

The old order, the sensible order, to which Jucundus belongs, includes not only the richness of empire but also the splendor of earth. A bountiful nature, the very principle of plenitude, furnishes his table, but Cyprian offers Agellius another interpretation of the same rich earth. Cyprian is already an exile; he has already crossed the Alps when we meet him, and he testifies not only to the loss but also to the giving back: " 'it is the compensa-

59. *Callista*, p. 86.

tion of my flight from Carthage that I am brought before the face of God.' "[60] He has already witnessed the breaking of the form and has discovered the invisible world beyond the veil; in short, he has learned, and he teaches Agellius, that principle of the economy of which Jucundus and the establishment have never so much as dreamed. With reference to the earth's beauty, he says that " 'these sights are the shadows of that fairer Paradise which is our home, where there is no beast of prey, no venomous reptile, no sin.' "[61] As though to prove the transitory nature of all visible things, the locusts descend and denude the earth, famine replaces plenty and discord, order. In the adventures which follow, Agellius and Callista follow Cyprian out of the city to seek that "fairer Paradise," our real home. When Agellius comes at last to the Mass, it is the end of his voyage, "coming home to his father's house";[62] nor can all the lost richness of Jucundus's world compare with it.

Callista herself has already been uprooted, is already an exile, before her suffering begins; consequently, though she is at first a pagan, she has a certain advantage over Agellius, for God has allowed her no delusions about being at home in the visible world. She is a "child of Greece" and has no happiness in Roman Africa.[63] ". . . young as she was, she had become tired of all things that were seen, and had no strong desire, except for meditation on the great truths which she did not know."[64] Once she learns them, the way of martyrdom opens quickly before her, but she too is given back the old forms in a new way. The night before her passion she dreams of Greece, of home, and the dream makes clear to her that Greece, like Ham or Ithaca, is only a symbol or economy. "But in reality, though she called it Greece, she was panting after a better country and a more lasting home, and this country and home she had found. She was now setting out for it."[65] In the dream, the Greece she sees is "more sunny and bright than before." At first it seems lonely, for all the in-

60. *Callista*, p. 160.
61. *Callista*, p. 160.
62. *Callista*, p. 336.
63. *Callista*, p. 222.
64. *Callista*, p. 295.
65. *Callista*, p. 366.

habitants are gone, but then "suddenly its face changed, and its colours were illuminated tenfold by a heavenly glory, and each hue upon the scene was of a beauty she had never known." Out of caves and grottoes come "myriads of bright images," and she realizes now that home, the real Greece, is "a world of spirits, not of matter."[66] Thus when she is taken from prison to the rack, she says very simply " 'I am ready; I am going home.' "[67]

One can almost imagine Newman's having such a dream of Oxford, those "angel faces . . . / Which I have loved long since, and lost awhile." The "whole man" moves to certitude, to the "ultimate aim" of his being which is the knowledge of God in his conscience and his heart. There are halfway houses— Troy, Greece, Rome, or Oxford—but all of those must be regarded finally as no more than symbols or economies; emblems and anticipations of home, but not home itself, not the realization of the idea or the full embodiment of our deepest subjective intuition. It is only as we pass through these cities, however, first embracing them, then despairing of them, with "fallings from us, vanishings; / Blank misgivings of a Creature / Moving about in worlds not realized," that we come finally to those invisible worlds that are. These are apprehended deep within us, in that complex intuition by which we know both our own existence and through it the existence of God. The painful breaking of the flesh and the subsequent memory of that moment when the light of sense goes out is the way to that apprehension.

66. *Callista*, p. 354.
67. *Callista*, p. 357.

PART THREE

Newman's Modernism: A Theology of Safeguards

We now have before us two facts about Newman, one or the other of which is often ignored: he was thoroughly conservative in his acceptance of Catholic dogma; but his philosophy and his characteristic modes of expression reflect the subjectivism and relativism of modern thought. The possession of these two facts puts us in a position to study Newman's theology, for (as I have already suggested) the peculiarity of that theology lies in Newman's attempt to unite fundamentalism in dogma with "modernism" in philosophy. In studying such a theology, two things are necessary: first, to see how the apparently impossible union is attempted and, second, to test the validity of that attempt.

In spite of the prevailing tendencies of modern theology and of recent Newman scholarship, we must not overlook the possibility that such a union may indeed be invalid; that "one side of [Newman's] religion was based on principles which, when logically drawn out, must lead away from Catholicism in the direction of an individualistic religion of experience, and a substitution of history for dogma which makes all truth relative and all values fluid."[1] My suggestion is that Inge is correct and that the way in which Newman avoided the heterodox consequences implicit in his principles was by refusing

1. William Ralph Inge, "Cardinal Newman," in *Outspoken Essays* (London: Longmans, Green & Co., 1923), p. 202.

(consciously or not is beside the point) to draw them out "logically" to their conclusions; that, in fact, his theology, so far from proving that Catholicism and modern thought, Catholic teaching and the "new civilization," can be reconciled, is really a tissue of last-minute withdrawals from the logical consequences of "modernism." That is not to deny that those withdrawals, which I shall call Newman's "safeguards," are in themselves logically consistent and philosophically justifiable, so long as we assume Catholic doctrine to be true. Their presence does seem to indicate, however, that modernist philosophical assumptions, taken in their own right without Christian modifications, will lead to unchristian conclusions.

The obvious standard or measure by which to test the validity of Newman's attempted synthesis is the admittedly successful synthesis of St. Thomas Aquinas. That is so for two reasons: in the first place, as I have already indicated, Thomism is the most complete expression of the "tradition of fifteen hundred years," the tradition which Newman consciously relinquished; in the second place, Thomism has been regarded until very recently (and the change is due in part to Newman's influence) as the standard philosophy of the Church, as the only mode of thought which can simply be identified with Christianity.[2] That is because St. Thomas's Aristotelian principles, "when logically drawn out," lead to, not away from, Catholicism. Aquinas secures his orthodoxy by taking his philosophy to its logical conclusions; Newman defends his orthodoxy by stopping his scepticism, subjectivism, and relativism short of their inevitable consequences. The results in Newman's case are what I have called "orthodox subjectivism," "orthodox individualism," and "orthodox relativism." In each case the measure of the orthodoxy is the degree of negation of the modern "ism."

2. It is not an official change; Aquinas is still the official theologian of the Roman Catholic Church.

✣

Orthodox Subjectivism: Newman on Faith and Reason

W E murder to dissect"; "freezing reason's colder part" as opposed to "the heat of inward evidence"; "mere understanding" or "speculation" as opposed to the "philosophical imagination." These are typically nineteenth-century and, speaking generally, typically modern sentiments and distinctions; the first is Wordsworth's, the second Tennyson's, the third Coleridge's. It would be easy to compile a much longer list of such statements to the same general effect in major literary work from Wordsworth to the present. Each bespeaks a distrust of reason and a conviction that the way to the truth is both emotional and intuitive. Tennyson's "heat of inward evidence" carries both implications; the evidence of God's existence is *inward* or intuitive, and it is also emotional or warm. He tells us quite painly in *In Memoriam* that he did not find God objectively, in the external evidences which reason draws from nature and human experience, but in the feeling heart. As we have seen, this yoking of emotion and intuition is itself a sign of the times, probably a grafting of traditional idealist notions of intuition or illumination on the stem of late eighteenth-century sensationalist psychology. The consequence for the modern mind is that reason comes to be suspect on two counts: it is natural or worldly rather than ideal or intuitive and therefore not susceptible to divine illumination; and it is cold, for it goes on wholly in the mind and does not involve the heart.

It is interesting to note that reason's fiercest Christian champion (I mean St. Thomas) examined both the modern epistemological preferences, the sensationalist and the idealist, only to reject them. Consider, for instance, his question whether human intellect can know the future.[1] His answer reflects his whole concept of the intellect; that man can only know universals, never singular or individual things, for man knows only by abstraction. Knowledge of the future is a sort of test case, and Aquinas argues that man's reason can know the future only so far as it can ascertain those universals which apply to the future, that it cannot foreknow "things" or individual events, for those come to man only by his senses. In other words, the future can be known in its causes, for those are universals and the subject of the intellect's natural function. That function is to work from certain givens, from first principles which are "naturally known" by the *intellectus* and from the sense images which we receive from the objective, external world in which we move. Guided by first principles, the reason, moving from antecedents to consequents— reflecting, deliberating, abstracting—reaches from sense images to universals. Those universals are abstractions and, by definition, the opposites of the particular or singular things which the senses apprehend. As we have seen, however, St. Thomas never allows the abstract, universal conclusions of the rational process to be divorced from the sense images in which that process originates: "the proper object of the human intellect, which is united to a body, is a quiddity or nature existing in corporeal matter; and through such natures of visible things it rises to a certain knowledge of things invisible."[2] Those who attempt to "know" either by ignoring the senses or by resting wholly in them and denying the necessity for abstraction are misled.

One of these is the idealist error, the other the sensationalist; St. Thomas rejects each in its turn. The former is the Platonist notion to which Augustine appears to subscribe, that the soul has power of knowledge or fore-knowledge within itself; "hence when withdrawn from corporeal sense, and, as it were, concentrated on itself, it shares in the knowledge of the future." Aquinas admits that such a view would be reasonable if one were a Platonist in his philosophy, if he "were to admit that the soul receives knowledge by participating the ideas as the Platonists

1. *ST*, I, 86, 4.
2. *ST*, I, 84, 7.

maintained, because in that case the soul by its nature would know the universal causes of all effects and would only be impeded in its knowledge by the body; and hence when withdrawn from the corporeal senses it would know the future." As we have seen, however, that mode of knowing is not "connatural to our intellect," which, instead receives "its knowledge from the senses."[3] In short, there can be no purely "inward evidence," no suprasensible intuition of truth which is independent of the "living busy world" and of corporeal nature.

Nor, according to St. Thomas, can our evidence, our knowledge, be warm or emotional as opposed to abstract; we cannot rest for knowledge on feeling or imagination. The fact is that we are not "brute animals," and if the direct, intuitive apprehension of ideas is not "connatural" to us, neither is the mere arrangement of sense images by the imagination. The latter is the way of beasts, who, lacking reason, "have no power above the imagination" wherewith to order their sense impressions. Hence "their imagination follows entirely the influence of the heavenly bodies." In one sense, we might say that beasts have a certain advantage over men; they have an intuitive and prophetic capacity which man, *on account of his reason*, lacks. He does not need it, for he has a higher faculty to work with. "Thus from such animals' movements some future things, such as rain and the like, may be known rather than from human movements directed by reason."[4] For instance, all country people know that a rain crow caws before rain, and indeed some people, those in whom the power of reason is underdeveloped, have certain affinities with the beasts. "*For their intelligence is not burdened with cares, but is as it were barren and bare of all anxiety, moving at the caprice of whatever is brought to bear on it.*"[5] In either case, that of the beast or the simple man, the abeyance of reason may deliver the imagination into the power of "celestial impressions" so that the mind is moved directly by divine power rather than indirectly through a laborious process of abstraction from sense images.

3. *ST*, I, 86, 4.
4. *ST*, I, 86, 4.
5. *ST*, I, 86, 4. Italics in original; Aquinas is quoting Aristotle (*De Divinat. per somn.* ii).

It should be clear that these two denials of the rational process, the idealist and the imaginative or bestial, have a common term. In both, knowledge is conceived as being apprehended immediately and directly without the interference, as it were, of reason. Whether one goes directly to ideas within the soul or to celestial impressions planted immediately in the senses and imagination (or, in nineteenth-century terms, to some fusion of the two), either way he avoids the labor of abstraction. One way is that of the angels and of the saints in heaven; the other is that of primitives, infants or beasts. Neither, however, according to Aquinas, is the way connatural to civilized man in this present life. Here, however, one other question demands attention: Does St. Thomas allow for a legitimate mode of immediate, direct, intuitive knowledge in his concept of the *intellectus* as opposed to the *ratio?* C. S. Lewis seems to think he does and suggests that the modern concepts of intuition and illumination (and, we might add, Newman's "conscience" and Coleridge's or Wordsworth's "imagination") are finally only substitutes or, perhaps, just new names for the scholastic *intellectus.* "*Intellectus* is that in man which approximates most nearly to angelic *intelligentia*; it is in fact *obumbrata intelligentia*, clouded intelligence, or a shadow of intelligence." Lewis quotes Aquinas, apparently to that effect, that " 'intellect (*intelligere*) is the simple (i.e. indivisible, uncompounded) grasp of an intelligible truth, whereas reasoning (*ratiocinari*) is the progression towards an intelligible truth by going from one understood (*intellecto*) point to another.' "[6] From that distinction, Lewis concludes that Aquinas did allow, for man, an approximation to angelic intuition; something like the nineteenth-century concept of an idealist or subjective mode of knowing God.

When we examine St. Thomas's statement in context, however, it appears that the way Lewis presents the argument is slightly misleading. In fact, the article in question is whether *intellectus* and *ratio* are distinct powers, and Aquinas's answer is that they are not.[7] It is not that the power of intellect appre-

6. *DI*, p. 157.
7. *ST*, I, 79, 8.

hends directly while the power of reason proceeds by syllogism. Rather, they are to be regarded as complementary functions of one and the same power. The "intelligible truths" which the intellect "intuits" are not ends in themselves, such as the knowledge of God "in my conscience and my heart," but those first principles of reason on which the function of the *ratio* depends. In other words, we might say that the *intellectus* inaugurates, sustains, and completes the rational process, but it never supersedes that process. The angels have no need of *ratio* because they "apprehend the truth simply and without mental discussion" but man "arrives at the knowledge of intelligible truth by advancing from one thing to another." "Reasoning, therefore, is compared to understanding, as movement is to rest, or acquisition to possession";[8] not as though one power of the soul rested perpetually while another moved endlessly or that one revelled forever in possession of its object while the other labored ceaselessly to acquire it, but rather that the same power, the reason, moves to its end and rest as it proceeds from those first principles which the *intellectus* does grasp directly and from sense images, by way of the syllogism, to an acquisition, by abstraction, of intelligible truth.

At first glance, St. Thomas's insistence upon the syllogism is somewhat less than appealing. There is something very attractive about the notion of direct knowledge, whether in the soul or in the senses, and the nineteenth-century yoking of the two makes the best of both worlds. All of us long for a direct knowledge of God, for the "heat of inward evidence"; so much so, in fact, that we envy those children and those simple or primitive people (Wordsworth even envied idiots) whose rational faculties are underdeveloped and who are therefore more nearly capable of that immediacy. It is not surprising that we should long for it because, as St. Thomas shows, it will be natural for us to have it when we are in heaven, and we cannot help yearning for that which will ultimately complete our nature. Our error, however, at least in Thomist terms, is our impatience. The only mode of knowledge "connatural" to the corporeal condition in which

8. *ST*, I, 79, 8.

we now find ourselves is the rational one, and to ignore that fact is to ignore our human condition and the responsibilities it entails. However, in intellectual circumstances such as those which have prevailed for the last century and a half, one can understand why many of St. Thomas's restrictions are likely to be ignored and why peasants and children should be viewed as our philosophers. For if the desire for an immediate knowledge of God is common to all men at all times, it is particularly so in an age when the rational process has itself become suspect, when men doubt whether the work of reason *can* ever find its rest in the possession of intelligible truth. Indeed, that doubt probably accounts for the fact that Newman rested his defense of orthodoxy on an epistemology which is far closer to Wordsworth's and Coleridge's than to Aquinas's.

Newman's position, however, is more difficult than that of those secular exponents of the "spirit afloat," for as a defender of Catholic orthodoxy he was faced with something more serious than a simple doubt about reason's capacity. In the century that preceded the Oxford Movement, in the work of such men as Tindal and Toland, the ratiocinative process had been used successfully against Christianity. In fact, it had become the chief weapon of a militant atheism, and we know that Newman from his early years was exposed to its anti-Christian use. He knew Gibbon and Hume, and since he possessed such knowledge it is neither surprising that he should become suspicious of reason's prerogatives nor that he should seek for Christianity other, more direct and more immediate modes of knowing God.

Nor was Newman's situation in any sense unique. A question of Carlyle's in *Sartor Resartus* puts both the modern difficulty and the attempted solution in the clearest possible light: "Is the God present, felt in my own heart, a thing which Herr von Voltaire will dispute out of me; or dispute into me?"[9] The implied answer is, of course, a negative, and the logic is essentially Pascal's; "the heart has its reasons that the reason knows not of." Behind both statements lies the assumption that whatever is sub-

9. Thomas Carlyle, *Sartor Resartus*, ed. Charles Frederick Harrold (New York: The Odyssey Press, 1937), p. 194. Hereafter cited as *Sartor*.

mitted to the judgment of reason can be destroyed by disputation, while what rests in the heart, what is felt upon the pulses (as Keats says), what is apprehended subjectively by a "complex intuition," is proof against the world's logic. "Feel it in thy heart," Carlyle adds, "and then say whether it is of God! This is Belief; all else is Opinion."[10] Such a sentiment discounts at the start the rudimentary Thomist and Caroline assumption that reason, duly exercised on the basis of true premises, is *bound* to reach conclusions harmonious with those of faith. Nor do the Schoolmen or the Laudians know anything of the heart in Carlyle's or Pascal's sense; for them the reason is the central ethical and spiritual faculty, and our knowledge of God depends on right reason rather than a good heart.

Lewis's comments on this matter of the heart are particularly appropriate to our present concerns, for he develops the idea in such a way as to lead directly to Newman. He notes that Hooker maintains the traditional view, that " 'Reason is the director of man's will, discovering in action what is good.' " With Hooker he groups "nearly all moralists before the eighteenth century" who regarded "Reason as the organ of morality" and saw the central moral struggle as that between reason and passion.[11] In this connection, it might be worth adding to Lewis's comments that, in the old view, unbelief is regarded as a sin of the heart or a victory of the passions over the reason; man may be led into apostasy by feelings or vain imaginations, but so long as he follows the dictates of right reason he will be directed to belief in God and in all the articles of the Catholic Faith. However, "the eighteenth century witnessed a revolt against the doctrine that moral judgements are wholly, or primarily, or at all, rational,"[12] and Lewis makes the interesting suggestion that "conscience," considered as an epistemological faculty, was a concept which rose to take the place of reason. By way of illustration, he alludes to Butler's *Sermons*, but, of course, he might have taken the next logical step, to Butler's greatest disciple; for it is with Newman, as we have seen, that the doctrine of "conscience" truly comes into its

10. *Sartor*, p. 194.
11. *DI*, p. 158.
12. *DI*, p. 159.

own. Newman would, I think, agree with Carlyle that "the God present, felt in my own heart" is the only proof against unbelief; but his more characteristic way of phrasing it (after all, he distrusted Evangelical emotionalism) would be to speak of "the God present, felt in my own *conscience*." Of course there are important differences between Carlyle's "heart" and Newman's "conscience," as we shall see directly.[13] Suffice it for the present, however, to consider them both as responses to the rationalistic atheism of "Herr von Voltaire" and, generally, to the whole process of secularization to which we have already alluded, which separates Newman from Hooker and the whole ethos of modern theology and literature from that of the middle ages and, in England at least, of the Renaissance.

The question now before us is how Newman safeguards his subjectivism from the heterodoxy which attends Carlyle's similar appeal. Among major writers in nineteenth-century England, Newman is the exception who proves the rule, for in most cases the appeal to the heart, while it may have buttressed religion in the broad sense, proved hostile to Catholicism. The Wesleyan movement and the Evangelical party are both indications of that fact, and we find it borne out again and again in Romantic and Victorian poetry. In the passage I quoted from *Sartor Resartus*, before Carlyle's query about the heart, there is another question which puts the contrast between feeling and reason into an anti-Christian context: "Meanwhile what are antiquated Mythuses to me?"[14] Orthodox Christianity, for Carlyle, is just such an "antiquated Mythus," and when we realize that fact we see immediately that if the felt presence of God in the heart is proof for him against unbelief, it is certainly no guarantee of Christian dogma. In fact, he is obviously not interested in guaranteeing that dogma, for he evidently regards a religion of the heart, not merely as a substitute for orthodoxy, but as superior to it; and here we see the danger, for Christians, in attempting to find some more direct, surer, or more immediate way to the knowledge of God than that which reason provides.

13. See below, pp. 165–166.
14. *Sartor*, p. 194.

The danger lies in the fact that the heart bears witness only to what it feels. Therefore, if we trust the heart to the exclusion of the reason, we shall soon find ourselves believing to be true only those articles of religion which we feel intensely and surely. For instance, if we feel no intense sense of our Lord's presence in the Sacrament, we are likely to deny that presence. We cannot imagine it; and we do not trust our reason to demonstrate it. In fact, if the heart alone has its reasons, we shall soon find ourselves discarding as "antiquated Mythuses" the whole rational, dogmatic structure of Christian theology; and unless there were some way to guarantee that the heart would always feel constantly and intensely, have a deep "inner conviction" about, every article of the Catholic Faith, from the Virgin Birth to the Lady's Assumption, it would seem impossible to defend Christianity by a simple appeal to the heart. In fact, the heart inevitably generates a religion of its own which may appear to be more "immediate" than orthodoxy and which, because the range of our feeling is limited, will surely be simpler. On both counts, it may give the impression of being "purer" or "higher" or more "ideal" than old-fashioned Catholicism. Consequently, the appeal to "inward evidence" issues in an attack upon Christianity which comes from a different quarter but which is finally no less devastating than the purely secular, rationalistic attack of Tindal's, Toland's, Hume's, or Gibbon's sort. Catholics can scarcely regard the religious Carlyle as a closer friend than the sceptical Voltaire.

As we have said, Newman is the exception who proves the rule. His conclusions are different from those of his contemporaries, even though his premises seem to be very nearly identical to theirs. In making terms with "modernism," he joins their retreat before the advance of scepticism and makes common cause with them against the mockery of Voltaire and Rousseau. With them he turns to the reasons of the heart; yet, in his case—and he is virtually alone in his day—"inward evidence," the complex intuition whereby we know God in the conscience and the heart, testifies to Catholic orthodoxy. How did he escape the popular iconoclasm, the conclusion that some religion presumably purer and more ideal than Catholicism was demanded by the heart? Had he begun with Aquinas's philosophy and made no conces-

sions to modern thought, his opposition to the heresies of the
times would have been clear and precise. As it is, the distinctions
are involved and complex.

The starting point for a discussion of the matter is actually a
digression; for before we can say precisely what Newman's position is, we must explain his terminology and reconcile various sets
of terms with one another. We must decide, for instance, whether
he means the same thing by "implicit reason" as by the "illative
sense" or whether "idea" and "image" may under certain circumstances be used interchangeably. I begin with a series of contrasts,
each of which is similar to, though not identical with, the rest
and in each of which one term suggests immediate or intuitive (subjective) knowledge—inward evidence—the other a rational, "scientific," or external mode of knowing. Take, for instance, *faith* and *reason*. "Faith, then, and Reason, are popularly
contrasted with one another; Faith consisting of certain exercises
of Reason which proceed mainly on presumption, and Reason of
certain exercises which proceed mainly upon proof."[15] Faith is an
activity of "the illuminated mind"; Christ is manifested "not to
the eyes of the flesh, but to the illuminated mind, to their
Faith."[16] As such, faith is clearly distinct from reason, neither to
be equated with the latter nor judged by the same standards;
"in the minds of the sacred writers, Faith is an instrument of
knowledge and action, unknown to the world before, a principle
sui generis, distinct from those which nature supplies, and in
particular . . . independent of what is commonly understood
by Reason." In other words, faith is not simply a matter of "be-

---

15. *OUS*, p. 223. Vargish presents a clear analysis of what Newman means
by "reason"; see pp. 33–43. For full discussions of Newman's conception of
faith see Thomas L. Sheridan, *Newman on Justification* (New York: Alba
House, 1967); David A. Pailin, *The Way to Faith* (London: Epworth Press,
1969); Philip Flanagan, *Newman, Faith and the Believer* (Westminster, Md.:
The Newman Bookshop, 1946); A. J. Boekraad, *The Personal Conquest of
Truth* (Louvain: Nauwelaerts, 1955); and A. J. Boekraad, *The Argument
from Conscience to the Existence of God* (Louvain: Nauwelaerts, 1961);
subsequent references to "Boekraad" are to the last-named work. See also
J. H. Walgrave, *Newman the Theologian*, trans. A. V. Littledale (New York:
Sheed & Ward, 1960).
16. *OUS*, p. 176.

lieving upon evidence, or a sort of conclusion upon a process of reasoning";[17] it proceeds in a different fashion. It is "independent of processes of Reason"; it "simply accepts testimony" and is distinct from reason by the same measure that "testimony is distinct from experience."[18]

Granting these distinctions and granting too the central Christian thesis that "the Gospel does not alter the constitution of our nature, and does but elevate it and add to it"[19] and that, therefore, the demands of reason must still be acknowledged within their limits, "how," asks Newman, "is it comfortable to Reason to accept evidence less than Reason requires?"[20] How, in other words, are we to justify living by those dictates of the heart, that principle of knowledge which is *sui generis* and, consequently, impervious to the "reasons" of the atheists or the Latitudinarians? If we were simply Evangelical enthusiasts, there would be no problem, for those people believe "that faculties altogether new are implanted in our minds, and that perceptibly, by the grace of the Gospel."[21] It is one thing to believe in a new *principle* of knowledge bestowed by grace upon our natural faculties; quite another thing to believe that new *faculties* are given. Newman, as a Catholic, is committed to the former rather than the latter view. It is the same old human heart which has its reasons, though those reasons may be given in a special way and be clearly distinct from the mundane ones which derive by syllogism from sense experience. Therefore the constitution of human nature must be respected, and faith, though it cannot really be measured in the same terms as reason, must at least be compared with it. Hence the question: How is it reasonable to proceed on faith, to believe on less evidence than reason requires?

The answer is that faith has "its life in a certain moral temper," whereas the "argumentative exercises are not moral; Faith, then, is not the same method of proof as Reason."[22] Newman glosses his phrase, "moral temper," with the note that "the intellectual

17. *OUS*, p. 179.
18. *OUS*, p. 180.
19. *OUS*, p. 181.
20. *OUS*, p. 187.
21. *OUS*, p. 181.
22. *OUS*, pp. 179–180.

principles on which the conclusions are drawn, to which Faith assents, are the consequents of a certain ethical temper, as their *sine quâ non* condition."[23] In other words, faith reaches its conclusions, not as those conclusions or consequents follow *logically* from their grounds, but as they follow *morally*. Under certain circumstances we "jump" to conclusions, and those conclusions prove, in practice, to be true, even though we were unable to prove their truth by logical process in advance. We "jump" because we are inclined to a certain conclusion by various forces other than, or in addition to, the purely logical or rational ones. In other words, faith "is mainly swayed by antecedent considerations," and in that respect, primarily, the principle of faith is distinguished from that of reason. "Faith is influenced by previous notices, prepossessions, and (in a good sense of the word) prejudices; but Reason, by direct and definite proof. The mind that believes is acted upon by its own hopes, fears, and existing opinions."[24] Such "previous notices" are not allowable in strict reasoning, which "rejects every thing but the actual evidence producible" in favor of its conclusions.[25]

Newman calls those prepossessions "inducements to belief which prevail with all of us, by a law of our nature,"[26] and faith is called a "moral principle" because these prepossessions constitute "probabilities." These "probabilities" are *moral* as opposed to *logical*, for they "have no definite ascertained value, and are reducible to no scientific standard, what are such to each individual, depends on his moral temperament."[27] These remarks bring us to the very heart of Newman's whole conception of faith. They explain in the first place how it is possible for him to maintain that though faith is a principle, *sui generis*, distinct from rea-

23. *OUS*, p. 179, n. 4.
24. *OUS*, pp. 187–188.
25. *OUS*, p. 188.
26. *OUS*, p. 189.
27. *OUS*, p. 191. For Newman's important distinction with regard to his use of the word *probable* see his correspondence with J. D. Dalgairns from Rome in December of 1846 in *Letters and Diaries*, XI, 288ff. See also the correspondence with Edward Healy Thompson (October 1853), XV, 464–466.

son, it is also, in one sense, a legitimate "exercise of Reason."[28] The apparent contradiction resolves itself when we realize that both activities proceed from premises to conclusions and that in that respect both are rational. In other words, faith is as distinct as reason from the intuitive grasp of God's existence in our conscience, for, as we recall, that original intuition of being is not subject to the "sceptical principle." Since, however, faith and reason proceed to their conclusions on different grounds, the former depending on presumptions and probabilities rather than on proofs, faith really can be said to be an epistemological activity distinct from reason. Though rational rather than intuitive in its nature, faith is nevertheless drawn toward the latter character of experience, for the presumptions on which it proceeds are supplied by those intuitions of the conscience and the heart. Thus Newman can legitimately argue that faith perfects our natural knowledge rather than destroying it, for it conserves the familiar rational process. It does that, however, by translating it into a new mode, by giving it moral, subjective, or "spiritual" as opposed to logical, objective, or "scientific" grounds.

Moreover, the distinction between logical and moral grounds enables us to see how faith may be regarded as a theological virtue (though Newman does not use the term, as such, in this context) or, as he says, a peculiar gift of the Gospel, "an instrument of knowledge and action, unknown to the world before,"[29] without taking the "enthusiastic" view that faith gives us new faculties of apprehension. Moral judgment in itself is no new faculty; on the contrary, the intuitions of the conscience which supply the grounds for that judgment are "possessed by pagans as well as Christians,"[30] and, once those grounds are supplied, it is a "law of our nature" to proceed from premises to conclusions on the basis of "previous notices" or "probabilities" rather than upon strictly scientific proofs. However, "when the probabilities we assume do not really exist, or our wishes are inordinate, or our opinions are wrong,"[31] then our conclusions will be invalid and

28. *OUS*, p. 207.
29. *OUS*, p. 179.
30. Sillem, II, 67.
31. *OUS*, p. 189.

instead of faith we have "weakness, extravagance, superstition, enthusiasm, bigotry, prejudice, as the case may be."[32] Faith is distinct from these in being a *right* moral judgment, based on valid presumptions, and what Christianity gives us is the proper moral disposition to distinguish what is really probable from what is not. Or, to put the matter another way, the grace given in the Christian dispensation refines the intuitive perceptions of the conscience and secures their validity. "A good and a bad man will think very different things probable,"[33] and Christian grace makes bad men good. Thus the man who lives by grace, according to God's will as it is revealed in Christ Jesus, will be furnished with a just estimate of probabilities and presumptions and, consequently, with valid moral grounds for his conclusions. Thus a man is morally responsible for his faith or lack of it, "because he is responsible for his likings and dislikings, his hopes and his opinions, on all of which his faith depends."[34] Thus Newman sometimes contrasts conscience and reason in the same way in which he contrasts faith and reason; for though faith and reason both differ from conscience in being deductive rather than intuitive, nevertheless conscience is so necessary to faith as the source of its moral judgments that for all practical purposes the two may be referred to interchangeably.

Another analogous distinction which we have already touched on in another context is that between *implicit* and *explicit* reason. That is the language of the *University Sermons*; in the *Grammar of Assent* Newman refers to the same processes as *informal* and *formal* inference. Explicit reason or formal inference are both names for the logical principle. In other words, they both signify essentially the same thing that Newman means by the simple term *reason* when he contrasts it with faith. Both denote the process of the mind from grounds to consequents, and their conclusions are necessarily abstractions or deductions. In that respect they are both "scientific" and therefore of limited use, so far as Newman is concerned, in questions of the knowledge of God; Paley's search for evidences is, in fact, a

32. *OUS*, pp. 189–190.
33. *OUS*, p. 191.
34. *OUS*, p. 192.

good indication to Newman of how little explicit or formal inference can do to help us in our exploration of religious mysteries.
"No analysis is subtle and delicate enough to represent adequately
the state of mind under which we believe, or the subjects of
belief, as they are presented to our thoughts."[35] For that reason,
Newman calls formal inference "explicit"—it is, at best, only the
outward manifestation, reduced to dubious simplicity, of the
mysterious operation which actually takes place within the mind.
At best, logic is an economical representation of inner mysteries, and we know enough already about Newman's subjectivism, his distrust of realist epistemology, to doubt for a moment
what his attitude toward the merely "explicit" will be. In fact no
language, not even that of Holy Scripture, gives adequate expression of the truth of God. Inspiration "uses human language,
and it addresses man; and neither can man compass, nor can his
hundred tongues utter, the mysteries of the spiritual world, and
God's appointments in this."[36] In attempting that impossible task,
logic murders to dissect; "nor does any real thing admit, by any
calculus of logic, of being dissected into all the possible general
notions which it admits, nor, in consequence, of being recom-
posed out of them."[37]

Implicit reason or informal inference avoids these difficulties.
Like faith, this type of reason is swayed primarily by probabilities
and, thus, involves the heart and moral nature, "the whole man,"
rather than simply the mind; "many of our most obstinate and
most reasonable certitudes depend on proofs which are informal
and personal, which baffle our powers of analysis, and cannot be
brought under logical rule, because they cannot be submitted to
logical statistics."[38] In other words, implicit reason, like faith,
rests its conclusions on a moral or personal, as opposed to a rational, judgment. Like faith, it comes to its conclusions imme-

35. *OUS*, p. 267.
36. *OUS*, p. 268.
37. *GA*, p. 215. Several of Newman's commentators have raised serious
objections to the nominalist tendencies of these theories. Two representative
studies are M. C. D'Arcy's *The Nature of Belief* (St. Louis: B. Herder Book
Co., 1958), pp. 102–111, and Fr. T. Harper's "Dr. Newman's *Essay in Aid
of a Grammar of Assent*," *Month* XII (1870), 599–611, 667–692.
38. *GA*, p. 229.

diately, almost instinctively, nor can it justify its proceedings by giving the world a full account of its procedures. Newman's best illustration of that instinctive and mysterious capacity of the implicit reason is the image of the cliff climber to which we have already alluded. The mind "makes progress not unlike a clamberer on a steep cliff, who, by quick eye, prompt hand, and firm foot, ascends how he knows not himself, by personal endowments and by practice, rather than by rule."[39] To move by rule is to move by explicit or formal inference; to proceed "by personal endowments and by practice" is to operate on the basis of personal or moral judgment.

If I understand him correctly, Newman means virtually the same thing by the "illative sense" that he means by implicit reason or informal inference. The image of the climber, the principle that the whole man reasons, by instinct rather than by rule, suggests the similarity. "It is the mind that reasons, and that controls its own reasonings, not any technical apparatus of words and propositions. This power of judging and concluding, when in its perfection, I call the Illative Sense."[40] He calls it a "rule to itself" which, like implicit reason, is independent of purely logical constraints, appealing "to no judgment beyond its own."[41] It "attends upon the whole course of thought from antecedents to consequents, with a minute diligence and unwearied presence, which is impossible to a cumbrous apparatus of verbal reasoning,"[42] the latter, of course, being explicit or formal. Likewise, its end is belief or "certitude" rather than formal proof, and it is thus akin to faith in opposition to reason. Therefore it seems reasonable to offer the distinction between the illative sense and formal inference as another cognate in the series we are developing.

How, then, if at all, do *implicit reason, informal inference,* and the *illative sense* differ from *faith?* Newman, so far as I can see, never makes the distinction completely clear, and in some respects, as we have seen, the terms can be used interchangeably.

39. *OUS*, p. 257.
40. *GA*, p. 268.
41. *GA*, p. 274.
42. *GA*, pp. 274–275.

On the other hand, he never simply identifies them, and even when he suggests their similarity, he keeps them distinct. For instance, he grants that "the reasonings and opinions which are involved in the act of Faith are latent and implicit,"[43] and that faith is complete without any application of explicit or formal reason; the language here, however, suggests that the "act of Faith" is still distinct from the "reasonings and opinions," even the implicit ones, which "are involved in" it. The difficulty can be resolved, I believe, by reference to Newman's discussion of assent and inference. As I understand his terminology, he means the same thing by an act of assent and an act of faith, and both are conceived as distinct from the inferential or illative process. Indeed, it is the difference between an *act* and a *process*; and, even when the latter is implicit and, consequently, involved with the former, the two remain formally distinct. That is because a process is, by definition, a movement, whereas assent is an act of completion or of coming to rest. One is a line; the other a point. It may be impossible to talk about faith in operation except with reference to the process of moral or personal inference or the functioning of the illative sense which is bound up with it; on the other hand we must not forget that assent, when it is made, is independent, even of the moral or implicit grounds, not to mention the merely logical or explicit ones, on which it is based. Newman is quite adamant on this point: "I lay it down, then, as a principle that either assent is intrinsically distinct from inference, or the sooner we get rid of the word in philosophy the better." An assent is "a substantive act" and "may endure without the presence of the inferential acts" which elicited it.[44]

It appears, therefore, that we may divide Newman's concept of faith or assent into two parts or stages—the *process* of implicit reason and the *act* of assent to which that process leads. Under either aspect, faith is opposed to explicit or formal or "scientific" reasoning, for both the informal inference and the act of assent are predicated on activities of the heart and conscience, of the whole man, transcending the ordinary laws of thought. In other

43. OUS, p. 277.
44. GA, p. 125.

words, faith considered as a process or as a special type of reasoning is opposed, as we have seen, to reason in general. Considered simply as an act, however, faith is distinct even from the implicit reason or informal inference which is "involved," "latent and implicit," in it. Therefore when we speak of the differences between faith and reason, we may be talking about the distinction between, on one hand, the complex activity of informal inference and its culmination in assent and, on the other, formal or explicit inference. However, faith may also be opposed to reason in the much stricter sense in which we consider the act of assent as distinct from and ultimately independent of any process of inference of any type, even the implicit or informal. In either case, in varying degrees, faith is considered as subjective, intuitive, and personal; reason as objective, scientific, and dependent on general laws. Therefore we see that we may legitimately add the distinction between faith and implicit reason to our list of contraries, though, for obvious reasons, Newman does not often insist upon it.

These considerations introduce another set of opposites to which we have already alluded—the *real* and the *notional*. These terms differ from the others we have been considering in that Newman applies them, primarily, to the objects of apprehension and assent rather than to the faculties and principles. Real assent is the assent to things or images; notional assent is to conclusions and abstractions. Thus we see immediately that notional assent is virtually inseparable from explicit reason or formal inference and that real assent is akin to implicit reason. Of course, we must remember that in either case assent is distinct from inference, even from informal inference, and Newman allows the possibility of a genuine assent to notions. We can conceivably reason our way to an abstract proposition and then give our assent to it, but such notional assent lacks the power of the real. "In its Notional Assents as well as in its inferences, the mind contemplates its own creations instead of things; in Real, it is directed towards things, represented by the impressions which they have left on the imagination. These images, when assented to, have an influence both on the individual and on society, which mere notions cannot exert."[45] Thus, without denying the integrity of notional assent, Newman generally speaks in terms of a broad contrast between real assent or belief and notional assent which is also belief but less intense and compelling.[46] We see immediately that the distinction is parallel to the others we have drawn, for real assent in its very vividness is like an intuition, while notional assent acquires the smell and taste of reason. Notional assent, like formal inference, "is necessarily concerned with surfaces and aspects . . . it does not reach as far as facts." "Belief, on the other hand, [is] concerned with things concrete, not abstract, which variously excite the mind from their moral and imaginative properties." Real assent is to "objects which kindle devotion, rouse the passions, and attach the affections,"[47] and Newman's sympathy is clearly with "reality." "No one, I say, will die for his own calculations: he dies for realities."[48] Real assent, the sort of belief that makes martyrs, demands that we accept the doctrine of God "with an apprehension, not only of what the words of the proposition mean, but of the object denoted by them."[49]

This insistence upon "reality" seems, at first glance, to contradict what we have said earlier about the idealist or subjective bent of Newman's thought, but, as a matter of fact, the two suppositions are closely linked. The bond between them is Newman's concept of the "image." Real assent, he says, "is directed towards things, represented by the impressions which they have left on the imagination." In notional assents, on the other hand, "the mind contemplates its own creations instead of things."[50] The distinction is very important, for it throws Newman's whole epistemology into a clear light. He obviously regards images as more reliable and more compelling than reasons (and here is another set of opposites analogous to the rest) because the former are di-

45. GA, p. 57.
46. GA, p. 68.
47. GA, p. 69.
48. GA, p. 71.
49. GA, p. 90.
50. GA, p. 57.

rect impressions while the latter are necessarily abstractions from what is direct. These images are what Newman means by *ideas*, and it follows that by turning inward to these ideas, one comes to a much more immediate and more nearly intuitive sort of knowledge than if one proceeded to acquire intelligible species from sense impressions.

Thomist terminology may help us to clarify Newman's position by contrast. In St. Thomas's language, these ideas or images of divine reality which reside in the mind independently of the senses are identified as either *infused* or *innate* as opposed to *acquired* species. Man does not acquire them by rational abstractions *a sensu*. He may have been born with them or they may have been impressed upon him directly by God; the former, of course, is the Platonist notion of innate ideas, the latter what Aquinas conceives to be the Augustinian concept of infusion. St. Thomas himself rejects both concepts, for though when the soul is separated from the body it will understand by "infused species," by "participated species arising from the influence of the Divine light,"[51] nevertheless, in this present life "to understand through a phantasm [a sense image] is the proper operation of the soul by virtue of its union with the body."[52] As we have seen, it is not accurate to say that Newman taught a doctrine of innate ideas (or, for that matter, of infused ideas); but, as we have also seen, the practical consequences of his emphasis on the conscience as an epistemological faculty are very much the same as those that follow from belief in innate or infused species. What the two doctrines have in common is that the idea of God which man holds is independent of the senses and of the abstracting power of the reason. Therefore, we might say that Newman demonstrates his affinity with the Platonic and Augustinian, rather than with the Aristotelian and Thomist tradition when he contrasts the *real*, not with the *ideal*, but with the *notional;* for the image or species or idea of God produced by the conscience has an immediacy, a "reality," which the abstractions of the reason, the acquired species, lack.

51. *ST*, I, 89, 1.
52. *ST*, I, 75, 6.

It is for this reason that Newman suggests a parallel between the conscience and the instinct, for each provides immediate as opposed to abstract knowledge. "It is instinct which impels the child to recognize in the smiles or the frowns of a countenance which meets his eyes, not only a being external to himself, but one whose looks elicit in him confidence or fear."[53] By a parallel operation, the child begins "to learn about its Lord and God from conscience."[54] In neither case is the knowledge rational or notional; rather, it is direct and immediate and independent of abstraction. In the case of conscience, it is knowledge which comes directly from God, and hence provides grounds for assent to Him which Paley could never argue us into nor "Herr von Voltaire" argue us out of. It is by an "instinct of the mind" that man recognizes in the dictate of conscience "an external master" in a fashion parallel to that in which the mind discerns individual beings "under the shifting shapes and colours of the visible world."[55] Nor does that apprehension by conscience of the idea or image of God depend on reason, for the child and the peasant know Him as well or better than the philosopher; and "until we account for the knowledge which an infant has of his mother or his nurse, what reason have we to take exception at the doctrine, as strange and difficult, that in the dictate of conscience, without previous experiences or analogical reasoning, he is able gradually to perceive the voice, or echoes of the voice, of a Master, living, personal, and sovereign?"[56]

Thus we see that Newman's concept of reality in the act of faith or assent is tied very closely to his idealism or subjectivism. Reality means immediacy—the knowledge of God which is intuited directly, which is felt instinctively "in my conscience and my heart." It is a voice, or echo of a voice, not an abstract or impersonal conclusion from evidences. Such reality of assent to

---

53. GA, p. 48.
54. GA, p. 48. Among Newman's best-known twentieth-century commentators D'Arcy is probably the most outspoken in his objection to the imprecise use of such terms as *instinct* and *sense*, which, he remarks, "will make the philosophic purist wince." (*The Nature of Belief*, p. 102.)
55. GA, p. 84.
56. GA, p. 85.

God is the strength of the holy martyrs, and Newman concludes the *Grammar of Assent* with a stirring roll call of those men and women whose courage can only be accounted for by the fact that they possessed their Lord immediately, as an idea or image independent of all proof and disproof. Our Lord ascended into heaven, but He has not left His disciples comfortless. He has "imprinted the Image or Idea of Himself in the minds of His subjects," and it is this "imprinted" image or idea, this "Thought of Christ, not a corporate body or a doctrine, which inspired that zeal which the historian [Gibbon] so poorly comprehends."[57] Sustained by His presence as an image or idea, not merely as a notional teaching, men "faced the implements of torture as the soldier takes his post before the enemy's battery," for "no intensity of torture had any means of affecting what was a mental conviction; and the sovereign Thought in which they had lived was their adequate support and consolation in their death."[58]

Such, for Newman, are the fruits of faith as opposed to reason, of moral as opposed to merely rational judgment, of informal as opposed to formal inference, of reality as opposed to notions, of images as opposed to reasons. It is interesting, by contrast, to note that for Aquinas even faith, the faith of confessors and martyrs, is notional. He agrees with Newman that faith is an "assent of the intellect to that which is believed,"[59] rather than to that which the mind can prove, but such an assent does not imply, for St. Thomas, a direct, intuitive, or "instinctive" awareness of faith's object. On the contrary, he insists that the object of faith, just as fully as the object of reason, is "something complex" which we apprehend, not immediately but rationally, not in an "imprinted" image but in an abstraction, "by way of a proposition."[60] Newman might well have subscribed to the various objections to the article in question [II (2), 1, 2]. The first is that since the "object of faith is the First Truth," the personal living God, and since that "First Truth is something simple," the object of faith

57. GA, pp. 353–354.
58. GA, p. 364.
59. ST, II(2), 1, 4.
60. ST, II(2), 1, 2.

must likewise be simple and direct rather than complex or abstract; Newman says almost exactly that with reference to the
martyrs. The second objection is that the "exposition of faith" is
contained in a symbol and that that symbol does "not contain
propositions [notions], but things"; consequently "the object
of faith is not a proposition but a thing." The third objection is
that since "Faith is succeeded by vision," and since the "object
of the heavenly vision is something simple, for it is the Divine
Essence," then the faith which anticipates that vision must also
have something simple for its object.[61]

St. Thomas answers all three objections on the grounds that
"the thing known is in the knower according to the mode of
the knower," not according to the mode of the thing known.
That means that the object of faith is in man in the same way
that the object of reason is, for both are ways of knowing and
have as their common ground the human faculties of knowledge.
Therefore faith has no more capacity than reason does to apprehend its object simply and directly, even though its object,
God, may be, in Himself, simple. In other words, all assent must
be notional because the means of apprehension "connatural" to
man's condition in this world are notional; "now the mode
proper to the human intellect is to know the truth by synthesis
and analysis." Only in heaven will it be possible to have real
assent. Thus, in answer to the objection that faith's apprehension
of God must be simple because God Himself is simple, St. Thomas
replies that "things that are simple in themselves, are known by
the intellect with a certain amount of complexity." To the objection that the symbol or exposition of faith contains not
propositions but things, he agrees that faith, like all knowledge,
does terminate in things, but that propositions or "acquired
species" are our necessary means for coming to the knowledge of
those things. To the third objection, that since our heavenly
vision of the Divine Essence must be simple, the faith which
precedes it must likewise be simple, Aquinas replies that "the
comparison fails" because, as he has shown, faith does not ap-

61. *ST*, II(2), 1, 2.

prehend God as He is in Himself but according to the mode of the knower—that is, by means of propositions, abstractions, and notions.[62]

It therefore appears that St. Thomas would not agree with Newman in ascribing those glorious martyrdoms to faith considered *sui generis* as a principle or mode of assent which differs from the rational and which serves to make God's image or idea real to us. "Whence," asks Newman, "came this tremendous spirit, scaring, nay, offending, the fastidious criticism of our delicate days? Does Gibbon think to sound the depths of the eternal ocean with the tape and measuring-rod of his merely literary philosophy?"[63] Of course he could not; but then the question arises whether Aquinas was able to "sound the depths of the eternal ocean" with his "merely" Scholastic philosophy, and it appears that he could and did. Moreover, it is Thomism rather than Newmanism which is capable of meeting Voltaire or Gibbon on their own rational ground, and one imagines that St. Thomas would have recognized, as Newman does not, that Wordsworth, Coleridge, or Carlyle were ultimately as great enemies of Catholicism as was Gibbon. Though Newman's conclu-

62. *ST*, II(2), 1, 2. Jacques Maritain gives a brilliant statement of the same Thomistic thesis: "It is indeed, God as He knows Himself, the divine transintelligible insofar as it is, in itself and by itself, object—to Himself and to the blessed—insofar as it offers itself to their apprehension, which is attained by faith. But nevertheless, for all that, we do not yet hold Him in our grasp; He does not become in Himself and by Himself object for us; we do not see Him as the blessed do. He is constituted object for our understanding only according to the ananoetic or specular mode—*per speculum in aenigmate*—of which the metaphysical knowledge of God has already furnished us an example, i.e., by means of the objectification of other subjects which fall under our senses and which are intelligible in themselves for us, and whose attributes have in the deity their sovereign analogate." Thus Maritain, following St. Thomas, regards faith not as something wholly distinct from philosophical analogy but rather as a "superanalogy." "The mode of conceiving and of signifying is just as deficient in it as in metaphysical analogy, but what is signified . . . is this time the deity as such, God as He sees Himself, and who gives Himself to us—obscurely and without our laying hands on him yet, since we do not see Him." [*The Degrees of Knowledge*, trans. Gerald B. Phelan (New York: Charles Scribner's Sons, 4th ed., 1959) pp. 241–242.]

63. *GA*, p. 368.

sions are orthodox, his view of faith as a principle distinct from and, in some degree, opposed to reason, his ultimate recourse to the heat of inward evidence—in fact, the whole series of parallel oppositions which we have been examining—unite him in sympathy with one "form of infidelity of the day" even while they provide him with weapons against another.

What then are Newman's safeguards? Abjuring reason in favor of immediate, intuitive awareness, abjuring acquired species for the image of God imprinted directly on the conscience, how was he able to prevent himself from falling into pure subjectivism and relativism and denying all objective truth? To state the question in terms we have used already: How did Newman manage to make himself an exception to the general modern rule that subjectivism and antirationalism engender heresy? How was he able to separate himself from traditional modes of Catholic thought, from the "tradition of fifteen hundred years," without compromising Catholic dogma? On what terms could he embrace the modern mind without forfeiting the old religion?

The answer lies in Newman's concept of the conscience; for we are faced with the curious circumstance that the very faculty which serves as the foundation of his subjectivism is also the faculty which insures the orthodoxy of his subjective apprehensions. As we have seen, he regards conscience as the medium by which divine images or ideas are impressed upon the mind; and in allotting that cognitive function to the conscience he immediately distinguishes his own epistemology from the idealism of purer Platonists such as Clement and Origen and allies himself with the synthesis of idealism and sensationalism which characterizes the views of his contemporaries. The "whole man reasons"; which means that the passions and affections of the heart are involved in the intuition of truth. Those affections, however, as Newman conceives them, always involve our sense of right and wrong; and at that point he qualifies the Romantic epistemology. At the risk of oversimplification, we might say that for Clement and Origen the mind, properly instructed in Apostolic doctrine and in the disciplines of recollection and contemplation, is the primary faculty for the intuitive apprehension of God and the invisible world. Those supernatural realities are present to man as innate ideas to be remembered, or as infused ideas to be discovered, in a sense to be *uncovered* by what revelation teaches economically (and Augustine takes a similar position). For Coleridge, Wordsworth, Carlyle, and Tennyson, in varying degrees, the heart, by which I mean the complex of feelings and passions, *but without any particular moral reference,* is the organ of intuitive apprehension. Therefore, as we have seen, Clement and Origen admire the "gnostic" or the knower while the modern poets admire the man of feeling.

Because for Newman neither the mind nor the feelings, pure and simple, are the primary faculties of apprehension, but rather what we might regard as the union of those faculties in the complex intuition of our existence as men, his admiration is extended to what he considers man's distinguishing feature, his ethical and religious capacity. Thus he admires supremely neither the gnostic nor the man of feeling but, as we have seen, the earnest man, the man who seeks in all things to do God's will. For Newman the source of our knowledge of God is not simply the heart but a "right heart," or a clear conscience, and in that distinction (we reach the point at last) lies the safeguard of his Catholicism and the reason why his subjectivism remains orthodox.[64] Why does the conscience provide a clearer and more reliable view of supernatural truth than either the mind or the heart considered as faculties independent of the moral sense? The answer is that conscience imposes upon us a keen sense of ethical responsibility for our opinions. The idea or image of God which it conveys to us is that of a moral governor, a stern judge, to whom we are answerable for all our thoughts, words, and deeds. Before the image of such a deity we relinquish all "liberty of speculation" and seek instead the "safe course." That means we seek authority of the sort which only the Church provides and submit all our theological speculations or intuitions to her orthodox and infallible judgment. Tennyson's or Carlyle's

64. As Przywara says, Newman's emphasis on conscience saves him from the "pure interiority" of Hegelianism, for conscience "belongs to the domain of ethics, and ethics simply as such lies within the sphere of 'practice.'" *Saint Augustine,* p. 283.

intuition of God can never have the same consequences, for the heart does not expose God to us in His role as judge nor constrain us, as the conscience does, to relinquish our liberty of thought to Him. Conscience, we recall, "involves the recognition of a living object, towards which it is directed." It teaches us that "there is One to whom we are responsible, before whom we are ashamed, whose claims upon us we fear."[65] Such is the idea of God, perceived *really*, upon which Newman's theology rests; and if, in one sense, Newman and his contemporaries agree that religion must be intuitive rather than rational, it is quite clear that the intuition of God which the conscience provides as the foundation for religion is totally different from that which derives from the heart.

Newman was fully aware that the traditional conception of conscience was being compromised by the reigning subjectivism of nineteenth-century philosophy, and the distinction he draws between the "real thing" and the modern copy serves very nicely as an index to where he stood in relation to the heresies of his day. "We are told," by modern philosophers, "that conscience is but a twist in primitive and untutored man; that its dictate is an imagination; that the very notion of guiltiness, which that dictate enforces, is simply irrational."[66] In other words, conscience is reduced to a simple matter of feelings, devoid of *real* moral significance and therefore in no way absolute in its dictates. Consequently, in popular usage, conscience no longer implies "the presence of a Moral Governor . . . [and] when men advocate the rights of conscience, they in no sense mean the rights of the Creator, nor the duty to Him, in thought and deed, of the creature; but the right of thinking, speaking, writing, and acting, according to their judgment or their humour, without any thought of God at all."[67] Thus considered, conscience is simply another name for the feelings and provides no safeguard for orthodoxy whatever. In fact, in the name of such a conception of conscience any sort of heresy whatever can be justified by an appeal to the feelings. However, when we recognize what

65. GA, p. 83.
66. *Diff.*, II, 249.
67. *Diff.*, II, 250.

conscience really is and that "He who acts against his conscience loses his soul" because he acts directly against God, we see that the right of conscience is no mere "right of self will" but a personal obligation to our Creator and Judge. Thus, properly understood, the principle of conscience, though it remains subjective and intuitive in nature, secures itself, by its very nature, from the dangers of heresy and atheism. Neither the mind nor the heart as cognitive faculties carries such built-in safeguards.

Newman's concept of natural religion provides us with another good index to his position. To orthodox theologians in the Scholastic or Caroline tradition, natural religion is that body of conclusions about God and supernatural matters to which we attain by right reason; Paley's position might be regarded as a latter-day, attenuated survival of that view. Since, in Scholastic thought, right reason *must* lead to the Catholic Faith, the beliefs of natural religion, though incomplete, are always potentially in accord with what revelation and the infallible Church teach and with what faith apprehends. Newman takes a radically different view of the subject. He conceives the origin of natural religion to be in the conscience rather than in the reason, and though he admits the existence of a purely rational natural religion, he dismisses such as a mere "intellectual religion," a "philosopher's, a gentleman's religion," which substitutes "taste for conscience" and "intellectual culture" for the fear of God.[68]

It is not that Newman denies "external" sources for our knowledge of God, from "the voice of mankind, and the course of the world"; he does, however, insist that natural religion is founded primarily on "our own mind, whose informations give us the rule by which we test, interpret, and correct what is presented to us for belief, whether by the universal testimony of mankind, or by the history of society and of the world."[69] Moreover, since the particular faculty of our mind which gives us that rule is the conscience, and since the conscience "teaches us, not only that God is, but what He is; it provides for the mind a real image of Him, as a medium of worship; it gives us a rule of right and

68. *Idea*, p. 193.
69. *GA*, pp. 295–296.

wrong, as being His rule, and a code of moral duties."[70] The consequence is a natural religion with an idea of God in which all his other attributes are subordinated to that of "justice— retributive justice." Therefore the effect of natural religion, so far from encouraging us to rest comfortably in our subjective impression of God, as a religion of pure heart or even pure mind might do, is to "burden and sadden" us and to convince us of a "fearful antagonism" between ourselves and our Judge.[71] Thus man is led to adopt sacrificial rites as means of atonement, to consecrate priests to serve at his altars, and submit his mind and will to God in fear; and in all these ways he is drawn toward orthodox Christianity.

Had Newman made the distinction between his own position and that of his contemporaries, between himself and Coleridge or Carlyle as well as between himself and Gibbon, he would probably have added that a natural religion which is simply of the heart could not lead to orthodoxy. However, focusing as he does on one form of infidelity and more or less failing to recognize the other, he defines his religion of conscience largely in contrast to Gibbon's "literary philosophy," the "religion of so-called civilization,"[72] the philosopher's or gentleman's religion, which, being mainly a development of the ratiocinative faculty, either ignores ethical considerations altogether or merely pays lip service to them. A superstitious or barbarous religion is, in Newman's view, finally superior to the philosophy of ancient Athens because, inspiring a fear of God, it is more nearly susceptible than the other to Christian conversion. A natural religion formed upon the dictates of conscience gives us "those frightful presentiments which are expressed in the worship and traditions of the heathen"[73] and which can only be soothed and calmed by the promise of grace and mercy, on the authority of Holy Church. No religion which inspires confidence in our rational capacities or in the goodness of nature could, in Newman's view, effect such an issue.

70. GA, p. 296.
71. GA, p. 297.
72. GA, p. 301.
73. GA, p. 301.

Thus we see that Newman's appeal to the immediate knowledge of God in the conscience, however closely it may resemble
his contemporaries' invocation of "inward evidence," is sufficiently distinct to account for the orthodox nature of his theological conclusions. The idea or image that conscience gives us of
God corresponds, so far as it goes, to what God *really* is, whereas
the heart, untutored by the conscience, is wicked above all things
and may easily deceive us. The feelings may provide us with an
idea of God but, because they exert no moral constraint upon
us, they can never force us to accept responsibility for that idea.
The conscience, on the other hand, communicates, in union
with the idea of God which it perceives, fear for the disposition
of our immortal souls. We may dally with our feelings, with the
knowledge of the heart, but the conscience terrifies us into
earnestness. Therefore, though we may rest comfortably in what
we *feel*, conscience compels us to seek for some relief from our
fear of God in the amendment of our lives, and it thereby dis-
poses us to recognize and embrace salvation when we finally
encounter it in the sacraments and doctrines of Holy Church.
Therefore we must never confuse the conscience with "what is
sometimes improperly termed, 'feeling';—improperly, because
feeling comes and goes, and, having no root in our nature, speaks
with no divine authority."[74] Conscience, because it does speak
with divine authority, must *necessarily* agree with the authority
of the Church, which is the external, institutional complement of
the inward faculty. God speaks in both, and He cannot contradict
Himself. Thus any man who has learned to attend his conscience
and obey its dictates will recognize in the Church Him whom he
has always known in his own mind. Conversion to the "one fold
of Christ" is, therefore, the logical, objective, and external consequence of what began in each of us as soon as we could distinguish what "ought" means. Feelings may possibly lead us to the
same conclusion, but then our course would be accidental rather
than inevitable. On the contrary, if we obey our consciences, we
must become Catholics; which, of course, the other "subjectivists"
of Newman's day failed to do.

74. *OUS*, pp. 59–60.

One other problem confronts us: distrusting ratiocination as
he does, how does Newman justify its use in the development
of Catholic theology? This question is distinct from and logically
subsequent to that of how he arrives at an objective religion
through the means of a subjective experience. Having left Littlemore and having arrived at last in Rome, and having traveled
all the way by means of moral intuitions rather than metaphysical
proofs, implicit rather than explicit reasons, how can he now
accept the logical and explicitly notional structure of Catholic
theology, a theology which, at least in its language, is Thomist
and scientific and, apparently, far less sympathetic to Newman's
mind than the Anglicanism which he had left behind him?

Whether it was, in fact, less sympathetic is a matter of debate.
Suffice it to recall that Newman's concept of the conscience
demands a strongly authoritarian doctrine of the Church as its
complement. As we have seen, the emphasis on authority, on
the *jus divinum*, the positive divine commandment, increases in
proportion as confidence in nature, reason, and human custom
declines. The Council of Trent set the Church of Rome on an
authoritarian course which, though it appealed strongly to St.
Thomas and the Schoolmen, was foreign in its ethos to the
traditionalism and rationalism of medieval Christendom. Hooker
and his followers, as we have seen, preserved the medieval flavor
in the Church of England, and it is at least arguable that even
as late as the eighteen thirties and forties, thanks to the old High
Church party and even, in part, to the fact of the Establishment,
Canterbury was closer in philosophical temper to the middle
ages than was Rome.[75] If so, Newman's secession may be legitimately regarded as a move in the "modern" direction, away from
the "natural" harmony of faith and reason, *jus divinum* and *jus
humanum*, to the new dualism in which those traditional complements become warring opposites and in which faith and the

75. It is interesting that Louis I. Bredvold finds Roman Catholic apologetics in England in the seventeenth century to be far more strongly influenced by scepticism and fideism than Anglican theology was. It appears
that the situation in the nineteenth century was not vastly different. See
Louis I. Bredvold, *The Intellectual Milieu of John Dryden* (Ann Arbor: The
University of Michigan Press, 1934).

apprehension of divine law come to be conceived as essentially subjective experiences and therefore in need of an infallible external authority for their sustenance.

Even though we may interpret Newman's conversion in this light, however, and though we may tend to discount in some degree the dependence on right reason in post-Tridentine Catholicism, we are still faced with the fact that Newman himself felt obliged to give a rational account of doctrinal developments. Therefore, our original question of how he reconciles that account with his distrust of ratiocination persists. The answer, I believe, lies in his distinction between faith and "philosophy" or faith and "wisdom," which he develops first in the *University Sermons* and subsequently in the *Idea of a University* and the *Grammar of Assent*. Faith, we recall, is "an exercise of the Reason, so spontaneous, unconscious, and unargumentative, as to seem at first sight even to be a moral act" not unlike the immediate intuitions of the conscience. Wisdom, on the other hand, is "that orderly and mature development of thought, which in earthly language goes by the name of science and philosophy."[76] Though "science and philosophy" may be misused and thus become enemies of Christianity, the true "philosophical temper" was "enjoined by the Gospel," and if we are "in earnest in seeking the truth," if we take reason, not "in the light of an amusement" but as a "grave employment," then philosophical speculation may serve as a handmaid to faith.[77] The "usurpations of reason" occur when the intellectual principle is divorced from the moral, the latter, of course, being the foundation of faith.

Wisdom, however, if it is truly wisdom and no secular counterfeit, is never independent of faith; and we must never confuse it with the mere "literary philosophy," the shallow intellectual scepticism of a Gibbon or a Hume. On the contrary, Newman insists that in labeling wisdom as "the mature fruit of Reason" we must not suppose that he is denying "its spiritual nature or its divine origin."[78] On the surface, wisdom may look like mere philosophy, like mere ratiocination, and it may be subject to the

76. *OUS*, p. 279.
77. *OUS*, p. 7.
78. *OUS*, p. 281.

same perversions, but properly understood it is rooted in faith, not contradictory to it.[79] For wisdom, or true philosophy, is "Reason exercised upon Knowledge,"[80] and faith is the source of that knowledge. Assuming the facts to be given, "Reason is synonymous with analysis, having no office beyond that of ascertaining the relations existing between them [the given facts]. Reason is the power of proceeding to new ideas by means of given ones," and those that are given, at least in so far as they are ideas of God, are, in fact, given by faith. "Thus, from scanty data, it often draws out a whole system, each part with its ascertained relations, collateral or lineal, towards the rest, and all consistent together, because all derived from one and the same origin."[81] The consequent intellectual growth is rational, but its roots, clearly, are in faith.

Thus we see that theological dogmas are the fruits of wisdom or philosophy, and Newman says that these are the natural and proper results of faith. They are "propositions expressive of the judgments which the mind forms, or the impressions which it receives, of Revealed Truth." The ideas or images of divine realities which are impressed upon us by our conscience and which we apprehend by faith become, "spontaneously, or even necessarily . . . the subject of reflection on the part of the mind itself, which proceeds to investigate it, and to draw it forth in successive and distinct sentences."[82] "Inferior animals," children, and the Seraphim "who are said to be, not Knowledge, but all Love,"[83] may rest with the divine images or ideas, without rational reflections; but philosophy is natural to man. Lest we should confuse Newman's proposition with St. Thomas's, however, we must not forget that for Newman faith and conscience, and the image of God which conscience forms and which faith holds, precede all reason, whereas, for St. Thomas, reason serves to acquire those images. Presumably Newman would regard the latter view as a "usurpation."

79. *OUS*, p. 282.
80. *OUS*, p. 290.
81. *OUS*, p. 290.
82. *OUS*, p. 320.
83. *OUS*, p. 323.

Thus Newman calls wisdom or philosophy "the last gift of the Spirit, and Faith the first."[84] We begin with faith; we end with wisdom. Faith, as we have seen, is distinct from reason in the usual sense and therefore unable "to analyze its grounds, or to show the consistency of one of its judgments with another." Reason in the service of wisdom proceeds to that analysis and relates that particular assent to all previous and subsequent ones. Faith "views each point by itself, and not as portions of a whole," for all assents are "the instincts of a pure mind, which steps forward truly and boldly, and is never at fault." The fact that these various assents have not been connected by a wise use of reason is no prejudice whatever against each one of them individually; "a peasant may take the same view of human affairs in detail as a philosopher."[85] Neither, however, is there any prejudice against the philosopher's drawing these individual assents into a comprehensive system, at least not so long as reason does not meddle with the province of faith. In fact, the exercise of reason upon the various assents of faith is not only natural to us but necessary for the defense of faith against heretical attack. In that defense, as Newman showed first in his study of the Arians, lies the development of Christian doctrine.

Therefore we see that in spite of the subjective and antirational bias of his thought, there is no ultimate difficulty for Newman in accepting a rational or notional theology; for as he conceives the proper use of reason in religious matters, it must never venture upon the ultimate questions of belief. Indeed, "where the exercise of Reason much outstrips our Knowledge; where Knowledge is limited, and Reason active; where ascertained truths are scanty, and courses of thought abound; there indulgence of system is unsafe, and may be dangerous."[86] In a true development of doctrine, however, such an "outstripping" will never take place, for in a "wise" system, all reason's conclusions must be tested against the original knowledge which, in the individual, is the divine image or idea; in the Church, the *depositum fidei*. Considered in light of these remarks, the *Essay*

84. *OUS*, p. 294.
85. *OUS*, p. 304.
86. *OUS*, p. 295.

on the Development of Christian Doctrine is a proper philosophical as well as doctrinal prelude to Newman's conversion;
for it serves as a test, not only of whether Roman systems are
true developments from the knowledge which revelation gives to
faith, but also of the whole validity of a notional theology.
Having found both the thesis and the doctrine valid, there is
no further difficulty for Newman in taking the step he does; for
Rome's development of dogma may be regarded as the proper
objective, rational consequence of the various, distinct propositions of the original revelation which Newman had already
received subjectively in faith. In fact, so far from there being
difficulty in reconciling the subjective and objective aspects of
the experience, the two actually depend on one another. Since
we cannot all remain peasants or children, we are forced to use
a notional theology in defense of faith; for just as conscience
demands as its complement and fulfillment an infallible external
authority in the "living busy world," faith demands as its complement and defense a notional theology.

Newman deals with the same question in the *Grammar of
Assent,* distinguishing there between assent and certitude; and
I take that distinction to be analogous to the earlier ones between faith and wisdom, or faith and philosophy. Faith and
assent, as we have seen, are certainly the same act, and the state
of certitude is apparently analogous if not identical to that of
wisdom. Certitude is "reflex assent," knowing that we know. It
is always notional, for it is assent "given to a notional proposition, viz. to the truth, necessity, duty, &c., of our assent to the
simple assent and to its proposition."[87] Simple assent is instinctive and spontaneous; again he calls to witness "the generous
and uncalculating energy of faith as exemplified in the primitive
Martyrs."[88] In fact, simple assent, the individual act of faith, the
acceptance of that idea or image of God presented to our conscience, is "the motive cause of great achievements," for it grows
"out of instincts rather than arguments" and is "stayed upon a
vivid apprehension, and animated by a transcendent logic, more

87. GA, p. 162.
88. GA, p. 163.

concentrated in will and in deed for the very reason that it has not been subjected to any intellectual development."[89] Such a development, however, when it comes, is altogether justifiable, and though there is a danger that in the process the native hue of resolution may be sicklied o'er with the pale cast of thought, the consequences of a fully developed certitude make the risk worthwhile. For like a mature theological system in the Church, certitude in the individual combines the past with the present, our childhood with our maturity, the glory of primitive martyrdom with the peace of completed wisdom. Indeed, as we have seen in another context, Newman conceives of certitude as the end or completion of man. The "child is father of the man," and in certitude's "complete exhibition keeness in believing is united with repose and persistence."[90] Moreover, certitude, like the notional development of Catholic theology, is indefectible. "Assents may and do change; certitudes endure. This is why religion demands more than an assent to its truth; it requires a certitude, or at least an assent which is convertible into certitude on demand."[91]

Thus we see that while Newman joins his contemporaries in abjuring the exercise of reason in the proof or disproof of God's existence, he safeguards its use in Catholic theology by admitting it as ancillary to faith and in dependence from that knowledge which faith and faith alone, resting on the dictates of conscience, holds. Reason cannot take the place of our assent to the image of God which the conscience demands, but exercising itself upon that assent, it can give us a theological system as well as the personal gifts of wisdom and certitude. As we have seen, however, reason admitted on these rather limited terms is quite different from reason as it is conceived in the traditional Catholic sense. For the Schoolmen and the Laudians, reason's job is to perceive the intelligible in the sensible, to draw out a knowledge of the "invisible things" of God from "the things that are made." Newman never contradicts the Schoolmen or his Anglican forbears in so many words by declaring that inductive function of

89. GA, pp. 163–164.
90. GA, p. 164.
91. GA, p. 167.

the reason in religious matters to be invalid, but in practice he assigns that function to the instincts of the conscience. That leaves for reason, in theology, only the more limited job of drawing conclusions from the original "givens" of faith. Newman applauds Aquinas for making Aristotle "a hewer of wood and drawer of water to the Church,"[92] but he shows no recognition of the vast differences between his own and Aquinas's conception of reason's range.[93] Never, so far as I can see, does he contemplate the possibility that right reason is capable of reaching conclusions, independent of faith, which are nevertheless in perfect harmony with faith. Thus while he has secured the use of reason in theology, he has done so by restricting its traditional Catholic limits rather severely.

That restriction serves conveniently as a final comment on the subject of Newman's orthodox subjectivism. For it indicates, in effect, the price Newman had to pay for his "modernism." He secured his subjectivism against its logical, heterodox conclusions, but he was only able to do so by setting severe limits on the

92. *Idea*, p. 470.
93. Throughout this chapter I have pointed to important differences between Newman and Aquinas and have implied that Newman was not very well versed in Thomist thought. That implication seems to be a just one; indeed he acknowledged as much himself. Though the relationship between the two is alluded to frequently in Newman studies, surprisingly little attention has been given to the matter. Most commentators let the question rest with the assertion that Newman was not a Thomist and proceed to quote the familiar letter from Rome in 1846 (*Letters and Diaries*, XI, 279). Perhaps the most judicious and succinct statement of the case is by Boekraad (pp. 39–42). If there could be said to be any trends one way or the other in Newman-Thomist studies they would be these: On one hand there are a few critics who, like D'Arcy, raise objections, primarily to Newman's terminology, which presuppose Thomist categories. Fr. Harper's articles cited above (n. 37) fall into that category. On the other, there is a considerable body of critics, the majority of those who have written on the subject, who wish to stress similarities rather than differences. Flanagan and Vargish both fall in the latter category, though Vargish grants some important distinctions (cf. pp. 40 and 48). The fullest statement of similarities is by H. Francis Davis, "Newman and Thomism," *Newman Studien* (Nürnberg: Glock und Lutz, 1957), III, 157–169. Davis insists that the differences are essentially in matters of method, not in content. In pursuing that thesis it seems to me he overlooks some important distinctions, especially in the area of epistemology.

happy exercise of the mind in its ascent from the creation to a vision of the Creator. All human systems, even intellectual systems, are ultimately closed; and an expense in one area demands economy in another. In order to afford the luxury of an immediate, intuitive knowledge of God in the conscience and the heart, Newman must sacrifice a part of creation's intellectual good. Moreover, that sacrifice entails further sacrifice—of those other aspects of a Christian polity which depend on the "Aristotelic-scholastic" conception of the intellect. Meanwhile, the ironic possibility persists that the intuitive or subjective mode of knowing for which the sacrifice is made may be, in the final analysis, an epistemological illusion, at least so Aquinas and the philosophical experience of the medieval schools would seem to indicate.

✤

CHAPTER IX

Orthodox Individualism:
The Individuality of Certitude

IF Newman's subjectivism and anti-rationalism prove potential threats to Catholic orthodoxy and demand safeguards such as those we have been examining, his insistence on individuality appears to be equally dangerous. All of us know from experience what the fruits of modern individualistic theories can be. If one man's meat really is another man's poison, and if the apprehension of the truth varies from individual to individual, how can we possibly maintain that any religious proposition is absolutely and everlastingly true for all men in all circumstances? Like the heroes of modern literature from Wordsworth to Joyce, we shall be forced to seek our own truth in our own way, leave Ireland and the Church behind us, and forego all hope of rest in absolutes.

It is obvious that Newman did not forego that hope, but it seems equally clear that his epistemological assumptions, had he not secured them by certain reservations, could easily have led him in that direction. Newman insists upon the individuality of religious experience in two senses: the most powerful source of religious knowledge is an individual thing or image or person, rather than a universal proposition; and the apprehension of the truth varies from individual to individual and depends on the factors which make the story of every life different from that of every other.[1] "Thus heart speaks to heart," the individual to the

1. Sillem, for instance, speaks of Newman's "doctrine of 'personalism,' " I, 19. In fact Sillem distinguishes *personalism* from *subjectivism* and rests a great portion of his treatment of Newman on the ramifications of that distinction.

individual, and the foundation of all religious experience is
" 'solus cum solo.' "²

Consider first the individuality of the thing experienced, of the
teacher or the thing taught. In the early days of the Oxford
Movement, Newman objected to Rose's and Palmer's notion
that the Church could be saved by a committee or a system.
"Persons move us," not programs; therefore Newman begins the
Tracts, which were based, he says, on the "antagonist principle
of personality."³ The teacher must be a person, not an organization; an individual speaking to individuals, not a doctrine or a
theory. He put that principle into practice in the *Parochial and
Plain Sermons*, and their effect upon the Oxford congregations
seems to prove its worth. He was teaching the Christian Faith
by allowing his person, his being, to move those various individual
beings who heard him, upon whom he worked his spell. Arnold's
subsequent description of those Sunday afternoons leaves no
doubt both how powerful and how personal that spell was, and
even reading those sermons makes the principle of personality
quite clear to us. Likewise, Newman conceived his role as tutor
at Oriel as that of pastor and father to his pupils. He sought
close personal relationships with them on the principle that only
through such relationships can knowledge be transmitted. Hawkins, failing to understand Newman's principle, thought he was
simply trying to build a party around himself, and the consequence of the misunderstanding was the end of Newman's
tuition.⁴

Many of his statements on the character of religious experience presuppose the same view. One great difference between
Christian experience and merely philosophical or rational experience is that "the philosopher aspires towards a divine *principle*;

2. *Ap.*, p. 177.
3. *Ap.*, p. 47.
4. For an account of Newman's experiences as a tutor at Oriel see the
appropriate sections of the *Autobiographical Writings* and also Professor
Culler's *The Imperial Intellect*, pp. 46–79. Culler stresses that "the rule of
personal influence" (p. 72) was the distinguishing characteristic of Newman's
approach to the tuition and the principal cause of his differences with
Hawkins.

the Christian, towards a Divine *Agent*." The Christian puts his faith not in a principle but in the person of his Lord, which conscience and heart, not reason, apprehend. He is called upon, not to subscribe to a thesis, but to dedicate his energies "to the service of a person."[5] Thus, what Newman calls the "method of personation" characterizes the teaching of revelation. A Christian seeks inspiration not from some abstract spiritual power but from the Holy Ghost, who is the third *person* of the Holy Trinity. Similarly, he does not fear some general principle of evil; he fears and wars against a *person* known as Satan. He is obligated, not to some mere theory of the Church or to a principle of Church government, but rather to the *person* of his pastor and his bishop. Most important of all, God Himself, to redeem the world, was born to us as a particular human being in a particular place in the *person* of Jesus Christ.[6]

It follows, therefore, that "personal influence" is the proper mode of "propagating the truth,"[7] nor is that truth "a mere set of opinions . . . which may lodge on the surface of the mind."[8] On the contrary, it is the truth of faith and conscience which must change the heart, and only a changed heart can change other hearts. Thus the teacher must not simply teach, he must *move* others; he is "thrown upon his personal resources, be they greater or less."[9] Newman even goes so far as to say that the "Inspired Word" is no more than "a dead letter . . . except as transmitted from one mind to another."[10] Men are converted to the truth of the inspired word not only because of the "likelihood of the message," which reason can judge and pronounce on, but also by "the word of its human messenger" which only the human heart, which receives both message and messenger, can judge. Thus, says Newman, St. Paul not only reasoned with the Athenians about the truth of the message he came to bring; he also presented his personal credentials: "he told his hearers that

5. *OUS*, p. 28.
6. *OUS*, p. 29.
7. *OUS*, p. 75 (title of Sermon V).
8. *OUS*, p. 86.
9. *OUS*, p. 87.
10. *OUS*, p. 94.

he came as a messenger from that God whom they worshipped already, though ignorantly, and of whom their poets spoke."[11]

Therefore Newman objects to reducing (he conceives it a reduction) the definite, concrete individual to the "*quidam homo, the individuum vagum* of the logician." No man, with flesh and blood, with a name and a history, can be regarded simply as representative of the species; and to discover who or what an individual is, we must do more than "refer to commonplaces."[12] Newman even takes to task the practice of representing men as "ideal personages" rather than as individuals, a practice common "in romances and dramas of the old school." "Tyrants, monks, crusaders, princes" and the like can never simply be reduced to type, for every tyrant, every monk, every crusader, every prince is himself alone.[13] Each has his own story to tell; each could write his *apologia*. Similarly with every "thing" in creation; nothing is quite like anything else. The universe is a vast conglomerate of unique beings, and classification according to genus and species, though a necessary tool for thought, must never be confused with an account of how things really are. In fact, such classifications, such abstractions from particulars, are economies in Newman's sense of that term—means of expressing and, in a sense, of controlling mysteries but by no means an adequate representation of those mysteries. Such too are all so-called laws —natural law, divine law, and so forth—which Hooker and St. Thomas and their respective schools take to be real. For Newman these laws are merely economical notions which the mind imposes upon the vast particularity of creation, not as an adequate means of describing or accounting for that creation, but simply as an economy and a necessary convenience. "General laws are not inviolable truths; much less are they necessary causes." We are forced to state such generalities, but we must never forget that those statements have little more than nominal validity. Whatever we may say about law, "each thing has its own nature and its own history," and "a law is not a fact, but a notion."[14]

11. *OUS*, p. 203.
12. *GA*, p. 26.
13. *GA*, p. 27.
14. *GA*, p. 213.

From Newman's point of view the danger is that the necessary convenience, unless we are careful, may become an unnecessary bondage and a cause of blindness to us. We "have two modes of thought," in one of which "we take hold of objects from within them, and in the other we view them outside of them; we perpetuate them as images in the one case, we transform them into notions in the other."[15] Thus we see that Newman's insistence upon individuality is consistent with his partiality to real assent; for the real "thing," as opposed to a notion or an abstraction from that thing, is always an individual. We can no more avoid notions than we can avoid a philosophical development of the ideas which faith apprehends, or than the Church, at war with heresy, can avoid theological development; but just as the original moral perception of the conscience remains the ground for all subsequent philosophical expansion of that perception, and just as the *depositum fidei* must always remain the foundation of later doctrinal development, so "real apprehension has the precedence, as being the scope and end and the test of notional . . ." and the apprehension of individuals as the "scope and end and the test" of our knowledge of the general.[16]

Again we find that Newman's position is clearly distinct from Aquinas's. As we have seen already, St. Thomas insists, repeatedly, that all knowledge is abstracted from sense impressions. It follows—and the contrast with Newman is striking—that man cannot *know* individuals, either things or persons. We can perceive individuals with our senses, we can hold their images in the memory, but we cannot *know* them. For the knowing faculty is our reason, and once the reason is set in operation, the individual becomes the member of a genus and a species. We *know* universals, not individuals. Consequently, there is no possibility in the Thomist system for real apprehension in Newman's sense —apprehension of an individual, knowledge of a person.[17]

Aquinas makes this matter quite explicit in talking about how the mind of man knows those things which are above it, namely God and the holy angels. We cannot, in this life, see God per-

15. GA, p. 27.
16. GA, p. 28.
17. See above, Chapter VIII, n. 59.

sonally, "through his essence." In fact, we are no more able to "see God through his essence" than we are to understand any other separate or individual thing in its essence. In contemplation, as we approach such a knowledge, we do so by the withdrawing of our minds from sensible things. It follows that "the mind which sees the divine substance must be completely cut off from the bodily senses, either by death or by ecstasy." Ecstasy, however, is a special gift and by no means our common mode of knowledge, and short of death we are bound to reason on the basis of phantasms. Hence follows the general rule that we cannot in this life know God as an individual being, in His essence. Man has a fuller knowledge of Him than lower creatures do; nevertheless, "the knowledge of God which can be taken in by the human mind does not go beyond the type of knowledge that is derived [by notional abstraction] from sensible things."[18] The "first object of our knowledge in this life is the *quiddity of a material thing*, which is the proper object of our intellect, as appears above in many passages." The *"invisible things of God are clearly seen, being understood by the things that are made"*;[19] that means that our intellect can derive a knowledge of God from those quiddities which are its proper object. That is our only means of knowing Him or of believing in Him, for we must not forget that though faith gives fuller knowledge than reason can attain to, the mode of that knowledge is identical with that of reason; that the thing known is in the knower according to the mode of the knower.

Newman's view of the matter, at least at first glance, is far more appealing than Aquinas's. There is an impassioned quality in his plea for the particular and the personal: "Let units come first, and (so-called) universals second; let universals minister to units, not units be sacrificed to universals. John, Richard, and Robert are individual things, independent, incommunicable."[20] Such language appeals to our modern notions of individual autonomy, but the very introduction of the word "modern" may prove the key to the difficulty. In any event, since it is the alleged

18. CG, III, 47.
19. ST, I, 88, 3.
20. GA, p. 212.

fact of Newman's modernity which is in question, we must not allow ourselves to accept his epistemological premises simply because they appeal to us. After all, we are modern men too. If we share with Newman the predisposition to take the individual —John, Richard, and Robert—as the test and measure of man, the particular as the measure of the universal rather than the other way around, there is the possibility that we may all be wrong together. When it comes to the question of how we know God, the idea of knowing Him directly and personally, as in ecstasy, is bound to move all men at all times in a way that the idea of abstract or rational knowledge never can; and, as we have already mentioned, such an epistemology seems even more appealing in an age such as ours when the validity of abstraction and the reliability of reason are distrusted. The fact remains, however, that both we and Newman may be wrong; what is appealing may not be true, and we may have been misled by the very fact of that appeal.

The contrast between Newman and Aquinas serves to show how the modern view, unless it is safeguarded, proves dangerous to orthodoxy. That danger lies in the fact that if the universal must minister to the unit rather than the other way around, if John, Richard, and Robert are to be the measure of what man is rather than man, the universal, the abstraction, being a measure of what John, Richard, and Robert are or ought to be, we can, in fact, never know what man is. If we were to take Newman's thesis to its logical conclusions (many contemporary existentialist philosophers do, in effect, just that) we should be constrained to give up absolutes altogether. We should find ourselves in the Sartrian dilemma in which it becomes impossible to justify, philosophically, those general laws of human nature and conduct which even Sartre himself agrees are, in fact, though he cannot see why, necessary to human existence. Or, if we turn our attention to the question of how we know God, if we make those images of His person which derive from the conscience the measure of our faith, how can we possibly know for certain that we are really believing in God at all? How can we be sure that our idea of Him corresponds with reality? Can we be certain that we are not giving our assent to a purely imaginary person or even, possibly, to a demonically inspired image, rather than to the true God? If we had the pure intelligence of angels, or if we were dead and our souls were functioning independently of our bodies, we could know essences reliably, but we do not need Aquinas to tell us that the knowledge of separate essences, much less the essence of God, is, in our present circumstances, largely a matter of guesswork. Who can really say he has known either John, Richard, or Robert as an individual rather than as an abstraction? Who, besides a few rare saints who have had ecstatic visions, can say they have known God personally in this present life? The very notion of saying so seems appallingly vain and recalls one of the least savory aspects of evangelical Protestantism. One suspects that Newman's own Calvinist experiences show very strongly in his insistence on such knowledge, nor does the traditional Christian view of martyrdom necessitate our believing that all those glorious martyrs of the primitive Church were sustained in their sufferings, as Newman believes, by such a knowledge.

I mentioned at the outset two aspects of Newman's individualism: the individuality of the thing or person known and the individuality of the knower. Having examined the one, we are now in a position to understand the other; for the two necessitate each other, and that which safeguards one from heresy also secures the other.

We have already stated (in another context) the central issue involved with the individuality of the knower: that since the "whole man reasons" the eccentricities of the particular individual are necessarily involved in the reasoning process.[21] Since no "whole man" is quite like any other "whole man," no individual reasons in quite the same fashion as any other individual. Thus, as we have seen, Newman can only explain the reasoning which took him to the Church of Rome by writing an autobiography. Moreover, it should be clear from what we have said about the moral nature of faith, or of "implicit reason," that Newman's conception of those acts also necessitates an emphasis

21. See above, Chapter VI.

on the individuality of the believer or reasoner. Faith is a moral judgment, and the implicit reason which it involves is directed by prepossessions or prejudices, rather than by strict logic. Therefore, since no one man's moral judgment is quite identical with that of any other man, the act of faith, and the implicit reason involved in it, will likewise vary from man to man. Since John, Richard, and Robert are individual beings (we consider them now as knowers rather than as the singular objects of knowledge), their prejudices and prepossessions differ, and the quality and intensity of their beliefs vary in direct proportions to those differences. In other words, the knowledge of units is determined to a considerable extent by the spiritual condition of the unit which knows.

Therefore, in the *Grammar*, Newman argues that real assent is from unit to unit, from person to person, while notional assent is an act of our common nature, rather than of our individuality. The latter has its place, as "a common measure between mind and mind";[22] but the particular remains the test of the common, for we live and believe as John, Richard, or Robert, not simply as "man." We can neither restrict the particular to the common measure nor lay down universal laws for the demonstration of God's existence; "real assent . . . is proper to the individual, and as such, thwarts rather than promotes the intercourse of man with man."[23] In other words, my real assent depends on me, yours on you, and no single account of knowledge can apply to both of us. If I believe in God and you do not, that is because I am who I am and you who you are. It is not that we are determined to be such, but that we are spiritually self-made. It probably means that I have attended to what my conscience directed while you have not, and that consequently what appear to you "weak reasons" or mere "presumptions" appear to me sufficient grounds for conviction. Under such circumstances it is clear that no single set of rational demonstrations can possibly work for both of us; for I am "spiritually minded" and you are not.

22. GA, p. 63.
23. GA, p. 64.

Therefore we must not conclude because many thousands of people hold to a common belief about God and about the divinity of our Lord that that belief is notional or scientific or the fruit of rational demonstrations which would be applicable to our common human mentality. On the contrary, in so far as the belief in each case is *real*, in so far as it is faith in the full sense of the word, in the person of God, it is individual, "being produced in different individual minds by various experiences and disposing causes, variously combined." Each of these thousands of believers comes to God out of a set of circumstances which is different from that of any other; no two of them could write the same *apologia*. "In each case the image in the mind, with the experiences out of which it is formed, would be a personal result; and, though the same in all, would in each case be so idiosyncratic in its circumstances, that it would stand by itself, a special formation, unconnected with any law."[24] Since there is no such law available to us, we can never account for why and when we give assent. Were it not for the principle of individuality, certain reasons would compel us to certain conclusions. As it is, we sometimes give assent on the very thinnest of rational grounds and sometimes withold assent to proofs which are rationally incontrovertible. Really, we can no more account for our own idiosyncrasies than we can for those of other people.[25]

From these considerations follows the proposition which we have discussed previously—that whereas certainty is a quality of propositions, certitude, considered here simply as the condition of believing, is a mental state, and the mental state of one individual is distinct from that of any other.[26] Since certainty rests in the propositions submitted in argument, it is necessarily a general condition, for presumably syllogisms have an objective force and are universally applicable. Therefore, if we believed according to a general law, our belief would rest upon the strength of the evidence presented in its behalf. But since in these matters each man is a law to himself, our certitudes differ, not in proportion to the strength of the evidences presented to us but in proportion

24. GA, p. 66.
25. GA, pp. 126–127.
26. GA, p. 262; cf. Ap., p. 498, and see above, pp. 107–112.

to our receptivity to those evidences. In other words "certitude is not a passive impression made upon the mind from without, by argumentative compulsion," but rather "an active recognition of propositions as true" which varies in its quality and degree from man to man.[27] It follows, conversely, that "ten thousand difficulties do not make one doubt,"[28] for if probabilities cannot compel us to belief, neither can difficulties, as external forces, compel us to unbelief. Therefore, just as the strength of evidences and the strength of certitudes are incommensurate, so too are difficulty and doubt; for both certitude and doubt are states of mind and therefore depend upon the individual believer or doubter.

Again Thomist comparisons are revealing, and on this matter of individuality in the knower or believer Newman departs from Aquinas more radically, I think, than at any other point. In the first place, the whole Thomist conception of man militates against the proposition that the whole man reasons and, consequently, against Newman's emphasis on idiosyncrasy in the rational process. According to St. Thomas, all men are on common ground where their intellectual activities are concerned; for man is a composite of form and matter in which the intellect is a power of the form, whereas matter, not form, is the individualizing principle. Therefore, we are not only constrained by our nature to know universals rather than particulars; we are also constrained to know according to universal laws. That is because matter, which gives us our individuality, does not have an intellectual function. John, Richard, and Robert differ from one another because of the "signate matter" which is bound up in union with their intellectual form. However, when each of them reasons, if he reasons as he should, he reasons precisely as do the other two; for the rational form of man is common to our whole species and what gives us individuation within that species is the material opposite of our rational faculty. Therefore, from a Thomist point of view it is simply, explicitly, false to say that the "whole man reasons"; for, in fact, only his formal or intel-

27. GA, p. 262.
28. Ap., p. 214.

lectual part does so, and when the principle of totality is sacrificed, the principle of uniqueness goes with it.

It is interesting to note that Aquinas anticipates and denies
Newman's whole position on this matter, Granting that "my
intellect is distinct from your intellect" and granting also that
"whatever is received into anything must be received according
to the condition of the receiver," it would seem to follow that
"the species of things would be received individually into my
intellect, and also into yours" which would make the knowledge
of universals impossible.[29] We see here, immediately, that Aquinas
is confronting both aspects of the problem which Newman presents. Newman argues for a knowledge of units by units; Aquinas
raises the question whether if we know simply as a unit we
can ever know anything but units, and thus whether universal
knowledge does not become an impossibility: "If, therefore, my
intellect is distinct from yours, what is understood by me must be
distinct from what is understood by you; and consequently it
will be reckoned as *something individual,* and be only *potentially
something understood.*"[30] Of course, according to Thomist defini-
tions, nothing can be *understood* as an individual but only by
abstraction. How, therefore, if my intellect is distinct from yours,
can either intellect be considered "as distinct from the imagination"?

St. Thomas's answer to the question is simply to reiterate that
matter, not form, is the individuating principle in man. That does
not mean that all men have one form; for since form is the
principle of being, that would mean that all men would have
one being. The intellectual soul of man is not itself material but
it *is* "the form of a certain matter" and, therefore, "according to
the division of matter, there are many souls of one species."[31]
Moreover, the essence of a composite being such as man involves
both form and matter. However, because matter, which is irrational, is their principle of individuation, these distinct intellects
do not differ in their mode of knowing. Therefore, "whether the

29. *ST,* I, 76, 2.
30. *ST,* I, 76, 2; italics mine.
31. *ST,* I, 76, 2.

intellect be one or many, what is *understood* is one."[32] That is because the intellect, mine or yours, understands a thing, "not according to its own nature, but according to its likeness"; that is, according to the acquired species which the intellect abstracts from the sense impression of the thing. Therefore a thing's "mode according to which it exists outside the soul," which the senses and imagination of individual men receive and which differs consequently from individual to individual, "is not the mode [of being] according to which it is understood" by the intellect. That latter mode, that of the abstract species, does not differ from man to man; "for the common nature is understood as apart from the individuating principles"[33] and the mode of knowing by which the individual intellect understands that common nature is likewise common and likewise independent of the "individuating principles."

We can therefore imagine that, had Aquinas read Newman on these matters, his response would have been that Newman was both consistent and consistently wrong. Newman is consistent in that he attributes the knowledge of individual things to the individuality of the knower, wrong in that he believes individuality on either score either possible or desirable. He is consistent too in linking individuality in either knower or object of knowledge to the principle of the whole man, for, in both subject and object, matter is the principle of individuation. The intellect, according to St. Thomas, cannot know individuals, for it knows only species abstracted from matter, not matter itself. Moreover, the reason it can only know species is, as we have just seen, that the principle of distinction between intellects is not in their mode of knowing but in the nonrational matter of which they are the "acts" or forms. For an intellect to know an individual it would have to become something like Newman's concept of "the whole man." Then it would cease to be an intellect *per se;* it would become mixed with matter, and thus lose its greatest power which is to know universals. "For if the intellectual soul were composed of matter and form [that is, if it were a "whole

32. *ST*, I, 76, 2; italics mine.
33. *ST*, I, 76, 2.

man"], the forms of things would be received into it as individuals, and so it would only know the individual."[34] It follows that the only point on which Aquinas would probably find Newman inconsistent would be in his conceiving the possibility of both individual and universal knowledge. If the whole man reasons, only the former is possible—which, from Aquinas's point of view, would be to reduce men to the level of beasts who, being purely sensual, do not *know* at all but only apprehend individuals.

There is another and less technical ground for Thomist objection to the principle of individuality—one that applies specifically to our knowledge of God. Again let us suppose Aquinas reading Newman, this time on the question of certitude; it seems inevitable that he would simply contradict Newman's distinction between certitude and certainty and argue instead that a state of mind *is* dependent upon the propositions which evoke it and cannot be finally regarded as a function of our individuality. He would maintain, I believe, that God can be demonstrated by propositions and syllogisms in such a fashion as to compel certainty in those who attend the argument. My grounds for ascribing such views to St. Thomas lie first in the simple fact that he undertook to prove or demonstrate the existence of God on a "scientific" or syllogistic basis. Why give rational demonstration of a point if rational demonstration can never elicit conviction? If certitude is a state of mind independent of the propositions which attempt to convince us, why offer the propositions in the first place? If Aquinas had believed, as Newman did, that evidences are of worth, not in themselves, but in their use by a mind which is already disposed to belief, I doubt that he would have offered evidences as he does, in proof of a proposition. Actually, Newman's position on the matter approaches tautology; for if sound reasoning convinces one man and not another, for the reason that one man is disposed to certitude and the other is not, it would seem to follow that the reasoning, itself, is of no final value other than to strengthen a conviction which is already a prejudice or a prepossession. In that case, the

34. *ST*, I, 75, 5.

individuality of the believer is sufficient cause of certitude, not the arguments which are presented to him. Therefore why argue? If God is self-evident to some and invisible to others, and if their respective individualities preclude any common ground in reason among them, proofs can be of no use—except, of course, the peculiar sort of "proof" from the conscience which Newman offers.

According to Etienne Gilson, whose knowledge of Aquinas seems sufficient warrant for believing his judgment, St. Thomas undertook the "proofs" in part at least to repudiate the principle of individuality in the proofs of his predecessors. From Augustine on, on account of an essentialist ontology, the assumption had been that man knows God by knowing being. (Newman's "proof from conscience" and from a complex intuition of our faculties has a certain similarity to the "essentialist" tradition.) It follows that God's existence is self-evident, for in so far as we have in our minds a consciousness of being we have, thereby, a consciousness of God. According to Gilson, however, Aquinas argues that all such arguments depend on a common error; "they mistake for God Himself what is only an effect caused by God."[35] In other words, they mistake essence for existence (*ipsum esse*), for the former is personally, individually, and intuitively knowable, while the latter, who is God, can only be demonstrated rationally. What Aquinas's Augustinian predecessors had taken for God was "at most an effect of God or His image stamped in our thought."[36] Immediately we see that Aquinas was in effect asking his predecessors the question which we have suggested he might have asked Newman: How do you know that the unit, God, which you, as a unit, John, believe you know, which you perceive by a complex intuition of your own existence, is really God? The only way we can *know* is by a rational demonstration which follows the laws of abstraction and which is applicable, equally, to all individuals. The image or idea of God which one particular conscience has received must be tested by such a

35. Etienne Gilson, *The Christian Philosophy of St. Thomas Aquinas*, trans. L. K. Shook (London: Victor Gollancz, 1961), p. 54. Hereafter cited as "Gilson."
36. Gilson, p. 54.

demonstration if we are honestly to speak of it as knowledge. Thus the reply which Gilson formulates for the Augustinians might apply equally to Newman: "If we say with the Augustinians that God can be immediately known by the intellect as light is immediately visible to the sight, or that God is more interior to the soul than the soul itself, it must be replied that the only beings directly accessible to our knowledge are sensible things. A demonstration is therefore necessary if the reason is to ascend from the realities thus given to it in experience to the reality of God who is not so given."[37] Once that demonstration is given, certitude considered as an individual state of mind gives place to certainty conceived as a proposition rationally demonstrated and hence universally binding. For Aquinas it is the latter not the former which is our only proper ground for belief; for only the latter, because it is universal rather than individual, can guarantee our certitude.

How, then, does Newman guarantee it? If God, and divine truth generally, are not subject to demonstration by reason, and if certitude is a state of mind which varies from individual to individual, how does Newman save himself from pure relativism? As we have seen, the general tendency of the individualist principle in modern literature and theology is to make every man the arbiter of his own truth and to call in question the possibility of absolutes. How does Newman avoid that danger? If each of the thousands of Christians in the world is, as Newman says, an epistemological law unto himself, how does it happen that they all believe the same things to be true?

One answer to these questions, though by no means a complete or genuinely philosophical one, is the simple assertion that the truth which is known individually is a common truth. If John knows God in his particular way and Robert knows God in his, even though the act of knowing or believing in either case is *sui generis* and not subject to the measure of abstract reason, nevertheless it is the same God which each knows and which draws each along his own particular path to a common center in

37. Gilson, p. 54.

the Catholic Faith. All roads lead to Rome, whether they begin in Britain or in Asia Minor, at Oxford or at Troy. From Newman's point of view it would be absurd to insist that the Greek Callista and the Roman Agellius submit themselves to the same set of proofs or evidences as the sufficient grounds of their certitudes, for each has his own story to tell, and those stories differ as widely as their race and nationality. However, since the object of their certitudes is the same Lord, their individual differences finally serve, paradoxically, to draw them together rather than to keep them apart. Those differences must be stressed rather than muted, for a man can only know God in his own way and on his own terms; however, since these various men know the same Lord, those very differences become the source of their bond with one another.

Newman makes the same point one way or another several times in the *Grammar of Assent*, as though he were anxious to avoid being understood as a mere relativist. Different minds throw different lights "upon the same theory and argument"; so, likewise, different minds believe in different ways upon the same God. Though they may "seem to be differing in detail," they are in fact "professing, and in reality showing, a concurrence" in their knowledge or belief. The value of any argument for Christianity is "a personal question," but that is "not as if there were not an objective truth and Christianity as a whole not supernatural."[38] The problem is not that the truth of Christianity is mutable or merely natural "but that, when we come to consider where it is that the supernatural presence is found, there may be fair differences of opinion, both as to the fact and the proof of what is supernatural."[39] Since these "fair differences of opinion" do exist, we cannot expect the same set of reasons to convince all men; on the other hand the truth which we approach individually is objective, supernatural and common to all. That truth *is*, and it is attainable, but "can any scientific common measure compel the intellects of Dives and Lazarus to take the same estimate of it?"[40]

38. GA, p. 235.
39. GA, pp. 235–236.
40. GA, p. 237.

One of Newman's illustrations of the point recalls Shelley's dome of many-colored glass. The principle of individuality in the knower does not mean that "any thing is truth to a man which he troweth." It does mean, however, that truth's "rays stream in upon us through the medium of our moral as well as our intellectual being,"[41] and that being differs from man to man. Thus, "though truth is ever one and the same, and the assent of certitude is immutable, still the reasonings which carry us on to truth and certitude are many and distinct, and vary with the inquirer."[42] Consequently "the Catholic religion is reached, as we see, by inquirers from all points of the compass," but that in no way implies the mutability or relativity of that religion. It does not matter where a man begins "so that he had an eye and a heart for the truth," for that religion is the truth and thus invariable.[43]

Newman makes the same assertion as a safeguard for the Catholic doctrine of the Church, for here, too, the principle of individuality raises a difficult problem. If the knowledge of God is *sui generis* in each man, if men approach Him from all points of the compass, how can Newman justify the traditional concept of the Catholic Church as a body in which believers are members rather than as a simple political structure in which they remain separate entities. It is quite a different thing to be the member of a body (St. Paul compares us to hands and feet) than to be an individual in the modern sense in which Newman appears to treat men. In fact, if men are individuals in this new sense, how can Newman justify the common forms of Catholic life— the offices, the Mass, and so forth? These make perfect sense if a man conceives his spiritual life, including his knowledge of God, not as a separate existence and individual mode of knowing but as derivative from the whole life and wisdom of the body of Christ; but how can these forms be accounted for if we approach them from the personal rather than the corporate direction? Again the simple assertion of a common truth, "one Lord, one Faith, one Baptism," serves Newman for at least a partial

41. GA, p. 237.
42. GA, p. 270.
43. GA, p. 287.

answer. We have alluded previously to the passage in which he says that God impresses the image or idea of Himself "in the minds of His subjects individually." Then he adds that "that Image, apprehended and worshipped in individual minds, becomes a principle of association, and a real bond of those subjects one with another, who are thus united to the body by being united to that Image."[44] Therefore, we see that the Church's corporate unity, like unanimity in faith, is a consequence of the many thousands of vastly varied assents to a common Lordship in Christ. It is not the other way around, which is the more nearly traditional Catholic view; the martyrs, whose blood is the seed of the Church, were not inspired, Newman says, by "a corporate body or a doctrine" but by "the Thought of Christ."

Newman's simple assertion that there is a common truth, a common object of belief, is convincing enough so far as it goes, and for some one who already believes the Catholic Faith it may be regarded as a legitimate safeguard against the heterodox tendency of individualism. On the other hand, because it is simply an assertion and not strictly an argument, it can only carry us as far as we are willing to believe it. Hence it cannot answer the sceptic's objection which is, "how are we to know in the first place that such a common truth exists?" It is all very well to say that if John pursues the truth in one way and Robert in another, their search will end at the same point, for God is the truth and there is only one God; but how, in fact, can we have that certainty to begin with? The sceptic might reasonably argue that if the phrase "search for the truth" has any meaning at all, it is that the truth is not already self-evident. If it is not, if we really are "searching" for it, we cannot say what or where it is or predict how our search will end. Therefore when a Christian allows individuality in reason and assent on the grounds that there is an absolute object of all true assent, it seems just to say that he has played unfairly with the argument and, indeed, has assumed the very thing he has set out to prove. It therefore appears that Newman's assertion of a common truth is invalid unless proved, and the question becomes one of whether it can

44. GA, p. 354.

be proved individually and personally rather than universally and objectively? Aquinas offered the latter proof; it is up to Newman, if his individualistic approach to belief is valid, to offer the former.

Does he? I believe he would say that he does—that the argument from conscience constitutes just such an individual and personal proof. If so, it means that his safeguard against individualism will prove to be closely related to his safeguard against subjectivism; and if we consider the matter closely we see that such a relationship is not at all surprising. After all, the problems are closely related; why shouldn't they be subject to similar solutions? How to guarantee that what the heart feels is objectively true? How to guarantee that what two different hearts apprehend and assent to as true will prove in fact to be the same truth? The problem of individuality haunts the problem of subjectivity, and the problem of subjectivity haunts that of individuality. As we have seen, abstract reasoning, if we are willing to rely on it, solves both problems at once, for it is neither personal nor subjective but transcends the limitations of the heart and of the single person. If, like Newman, however, we are not willing to rely for certitude on the syllogism, we must find some other solution for the joint difficulty in question, and if, in fact, the two problems are facets of the same one, the solution of one may prove to be the solution for the other.

As we have seen, conscience secures the knowledge of the heart against heresy, guarantees orthodoxy, by inspiring in us the fear of God and thereby forcing us to test what we believe and to take moral responsibility for our assents. According to Newman, such an approach to belief does not demand an unfair, a priori assertion that what we search for exists. In fact, he regards the argument from conscience as strictly empirical. It only asks us to take those steps which our conscience sanctions, each of which leads us toward an authoritarian religion which offers grace and certitude by infallible promise. Not only personal experience but the whole history of natural religion proves that tendency. In Newman's view, once a person so directed encounters the Catholic Church, he cannot resist recognizing there an echo of the same voice whose echo he has heard also in his own heart. From that point on, the proof of the pudding is in the eating, and no *a priori* assumptions about the truth of Catholicism are necessary. Thus the proof from conscience solves the problem of subjectivism, and a solution of the corollary problem of individualism follows hard upon. For if John, Richard, and Robert *each* obeys the sanction of his conscience, if *each* one does what his conscience demands, *each* will end his quest in the Catholic Church, no matter how diverse the modes in which their consciences originally spoke to them. Nor does that conclusion demand a prior assumption about what their ultimate destination will be, for the theoretical principle here gives way to the practical.

Of course, in a question of this sort, it is very difficult to divorce argument from faith, just as it is difficult in Thomist theology to draw a hard and fast distinction between what the philosopher proves and what the theologian believes. Whether we argue syllogistically or practically (that is from the dictates of the conscience), it is hard to ignore those conclusions which we have already accepted on faith in authority before we came to prove them. How can we be sure that conscience pure and simple can lead us to belief in God and to acceptance of Catholic doctrine when, in fact, we already believe that will be the end of the journey on which we are embarked? In other words, how can we be certain we are not still dragging some measure of presumption into our proof? Of course the answer according to Newman is that we never can be certain and that in fact we need not be. The very principle of implicit reason or moral judgment assumes from the outset that we cannot proceed in our reasoning without certain presumptions; indeed, how can we say those very presumptions are not sanctioned by the conscience? Therefore Newman does seem to regard the argument from conscience as an argument in the true sense, as a "proof" of theism, which is valid as proof, and, as it is applied indirectly to the problem of individuality, it would appear to serve as a legitimate safeguard for orthodoxy.

When we examine a course of reason retrospectively, it may be virtually impossible to exclude *a priori* assumptions from our explanation of it. If however, we give an account of ourselves when we are half-way up the cliff, when we have not yet reached a conclusion or destination, we are forced to rest on the terms of our argument in so far as we can make them explicit to ourselves and to others. When Newman wrote the *Grammar of Assent,* he had already followed conscience to a Catholic conclusion; therefore he seems simply to be asserting that if every individual obeys the dictates of conscience, however varied those may be, each will come eventually to believe what Newman believes. In 1841, however, in the well-known article on "Private Judgment," we find him in mid-journey, in the very process of following his conscience, by no means certain where it was leading him. The article, therefore, becomes for us an interesting test of Newman's safeguard, for it raises the very problem of individuality which we have been considering and attempts to solve it empirically rather than by stating assumptions. That solution, as we shall see, amounts to an application or adaptation of the argument from conscience.

Newman states the problem of individuality here in virtually the same terms in which we have broached the problem to him: "there is this obvious, undeniable difficulty in the attempt to form a theory of Private Judgment, in the choice of religion, that Private Judgment leads different minds in such different directions." Granting the necessity for respecting our individuality, and admitting that private judgment is therefore a duty and a virtue, how can we account for the fact that it leads men not only to different but to mutually exclusive conclusions? One man reasons according to the dictates of his particular character and circumstances, exercises his right of private judgment, and ends "in the Wesleyan Connexion." Another, following the same course, becomes a Quaker. Still another becomes a Roman Catholic. Had Newman lived in the twentieth century rather than the nineteenth he would have found most men maintaining that their personal moral judgments led them to various forms of atheism or agnosticism. In either case, however, the problem involved is the same: whether "exercises of mind, which end so diversely, [are] one and all pleasing to the Divine Author of faith."[45]

45. *Essays*, II, 336.

They are, Newman says, but only when safeguarded by one very important reservation: that a man must be willing to take responsibility for his decisions and, if necessary, to suffer persecution for them. Thus he calls the act of private judgment "in its very idea, an act of individual responsibility."[46] He does not mention the conscience as such in this connection, but it should be fairly clear that what he is offering here as a security against the dangers of individualism is analogous to what he suggests as the proof or test of mere feeling. In either case, moral responsibility is involved, and persecution is a valid test of whether we have made our judgments with a conscientious mind. I have said this argument is empirical, and it is this emphasis on the necessity for suffering which makes it so. If a man sets out to prove something logically, he necessarily trusts to the test of the syllogism. Likewise, when he embarks on a practical proof (and Newman insists repeatedly that faith is a practical principle), he trusts to the test of action or use. We cannot be sure how strong a house is until it has weathered a hurricane or, perhaps, failed to do so; neither does a man know how valid his principles are until they are tested by some crisis or other. Newman seems to be suggesting that religious judgments need to be submitted to a similar test of stress, and he is willing, evidently, to rely upon the consequences of that test. Suppose John decides to become a Quaker, Robert to become a Catholic. Let each be required to suffer for his decision, and Newman is convinced that only the valid choice will survive the agony. Let thousands of indivduals from all points of the compass embark upon a series of conscientious choices and let each be willing to suffer if necessary for his choices, it will follow inevitably that each will end in an assent to the truth (and of course truth is by definition one), for only the truth can bear the true test of practicality. "Our business is to ask with St. Paul, when arrested in the midst of his frenzy, 'Lord, what wilt Thou have me to do?'"[47] The way to be certain that we have asked that question in good faith and that we have really heard God's answer is to risk ourselves on the strength of

46. *Essays*, II, 338.
47. *Essays*, II, 343.

our conclusions.[48] If all individuals take that risk, exercise that responsibility in the face of suffering, there will be no danger of their being drawn to contrary conclusions about what is true and false.

Newman develops the same point in a sermon on "Human Responsibility." Who are the heirs for whom the kingdom of God has been prepared? "He tells us expressly, those who fed the hungry and thirsty, lodged the stranger, clothed the naked, visited the sick, came to the prisoners, for His sake." In other words, the way to faith in God is practical and involves testing and sacrifice, and it is interesting that the context of these remarks is an attack on the Calvinist notion of predestination. Newman is going to considerable lengths to show that we do, indeed, work out our own salvation with fear and trembling; that faith is not only tested, it is in some sense created in the very exercise of it. These commandments to work and suffer throw us "upon human agency and responsibility,"[49] for it is only by human acts, by keeping God's commandments at whatever cost to ourselves, that we come to know Him. This is in no way to deny that we live by grace not works, but the human mind has "a power of resisting grace" which means, in effect, that it has "the ultimate determination of its own fate committed to it, whether to be saved or rejected, the responsibility of its conduct, and, if it was rejected, the whole blame of it."[50]

One other point should be made here; namely, that we sacrifice ourselves in keeping commandments, not for the sake of the commandments as such but for His sake who gave them. Newman is fond of quoting, " 'If you love me, keep my commandments' "; or " 'Eye hath not seen the things which God hath *prepared* for them that *love* Him.' "[51] Newman's point is that no one "will die for his own calculations: he dies for realities,"[52] and those

48. For another statement of the same thesis see "The Ventures of Faith," *PPS*, IV, 295–306.
49. *PPS*, II, 321.
50. *PPS*, II, 322. For a fuller presentation of Newman's views on the relationship between grace and free will see his *Lectures on Justification*.
51. *PPS*, II, 322; italics are Newman's.
52. *GA*, p. 71.

realities, as we know, are individual and personal. Thus we come full circle, for we see that the practical test of private judgment, of individuality in assent, demands the other side of the coin we have been examining; namely individuality or personality in the object of assent. Newman believes it impossible that a man will sacrifice himself and suffer persecution for a universally acknowledged abstraction or rational demonstration; only personal fidelity to a person has power to stand such testing. Therefore, he is confident that when the act of private judgment is performed conscientiously and earnestly, when either the possibility or the fact of persecution is taken into account, the consequence must be a belief in God as person, as one come in the flesh. Thus we see that the roll call of martyrs at the close of the *Grammar of Assent* is a highly appropriate ending for that essay and, in a sense, the logical conclusion for Newman's whole concept of individuality. These martyrs vary vastly in age, background, and personality. Newman insists, in fact, upon that variety. However, their individual approaches to Christ in no way lead them to different Christs, for the image or idea of Him as person which each possesses individually has been put to the test of fire, beast, rack, and sword. Had Callista embraced a false image of Christ rather than the true one, her faith could not have endured the torture by which it was tested, and the reason it could not have endured would have been that she had rested it upon a notion rather than a person. It was her love for Him, heart speaking to heart, which sustained her—a deeply personal, highly individual religious experience which suffering proved to be identical in its object with the experience of St. Cyprian, Agellius, and all the other martyrs and confessors of the Church. All loved a person and suffered for that love, and we thus see that the test of conscience or of practicality becomes ultimately a test of personal devotion.

We had occasion to say earlier that Newman opposes the real, not to the ideal but to the notional, and here we see an illustration of that contrast. The image or idea of God which is imprinted on the conscience and apprehended by faith elicits, if respected, real activity and suffering in the physical world. In this respect, Newman's safeguard against individualism also distinguishes his subjectivism from the purer idealism of his Alexandrian and Augustinian predecessors. Influenced by Plato as they were, those ancient Doctors of the Church thought of being as essence and consequently of the innate or infused idea of God as the image of an essence. Consequently, for all of them in varying degrees, an approach to the knowledge of God demanded meditation on the concept of being. As a consequence, their idealism required knowing rather than acting, for, since God as perfect being is perfectly immutable, we approach Him most appropriately in the stasis of contemplation. Though the term had been abused before his day, Augustine, like Clement, admires the "gnostic."

Because Newman found the idea or image of God in the conscience rather than in the pure mind, the whole emphasis naturally shifts. As we have seen, the image that the conscience conveys is of an acting (commanding, judging) *person*, not of a static essence. Consequently our proper response to Him is the response of the whole man—not simply to know Him in contemplation but to risk our whole lives on doing what He commands. Moreover, it is worth remarking that, in this one respect, Newman is closer to Aquinas than to the Platonists of the ancient Church; for the Thomist emphasis on God as existence rather than as essence also demands that we know Him in act rather than in static contemplation. In fact, the Thomist concept of *compositio* or judgment is ultimately a principle of action; and it is in this action that the chain of abstract reasoning by which St. Thomas demonstrates God's existence comes to its proper completion. After we have arrived at concepts of God by reasoning on the evidence of our senses, it remains to affirm or judge that God is and is thus and so, for it is only by the *act* of judging that we acknowledge the *Act* which is God. "For although, as we have said, our intellect arrives at the knowledge of God through diverse conceptions, it yet understands that what corresponds to all of them is absolutely one." Therefore the chains of reason, with the various abstractions which are their fruits, such as the Unmoved Mover or the Uncaused Cause, must be completed by an act of the mind which "sets forth the unity of a thing by a composition [or judgment] of words."[53] Had St. Thomas wished

53. CG, I, 36.

to stress the principle of individuality, he might well have ended with something very close to Newman's test of conscience or practicality, in which a true knowledge of God for each of us comes to rest on the judgment or "composition of words" for which each of us takes an individual moral responsibility.

St. Thomas, however, did not stress the individuality of the act of judgment, for in his system, as we know, the reasoning upon which such judgments rest is a common activity depending on common grounds. Since he did not submit himself to Newman's individualistic premises, he was not constrained to adopt his safeguards. Presumably every act of judgment or composition must be an individual act, but there is no danger of diversity or of false judgments in different individuals, for that which is judged is not a subjective intuition but an acquired species. We *acquire* an image of God from objects common to the senses of all men and by a process of reasoning which moves according to universally acknowledged rules. Therefore, though the act of judgment might conceivably be a test of rationality, or even of morality, in the individuals who make it, it can in no way be regarded as a test of the intelligible species on which it is pronounced. For Newman, however, the latter has to be the case; or, to speak more precisely, we should say that the test of the individual who acts and suffers for his image of God and the test of the image for which he acts and suffers become inseparable. Because the image is implanted directly in each individual and is therefore perceivable to him alone, there can be no way to establish its universal validity save by the acts and the sufferings of that individual. Thus the test of the person and the test of the image are inseparably united.

Thus we return to the motif of the exile; for we may reason and even judge in the city, but the desert and the sea are the *loci* of suffering and testing. Newman's safeguard for orthodoxy against the latent danger of individualism may preserve the Faith of the Church intact and it may even provide the principle of union for those "solemn troops and sweet societies" of blessed saints and martyrs for whom the individual image of Christ, proved true by suffering, has become "a principle of association, and a real bond of those subjects one with another, who are thus united to the body by being united to that Image."

It is difficult to see, however, how Newman's principles allow for the city—for the static, traditional society in which the knowledge of God is the fruit of common reason rather than of individual testing. In fact the "modern" principle of individuality in religious experience, though it may be safeguarded against heretical excesses and, in a sense, "redeemed" for orthodoxy, still jeopardizes the whole idea of Christendom, of a "Christian Polity," of the "tradition of fifteen hundred years." For if our only true teacher is our conscience, if every individual must come, alone and in agony, to the fellowship of the apostles and prophets in the Catholic Church, then there is little need for those established forms and ceremonies which articulate the belief of the traditional community and make its transmission possible. Thus we are not surprised that Newman's subjectivism and individualism lead directly to a type of relativism, to his concept of the mutability of forms. We have touched on that matter already; now we must consider it in detail and examine Newman's orthodox safeguards.

CHAPTER X

Orthodox Relativism:
Newman on Faith and Form

L ET us begin by distinguishing three different uses of the word *form*. In the first place, we may speak of form in the sense in which we most frequently employ it, as the shape or structure of a physical object as distinguished from the matter of which that object is composed; thus we distinguish between the form of a tree, its shape and characteristics, and the wood which constitutes its matter. In the second place, we may speak of form as the shape, not of a physical object, but of a ceremony, action or institution; thus we refer to "forms of prayer" and to "forms of government." Finally, we may use the word *form* in Aquinas's sense, by which we mean that which gives being to a thing, whether that thing be a man, a tree, a ceremony, or an institution. Thus considered, form is logically distinct from matter, but there is no real distinction between a form and that of which it is the form. For instance, man's soul is the form of his body, and *"we need not ask if the soul and body are one, as neither do we ask if wax and its shape are one."*[1]

We see immediately that St. Thomas's use of *form* is no more than a metaphysical extension of the two common uses. The obvious similarity between the latter is that both have to do with external shape or configuration, for the second meaning is really only a metaphorical extension of the first. The form of a government is actually the "shape" of a government, in much the same sense that the form of a tree is its shape. Institutions might be said not to have shape in any true sense, but there is certainly

1. *ST*, I, 76, 7. Italics in original; Aquinas is quoting Aristotle (*De Anima* ii, I).

something very close to a physical configuration in the order or structure of a government. A monarchy even looks and sounds different from a democracy, and it seems little exaggeration to speak of these different orders of government as forms, by analogy with the forms or shapes of physical objects. Likewise, when we turn to the Thomist conception of form, we must also consider shape. Since "form is the cause of [a thing's] existence,"[2] it takes only a moment's reflection to see that form, thus defined, necessarily involves shape or configuration. Gilson makes the point very well in relationship to the arts: it is manifest, he says, that "we speak of a being only when we can grasp a plurality in a principle of unity which is precisely its form. This can be the form of a concept, of a mode of reasoning, of a tree, of an animal, or of a man; it can also be that of a work of art. To say that a symphony, a poem, or any book is 'formless' is tantamount to denying its existence."[3] In other words, that which makes man man is the particular configuration of being which distinguishes him from any other species, and that which constitutes a monarchy as a monarchy is the particular configuration which distinguishes it from any other type of government. In either case, the essence of a thing is inseparable from its form and that form, even in the metaphysical sense, implies shape or pattern.

Now let us consider another use of the word *form* which is clearly distinct from either the common or the Thomist sense. I refer to what we might legitimately call its usual "modern"

2. Aquinas makes this point again and again in a variety of contexts: in reference to causes and specifically to a thing caused we must consider "the form whereby it is a being" (*ST*, I, 5, 4); with reference to "mode, species and order" in the "essence of goodness," we must realize that "everything is what it is by its form" (*ST*, I, 5, 5); with reference to the question "whether an actually infinite magnitude can exist?" it is necessary to remember that "nothing is actual by its form" (*ST*, I, 7, 3); and with reference to the "immutability of God" and the whole matter of "corruption," the key to our understanding lies in the fact that "existence is consequent upon form, and nothing corrupts except it lose its form." (*ST*, I, 9, 2) Many more instances could be cited; indeed, the fact that "form is the cause of existence" stands at the very heart of Thomist metaphysics.

3. Etienne Gilson, *Forms and Substances in the Arts*, trans. Salvator Attanasio (New York: Charles Scribner's Sons, 1966), p. 4.

meaning, in which form is thought of as the shape in which a thing's essence is expressed but not as the giver or determiner of essence. In this sense, form means primarily a mode of expression which is not necessary to the being of a thing but in which that being manifests itself. Moreover, because there is no necessary link between form, thus considered, and essence, the form or expression can be changed without affecting the being of the thing expressed. Thus someone who uses form in this purely external or "expressive" sense may argue that the "forms of government" can be varied infinitely without affecting the essence of government; that democracy and monarchy are *essentially* the same. Similarly, in the nineteenth century it is customary for poets and philosophers to argue that the essence of Christianity is distinct from and independent of its forms,[4] and, as we have seen, Newman approaches such a view both in his general tendency to interpret all outward and visible things as economies and, particularly, in his treatment (in 1839) of forms as the mutable expressions of a common "spirit afloat."

This modern use of *form* is probably Platonic in its origins and in its *spirit*, though a curious reversal of terminology distinguishes the two. Plato, as we know, uses *form* and *idea* interchangeably; the form of a thing is separable from the thing itself and has a metaphysical existence antecedent to and independent of the thing. Hence the form can be known by the mind as an innate idea, even though the thing itself may never have been encountered sensibly. Thus for Plato there is a sharp distinction between form (idea) and shape, even when shape is taken metaphorically. It is the great accomplishment of the Aristotelian-Thomist philosophy that it bridges that gap and establishes an inseparable connection between the form of a being and that being's shape as a real existence "in the flesh." The modern view, on the other hand, seems to be a reversion to the Platonist separation but with the reversal of terms to which I referred above;

4. The most famous instance of that idea is Tennyson's statement that "The old order changeth yielding place to new, / And God fulfils himself in many ways." The sentiment is not unique to Tennyson, however: Arnold and Carlyle, among others, build their religious systems on the assumption that the forms of faith are separable from faith itself.

namely that in modern usage *form* comes to mean simply the external shape of a thing in time and space and is thus opposed to the thing's idea. In other words, Plato's opposition of form (idea) and shape is renamed an opposition between idea or essence and form, and one cannot help speculating that the change can be explained by the very force of the words in question. Both in Latin and English, *form* is so nearly inseparable in our thought from *shape* that, if we persist in thinking as Platonists, we naturally divorce *form* and *idea* and treat as opposites terms which Plato used indistinguishably. We do Plato no injustice in the process, however. On the contrary, it seems to me that the modern usage simply articulates in our normal vocabulary the opposition between idea and object, between intelligible and sensible reality, which is at the heart of all Platonist thought. On the other hand, if we are willing to think as Aristotelians and Thomists, we can use the word *form* to mean both idea *and* shape, for in the Thomist tradition the idea of a thing (or, metaphorically, of an institution) is ultimately *in* the thing, derivable only as an acquired species, by abstraction, from the composite entity, from the configuration or shape of being, in the sensible object. Thus Aquinas argues that a form is not a subsistent being in itself, but rather that it "is something *of a being*; for it is called a being, because something is by it."[5]

Let us pursue this distinction between form in the modernized Platonist sense, as mere external shape and therefore separable from essence or idea, and form in the Aristotelian-Thomist sense, as united with a thing's material being and as the cause, in that union, of the thing's essence. We may do so by exploring still further what we mean by "forms of government." Let us suppose, for instance, a medieval man who takes *form* in the Thomist sense and who believes that monarchy is literally the only possible type of government, that *government* and *monarchy* are synonymous terms. The philosophical ground of his argument would be that monarchy is the form (Thomist sense) of government, which would simply be another way of saying that a king is necessary to the essence of government; that without a king

---

5. *ST*, I, 104, 4. Italics are in original for the sake of emphasis.

there can be no government. (It is admittedly an exaggerated position, even for a staunch monarchist; Aquinas himself would probably not claim more for monarchy than status as an accidental form. However, the example should serve very well by way of illustrating the point.) Let us suppose that this hypothetical monarchist confronts in argument an opponent who takes the modernized Platonist view of form as mere external utterance or objectification of an idea and as distinct from a thing's or institution's essence. For the latter, several possible positions are available: he may regard the monarchy as the best possible form (new sense) of government, as the best possible objectification of the ideal essence of government, but still not necessary to that essence; he may regard it as a bad form of government but as a possible one; or he may regard it as good at certain times in history and under certain circumstances, bad or indifferent at others, depending on the particular conditions of human society in which men then find themselves. In any one of these latter attitudes we can say that the monarchy is regarded, in Newman's sense, as an economy, as a symbol in which the invisible or ideal essence of government embodies or expresses itself. The form in this sense, as the external shape or economy, may be good, bad, or indifferent; also, its worth may depend upon its time and place. Thus, one who views the monarchy economically may be either a stout defender or strenuous detractor, depending on his estimate of the form's truth-to-reality. The defender and the detractor have this in common, however: neither of them believes government to be impossible without a king. On the other hand, our hypothetical medieval gentleman, if he is to defend government at all, has no choice save to defend monarchy, for he thinks of the form, not as an economy or as visible symbol of an invisible, ideal essence, but as the very *shape* of what government is. In his view "to be a government" is, by definition, "to be a monarchy." Therefore, for him to speak "economically" either of replacing the kingship with a new form of government or of keeping the kingship because it is the best possible form of government is simply nonsense. It makes no more sense to him to separate kings from the essence of government than to separate the quantity four from the addition of two and two.

On the other hand, it is clear that the man who views the monarchy economically, as a form in the modernized Platonist sense, defines the essence of government in a less precise, literally a less *formal* manner. For instance, he might say that "to be a government" is "to be a source of order," or "to be a guarantor of freedom" or "to be a defender of the Faith," and that that essence, apprehended originally as idea, might be embodied or expressed in any number of different shapes—democracy, socialism, aristocracy, or even kingship. However, to change the form would not change the essence. In fact, a new form might express that essence better than the presently established one. Similarly, with regard to religious forms, one man may argue that "to be Christianity" is to be a religion which believes, among other things, in the Holy Trinity and in Transubstantiation; that these doctrines, along with others of equal importance, taken collectively, constitute the form (Thomist sense) of Christianity; that what might appear to a modern man to be merely the external or symbolic expressions of the Christian essence are really the determiners or causes of that essence and can no more be separated from that essence than fire can be separated from heat. On the other hand, the man who takes these doctrines as forms in the modern or economical sense may argue in their behalf that they are the best possible expression of the invisible essence of Christianity, or he may argue that they are poor, vastly limited economies which need to be replaced by new and better models. (The latter, of course, was the popular Victorian view from Carlyle to Matthew Arnold.) In either case, he has defined the essence of Christianity as "to be" something other than a religion which believes in the Holy Trinity and Transubstantiation. He may have defined its essence as "justification by faith alone" or as a mode of keeping the moral law. In either case, the forms (new sense) of doctrine in question are accepted or rejected, depending on whether they express properly what is considered to be essential and, therefore, ultimately independent of all expression.

Hence we see that the two views of form which I have been outlining, form considered as inseparable from, as cause of, the essence of a composite entity in the "real world" and form considered as the inessential and economical expression of an ideal essence, lead to two radically different views of all established institutions. The man who regards a particular form as essential to an institution's being, as the configuration of being which determines what it is, simply cannot conceive the institution apart from that form. For him, to speak of the government of England is to speak of the king, or to speak of Christianity is to speak of its traditional doctrines and practices; nor is it possible for him to conceive any discontinuity or separation between the two. They are related, in his view, as we have suggested, as heat is to fire. They necessitate one another as truly as the concave necessitates the convex. On the other hand, the man who believes that all forms are economies, mere external shapes without which a thing or institution would still retain its essence, conceives of the relationship between form (new sense) and essence as that between the curve and the asymptote.[6] However closely the economy may approach to the essence which it expresses, it can never quite become identical with it; thus no form can be defended as having absolute value, for form is not the determiner of being.

For the last century and a half, the Modernist-Platonist conception of form has prevailed. Revolutionaries have cut off crowned heads and liberal theologians have attempted to reform (quite literally *re-form*) the Church on the theory that the essences of Church and state exist ideally rather than really and are therefore separable from traditional structures, rites, doctrines, and establishments. They have generally agreed with Carlyle that the latter are "antiquated mythuses" and, on account of their very antiquation, have become veils to obscure rather than symbols to express their religious or political essence. Abbot Samson's society is, for its time and place, a proper, economical expression of the essence of a commonwealth. Since for Carlyle, however, the essence of society exists in the realm of the idea

6. Nédoncelle makes the same suggestion with reference to Newman; but he reverses the terms of the analogy: "Entre l'idée et ses aspects historiques, il y a le rapport d'une courbe à son asymptote; un excédent semble toujours subsister au bénéfice de l'idée, qui garde un résidu mystérieux et inconnaissable." (p. 239.)

and independently of all its expressions, and since no given form (new sense) is necessary to that essence, the forms may change as time and circumstance demand. Consequently, he does not advocate that we return to the world of Bury Saint Edmunds. On the contrary, he holds up an economy from the past, not as a model to be imitated, not as the form which is the cause of a thing's essence, but as a symbol, now outdated, in which the ideal essence can be seen. Once it has been seen and grasped, it can presumably be distinguished from the "antiquated mythus" and embodied in contemporary England in an adequate modern economy.

Tennyson is of the same mind about forms: Arthur tells Bedivere that the form (new sense) of the Round Table must be dissolved and that he, Arthur, the old form of authority, must depart, for only the breaking of past forms can set free the ideal essence of society and government, and unless that essence is in fact set free, it cannot express itself in new forms proper to a new age. There are many other Romantic and Victorian instances of the same notion, including the fundamental heresy of the age: that the forms of rite and doctrine which orthodox Christians have always believed to be essential to the Faith are no more than economies and therefore separable from the central religious idea which they embody. Thus a literal belief in the articles of the creeds, like an acceptance of monarchy as the "to be" of government, must be sacrificed so that Arthur can come again, both as "a modern gentleman" and "thrice as fair." Thomas Arnold, for instance, questions whether the doctrine of the Trinity is essential to Christianity or merely an arbitrary symbol in which that essence can be expressed,[7] and Matthew

---

7. Cf. Arthur Penrhyn Stanley, *The Life and Correspondence of Thomas Arnold* (New York: Charles Scribner's Sons, 1910), I, 34–35. Of course one can cite numerous examples of Arnold's relativism and heterodoxy. For instance his *Principles of Church Reform* (1833) assumes from the outset that the forms and dogmas of the Christian Church are not absolute and can therefore be modified or "re-formed" to meet the needs of the times. In fact the *Principles of Church Reform*, appearing in the same year that the Oxford Movement began, must also be regarded as a tract for the times. See also Lionel Trilling's discussion of Thomas Arnold in his *Matthew Arnold* (New York: W. W. Norton & Co., 1939), Chapter Two, "His Father and His England."

goes his father one better (or worse) by reducing all the dogmas of the Church to mere symbols of an ideal truth, whose worth as symbols are relative to their place in history.

The question then arises: What would be the logical, the obvious way for orthodox Christians to combat this typically Romantic and Victorian (and modern) view of rites and doctrines as a series of forms considered merely as expressions and inessential to the faith which they embody? Of course, one can simply assert that "to be Christianity" is to be creedal, apostolic, scriptural, and sacramental; and such assertions, being of faith, are the foundation of all further considerations. It may be possible, however, to second the assertions of faith with the reasons of philosophy, and the latter is our present concern. How, then, we ask, should a Christian philosopher attempt to refute Tennyson, Carlyle, or the Arnolds? (I am unaware that anyone has attempted to do so philosophically; indeed, it is one point of our present argument that Newman, who would have been the logical person to do so, did not.) Since their error is linked to the idealist presuppositions of their modernized Platonism, it would seem that the best way to refute them would be to question those presuppositions; to attack the whole conception that form is mere objectification and the consequent assumption that essences can be dealt with simply in the mind, as ideas in isolation from embodied forms. We see immediately that in this matter, as in the others we have been considering, the realism of St. Thomas serves us best as a foundation for orthodoxy and as a test of less thoroughly Christian philosophies.

The Thomist grounds for a refutation of Victorian liberalism are evident from what we have already said about form. Since a thing "is so in so far as it actually possesses form"—since form alone "actualizes" a thing, gives it its essence—mutation of forms means mutation of essence. Therefore, it is impossible to speak of an unchanged idea embodying itself in a succession of various forms. Indeed, it is impossible to speak of a thing's essence as idea except in so far as we abstract that idea from "shape" or "act" in matter. The Victorian liberals are guilty of what Aquinas calls the "Platonist error"; they assume that the essence of a thing exists as idea apart from the thing itself. In such a view, the only way to know what the essence of a thing is is to get past all its partial embodiments or economies. Thus to know the essence of Christianity one must transcend all the various historical manifestations of that essence and learn to regard those various manifestations as dispensable. Newman was by no means prepared to take the latter view to its logical conclusions; however, he was so deeply influenced by the "modernist" Platonist assumptions of his contemporaries that a clear-cut denial of their premises, such as that which Aquinas could have offered, was impossible for him. Instead of cutting to the root of the problem and undermining the metaphysical and epistemological propositions on which the liberal error rests, he accepts those propositions and modifies them to meet the demands of a fundamentalist approach to dogma. In those modifications consist his safeguards against relativism.

Lest there be any doubt that Newman did, in fact, accept the philosophical assumptions of his contemporaries, let a few passages suffice for illustration. He points, for instance, to what he calls "the internal consistency of such religious creeds as are allowed time and space to develope freely" and asks what guarantees this consistency among their various forms. He answers that in this respect the development of a creed is like the working out of a set of principles in the life of an individual; in both cases, the "internal consistency" is accounted for by the original ideas or prepossessions on which the development is predicated. For most men, "the principles which they profess guide them unerringly" and, whether they can articulate them or not, those principles provide them with "an instinctive sense in which direction their path lies towards" their particular goal.[8] In other words, ideas, images implanted in the mind, direct man's development; and though under varying circumstances those ideas may express themselves in a great variety of forms, may call forth actions or decisions which at first glance appear to be mutually contradictory, if we examine those forms of expression carefully we can discern their inner coherence—that they are all manifestations, articulations in thought, word, or deed, or the original ideas of the life in question. Just so, in the Church, the

8. *OUS*, p. 211.

"principles of the doctrine of Christ" give an internal consistency to the historical mutations of Christian dogma and ceremony. These principles never change, but the expression of them varies as the world varies, changing from age to age in their outward shape and color. In fact, as in the case of an individual, the degree of change is sometimes so considerable and the variety of forms is so vast, that "Faith alone is able to accept it [the original principle or idea] as one and the same under all its forms."[9]

Indeed, *faith* consists in part in keeping a firm hold upon the idea or image of God on which both the individual and the Church base their developments. If we have been attentive to our consciences and to what God has revealed in the Incarnation, if we have a secure grasp of the "principles of the doctrine of Christ," we shall have no great trouble in recognizing those principles under all their manifestations. Moreover, in order to keep a firm, subjective grasp upon the essence of Christianity, we must be careful never to confuse it with any of its economical manifestations. The "idea or vision of the Blessed Trinity in Unity of the Son Incarnate and of His Presence" is to be kept distinct from the forms which express it. As that "idea or vision" develops, as it expresses itself in various ways, it becomes the legitimate subject of "a number of qualities, attributes, and actions." If, however, we are to recognize the idea within those forms, the essence as distinct from the theological propositions or the rites which express it, we must never lose our original apprehension of God as "one, and individual, and independent of words." If we keep the two distinct and hold fast, subjectively, to the "essence" of the Faith, we shall never confound "particular propositions" which "express portions of the great idea vouchsafed to us" with the idea which these subserve and on which they depend.[10]

This "modern" distinction between essence and form is so deeply embedded in the very core of Newman's thought that it is very nearly taken for granted in all his theological work. At times, in fact, he intimates that theological development, the

9. *OUS*, p. 303.
10. *OUS*, p. 331.

descent of the ideal Christian essence into external form, is only to be accepted as a necessary evil. In the *Arians of the Fourth Century* he "avows" his belief "that freedom from symbols and articles is abstractedly the highest state of Christian communion, and the peculiar privilege of the primitive Church."[11] He implies a metaphorical similarity between the primitive stages of Christianity and the youth of man; in both situations, the ideas and visions of divine reality subsist in their purity, not yet divided or masked by those forms in which they must later embody and express themselves. The Fathers of the primitive Church, cherishing this freedom and innocence, were understandably "dilatory" in theological developments. "They were loth to confess, that the Church had grown too old to enjoy the free, unsuspicious teaching with which her childhood was blest."[12] He voices similar notions in the *Essay on Development.* In discussing papal supremacy as a legitimate development from the original "idea or vision" of Christianity, he is forced to admit that no such form of doctrine is found explicitly stated in Scripture or in the writing of the earliest Fathers. If it is there at all, it is only by implication. The explanation is that in the Church's youth the essence of the Faith was grasped subjectively or intuitively in the idea, and there was no need for expressing it by economical divisions and codifications. "St. Peter's prerogative would remain a mere letter, till the complication of ecclesiastical matters became the cause of ascertaining it. While Christians were 'of one heart and one soul,' it would be suspended; love dispenses with laws."[13] The principle is that "no doctrine is defined till it is violated";[14] no formal expression of the central Christian idea is required until the innocent and immediate apprehension of that idea is in some way impeded. "Thus, the holy Apostles would *without words* [without forms] know all the truths concerning the high doctrines of theology, which

11. *Arians*, p. 36.
12. *Arians*, p. 37.
13. *An Essay on the Development of Christian Doctrine*, p. 150. Hereafter cited as *Devel.*
14. *Devel.*, p. 151.

controversialists after them have piously and charitably reduced to formulae, and developed through argument."[15]

Thus we see that in the Church, as in the individual, development consists in "reducing" the original idea or principle into a complex system of forms or economies. Taken together, the Church's promulgations constitute her spiritual autobiography, her *apologia*. She too came trailing clouds of glory, with the clear image or vision of her Lord infused within her mind; and for a while she lived peaceably in the paradise of her original and intuitive knowledge of the Christian essence. But then the shades of heresy closed upon her, and she was forced to become conscious of herself, to go out into and to do battle with the "living busy world." In the process, she had to *define*, which means to limit or give form to, her original subjective impression or image of Christ. In doing that, she brought forth the series of forms which, taken collectively, we call Christianity, the faith and practice of the Catholic Church. However, being divine and indefectible, she has never confounded that faith and practice, important and, indeed, necessary though it is, with the still more important, the more truly necessary idea or image of God from which all Christian forms depend, from which they receive their life. She knows that all developments of doctrine are at best economical representations, "condescensions to the infirmity and peculiarity of our minds, shadowy representations of realities which are incomprehensible to creatures such as ourselves."[16] She knows, moreover, that that idea of God from which all forms draw their meaning is grasped by man directly from the conscience, not by abstracting reality from the forms; that the heart of Christian experience is " 'solus cum solo,' " a "homage of the heart to the Unseen"[17] with which no forms must be allowed to interfere.

If, therefore, the essence of Christianity is finally regarded as independent of all the forms which express it, and if a man's

15. *Devel.*, pp. 191–192; italics mine.
16. *Arians*, p. 75.
17. *Ap.*, p. 177.

proper knowledge of that essence is direct, intuitive, and likewise independent of those forms, how can the forms be justified as necessary, much less as sacred and everlasting? The Tennysonian, Arnoldian, or Carlylean view that they are dispensable and alterable seems at first glance a reasonable, even necessary, conclusion from the premises, and the question that confronts us is how Newman, apparently sharing those premises, reached exactly the opposite conclusion. If the doctrine of the Holy Trinity is an economical form in which we attempt to express the ultimately inexpressible nature of God, and if we apprehend an awareness of that nature, "without words," without abstracting understanding from the doctrine, how can the form, the doctrine, be regarded as necessary? Why should Newman not join his liberal contemporaries in maintaining that such a form was the product of the times in which it was articulated and in no way absolutely binding on Christians of subsequent and different times? In other words, what is Newman's orthodox safeguard against relativism?

The 1839 essay indicates that in spite of his orthodoxy he felt the pressure of his philosophical premises and that he had come to at least a half-conscious realization that his system needed safeguards. He talks rather freely there both about "changes in the moral state and (what may be called) *mind* of the Church" and about changes imposed on the Church from without by "the silent progress which society has been making, the revolutions of civil government, [and] the march of civilization."[18] Such remarks lead him to comment further that "we cannot, if we would, move ourselves literally back into the times of the Fathers: we must, in spite of ourselves, be churchmen of our own era, not of any other, were it only for this reason, that we are born in the nineteenth century, not in the fourth."[19] That statement could have been made by one of Newman's liberal contemporaries with little or no modification. Taken out of context and without any qualifying examples, it could be used to justify abandoning all the forms of orthodoxy.

18. *Essays*, I, 287.
19. *Essays*, I, 288.

Newman was apparently aware of that possibility himself, for, as we have seen, the footnote that he added to the 1871 edition of the essays attempts to guard against the danger.[20]

In that note he says quite candidly that "what is said above goes further . . . than I habitually went myself as an Anglican, and in my deliberate judgment." He adds that since 1839 he has "gradually acquiesced" in an "hypothesis about the *depositum fidei*" according to which doctrines develop or evolve "out of certain original and fixed dogmatic truths, which were held inviolate from first to last, and the more firmly established and illustrated by the very process of enlargement." By way of contrast to this later, more mature view, he describes the 1839 notion as a theory of "*metamorphosis* and recasting of doctrines into new shapes,—'*in nova mutatas corpora formas*,'—those old and new shapes being foreign to each other, and connected only as symbolizing or realizing certain immutable but nebulous *principles*."[21] We have already mentioned Newman's distinction between "immutable but nebulous *principles*" and "fixed dogmatic truths"; now, however, we are in a position to see that it is on precisely that distinction that his safeguard against relativism rests. In fact, Newman's very language establishes his orthodox qualifications beyond any question.

The only question is whether the force of language serves for more than simple assertion of a difference in attitude; is there anything in this qualifying note to suggest a genuinely philosophical modification of the original theory? With reference to what he says about the forms themselves, there seems to be very little more than simple declaration. He has come to prefer a theory of "enlargement" to one of "recasting," but is there anything here to indicate why one theory should be philosophically necessary and the other not? The only hint of a reason lies in his remark that in the recasting theory the old and new shapes are foreign to each other and connected only by virtue of their common role as symbols or economies of an identical, ideal essence. On the other hand, a "process of enlargement" suggests

20. See above, p. 67.
21. *Essays*, I, 288, note.

that new forms depend upon old ones and complete or fulfill rather than superseding them. We know, of course, that the latter was Newman's theory as he worked it out in the *Development of Christian Doctrine*, and yet the question remains there, as here, whether there is any philosophical coherency or necessity in the one view as opposed to the other. In other words, does Newman at any point indicate that some factor in the relationship between essence and form demands "enlargement" rather than simple "recasting"? If we can show that he does so, we can also show that he has refuted Arnoldean liberalism on its own ground.

We shall recur to the point in due course; however, it can only be dealt with in light of the other distinction Newman makes here between two views of the original Christian idea. The recasting theory goes hand in hand with the assumption that what is being recast are "immutable but nebulous *principles*." On the other hand, in the "process of enlargement," what is being enlarged is a body of "fixed *dogmatic truths*, which were held inviolate from first to last." Enlargement does not change these; rather, they are "the more firmly established and illustrated" in the process.[22] From this distinction rises a second inquiry: is there some reason why a fixed dogmatic truth necessarily demands expression by enlargement rather than by recasting, by the addition rather than the simple mutation of forms? Moreover, that query leads promptly to a third: can we, unless we speak as Thomists, speak legitimately of the essence (or idea) of Christianity as a body of "fixed *dogmatic truths*"; for is not dogma itself either an economical manifestation of the idea of Christianity or else its form or "act-of-being" in the Thomist sense?

The following, then, appear to be the issues on which the subject of an orthodox safeguard turns. The popular nineteenth-century notion, a revived Platonism, is that the essence of Christianity, whatever it may be, is possibly immutable in itself but certainly nebulous, existing for man in the realm of idea or subjective impression and hence capable of being expressed in a great variety of forms which may be reshaped or exchanged as time and circumstance demand and which are connected with one

22. *Essays*, I, 288, note.

another only in so far as they are symbols of the same idea, objectifications of the same essence. Newman accepts the basic assumption that the essence is subjectively apprehended and separable from the forms that express it, but he defines that essence as "fixed" rather than "nebulous." He maintains, moreover, that though a new form may be added for the due exposition of that essence, the old ones must not be discarded; for the new stand to the old, not in the relation of distant cousins or of cognate mutations from the same root stock, but as a new branch growing out of an old one and deriving its life, not directly from the idea, but through the channel of the older forms. Moreover, he hints, at least, that there is either something inherent in the archetypal relationship of ideas to forms or something peculiar in the relationship that his own doctrine of ideas presupposes, which demands preservation and continuity rather than recasting.

As to this latter matter, Newman gives us very little to go on, but it is none the less fascinating to consider the possibilities. Had he been less the ethical, practical man that he was and more the metaphysician, he might have undertaken to show how his own conception of the idea of Christianity differed from that of his liberal contemporaries; and in doing so his first step would probably have been to contradict the vagueness of their conception. He might even have questioned whether men like Tennyson, Carlyle, or the Arnolds really mean "idea" when they use the word, or whether they mean, instead, something like the Hegelian Absolute, what Newman calls a "nebulous principle" rather than a "fixed truth." The terms of Newman's contrast are apt; for a principle by its very nature is nebulous rather than fixed. Even though it may be an immutable or absolute principle, those conditions do not necessarily endow it with the equality of a fixed truth capable of a single dogmatic or formal articulation. "Principles are abstract and general, doctrines relate to facts"; "Personal responsibility is a principle, the Being of God is a doctrine."[23] If, therefore, when we speak of the "idea of God," we really mean instead the "divine principle" or the "Absolute," it makes perfect

23. *Devel.*, p. 178.

sense to say that we can express our so-called "idea" in a variety of ways. Thus a doctrine such as that of the Holy Trinity comes to be regarded as no more than a metaphor growing out of certain historical and intellectual circumstances of the first three centuries of the Christian era, a figurative or perhaps "mythical" expression of a "nebulous principle." Likewise, Christianity can be viewed simply as a religious principle, as no more than a set of attitudes, capable of any number of different embodiments.

On the other hand, if, when we speak of the idea of God or of Christianity we literally mean *idea*, we find ourselves speaking of a definite reality which has fixed limits and which can only express itself in certain ways. If God is a definite being as well as the principle of absolute being, the idea or image of Him which the true idealist believes he holds in his mind, either innately or by infusion, must be the idea of a definite being. Consequently, any expression of that idea in the forms of doctrine must correspond to the "shape" of the idea. Thus, if God in His essence is three persons in one substance, the idea of Him, if it is to be expressed in doctrinal form at all, must be expressed in the dogma of the Holy Trinity—as, for instance, in the Nicene or Athanasian Creeds. Similarly, if the essence of Christianity is of a real religion, a faith, a revealed deposit of truth, rather than simply a principle of thought and action, the objectification of it, as a form, must likewise be fixed and definite. Thus, if we really mean *idea* when we speak of the "idea of Christianity," we cannot agree with Matthew Arnold in making a radical distinction between that idea and what he calls the *fact*. Of course, what Arnold really means by *idea* is *principle*, and we may translate "idea of Christianity" to mean something like the "principle of religion." Thus, since a principle, as we have said, is nebulous, it becomes possible for him to speak of its various formal embodiments.

We have already discussed Newman's idealism at some length, and we have seen how closely he is drawn by that idealism to the mode of thought of his most illustrious secular contemporaries. However, if on one hand he seems to share their philosophical tenets, he distinguishes himself from them by taking those tenets more seriously than they do. If we can say legitimately that

Newman and Arnold are both idealists, we must add that Newman, in spite of his philosophical imprecision, is an idealist in
a more literal sense. Moreover, it should now be clear that the
very literalness of that idealism provided him with his necessary
safeguard against the heresies in which his less consistent contemporaries involved themselves. When they said *idea*, they obviously meant something vague, like *principle* or *attitude*. When
Newman said *idea*, he meant an image (or species) that corresponds to a fixed reality. In this regard, too, his emphasis on
conscience served him well; for, as we have seen, the conscience
speaks to Newman, not of a principle, but of a person. In fact,
the conscience by its very nature gives us definite information. It
does not simply teach us that God *is* but that God is just or that
God is a being who by His nature demands faith, worship and
righteous conduct. Consequently, the conscience impresses upon
us the idea of a fixed and definite religion as the necessary, as
the only possible response to the God whom it reveals. Therefore,
it prepares us to recognize Christianity as the true religion, for its
depositum fidei supplies what conscience demands.

The conscience as such, however, is not our immediate concern. My point in referring to it is simply to show that Newman's
emphasis upon it and his interpretation of its role, so important
as we have seen it to be in other aspects of his thought, serves
also to secure for him the effect of a genuine and literal idealism.
It is that effect which, in turn, secures his orthodoxy, and it is
the latter relationship[24] rather than the role of conscience as
such that we must now describe.

If we consider in retrospect the various illustrations of Newman's idealism and subjectivism that we have already offered, it
becomes clear enough that he habitually thinks of ideas as fixed
and definite. When he compares the ideas which underlie the
development of doctrine with the "principles" on which individuals build their lives, the term "principle" has little more than
a figurative sense. The "principles of the doctrine of Christ"
always signify for Newman something fixed and solid. Therefore,
though he maintains that the "idea or vision of the Blessed

24. I.e., between the effect of a true idealism and orthodoxy.

Trinity in Unity, of the Son Incarnate and of His Presence"[25] is distinguishable from any doctrinal form in which that vision may be expressed, the very language assumes that the vision itself is a distinct idea and not simply a principle in a general or nebulous sense. Therefore, though the idea may be independent of the dogma, Newman can see no reason for objection "against a general, natural, and ordinary correspondence between" the two. For "surely, if Almighty God is ever one and the same, and is revealed to us as one and the same, the true inward impression of Him, made on the recipient of the revelation, must be one and the same." It follows that "since human nature proceeds upon fixed laws, the statement of that impression must be one and the same, so that we may as well say that there are two Gods as two Creeds."[26]

All of Newman's distinctions between true and false developments rest on this assumption, that the idea of God in our minds corresponds to a definite reality and that the various formal statements of that idea must likewise correspond to that reality. A development is true or not depending on whether it is "faithful or unfaithful to the idea from which it started."[27] Such a proposition presupposes an original idea which is sufficiently precise in itself to serve as measure of what is true or false. That, we see immediately, is an entirely different sort of concept from something like the Hegelian Absolute or from any mere principle of religion or ethics. "If Christianity is a fact," as Newman supposes it to be, "and impresses an idea of itself on our minds," that idea must have all the definiteness of fact; and when in course of time it expands into a great variety of forms, each of these must be, in itself, "determinate and immutable, as is the objective fact itself which is thus represented."[28] If one of these developments should prove to be indeterminate or mutable, it can be identified immediately as being unfaithful to the fixed idea which gave it birth. Such are heresies—forms of doctrine or

25. *OUS*, p. 331.
26. *OUS*, p. 328.
27. *Devel.*, p. 41.
28. *Devel.*, p. 55

rites which are unfaithful to the idea from which they spring; and these invariably prove to be "barren and short-lived."[29] It is obvious that if the idea were not precise enough to define by contrast what was unfaithful to it, it would be impossible to say what was a heresy and what was not. The latter position is, of course, essentially that which Coleridge, Carlyle, Tennyson, the Arnolds, and Newman's other heretical contemporaries took.

It should be clear from these remarks that the definiteness of the idea also serves to guarantee the preservation of forms already established in the process of development. Since the idea has factual solidity and since, therefore, it serves as a measure to distinguish true from false, it is possible to say absolutely that this form of doctrine is true and that is false. Hence the idea itself preserves every true development of it, for what is true cannot be discarded. If that "form" known as the doctrine of the Holy Trinity is definably true, proved true when measured by the idea of God which conscience impresses on our minds, it assumes its place as an absolute among absolutes and can never be superseded. Any subsequent development of the idea of God must therefore presuppose the doctrine of the Trinity, for to ignore it or deny it is to deny the truth itself. Thus, integrity of the "old forms" serves Newman as a test of true development. He speaks, for instance, of the "preservation of type" as one "note of a genuine development";[30] that the parts of the developed form must correspond to its original rudiments. Likewise, any true development must exert a "conservative action on its past"; "for a corruption is a development in that very stage in which it ceases to illustrate, and begins to disturb, the acquisitions gained in its previous history."[31] The developments consist "in addition and increase chiefly, not in destruction";[32] but such a proposition makes sense only if the original idea is distinct enough to provide some proof that what is already established is, in fact, true.

Thus we see that Newman's idealism secures itself philosophically by its own consistency. It follows that the practical test

29. *Devel.*, p. 95.
30. *Devel.*, p. 171.
31. *Devel.*, p. 199.
32. *Devel.*, p. 200.

of true developments in the Church will resemble the test of various private judgments in the individual; for in each case the original idea of God is being tested as by fire. Just as martyrdom proves the individual's apprehension of God to be universally true, so the durability of forms, of doctrines and rites, under stress and persecution proves the Church's apprehensions to be valid. It may be impossible in an idealist and basically anti-rationalist system to demonstrate the truth of doctrine "scientifically" as Aquinas does, but what logic cannot prove, fire and sword will. Thus Newman does not offer us so much the logic of a form as its history, not the examination of a doctrine as an existing entity but rather an account of how its coming-to-be and its durability prove its validity. An idea is "elicited and expanded by trial"; it "battles into perfection and supremacy." In the process, the forms of its utterance are tested by that very trial and battle. Just as the martyr in his suffering is forced to resign all dependence on secondary things and rest on Christ alone, so an idea in its process of development is forced by the pressure and testing of historic circumstance to disengage itself "from what is foreign and temporary" and thus to present itself ultimately as a set of forms which constitutes a true economy.[33]

We have before us now three views of the relationship between "faith and form." One is the realist (Thomist) view in which the form of a thing is the cause of its being, of its "actuality." According to such a view we can no more talk of Christianity without its peculiar rites and doctrines than we can talk about a house without that shape which makes it a house and not simply a heap of building materials. In this view, the *idea*, so far from being a subjective image preceding the form and finding at best only partial or economical expression in that form, is an acquired species derived by abstraction from the composite entity which exists objectively in the real world. Accordingly, we can say that the essence of a thing is inseparable from its form and in no sense to be considered as simply ideal. Thus, according to Aquinas, the essence of a sacrament is *caused* by its formal

33. *Devel.*, p. 40.

element, namely the words which are imposed on the matter of water or of bread and wine, giving them shape in something of the same way that the form of the house gives shape to the matter which goes into the building of it; and in either case the form determines the essence, the "to be" of the thing in question. To be the Sacrament of our Lord's Body and Blood is to be a particular form, a particular set of words, nor can the essence really be said to exist as an idea prior to the form or act which gives it being. Another view is that which loosely speaking we call the idealism of the major nineteenth-century liberals, according to which what is called the relationship between the idea and the form of a thing is really the relationship between a principle and its various applications or expressions. In this view, the essence of an entity such as the Eucharist would be said to exist in some vague, general principle concerning the communion between God and man, a principle which, because of its very diffuseness, could be expressed in a variety of different and even, apparently, self-contradictory forms. A third view—Newman's—is a more precise sort of idealism in which, though the essence of an entity resides in the idea or subjective image rather than in the composite reality, that idea or image is, nevertheless, so definite and exact in its nature that it demands an equally exact formal objectification. The one question that remains for our consideration is whether there is, in the final analysis, any practical difference between Newman's position and the traditional, Thomist one.

The great metaphysical distinction between the two (we have already noted it) is that because, for Newman, the essence of an entity resides ultimately in the idea or subjective image rather than in the embodied form, we can apprehend the idea and consequently the essence independently of the form. In fact, this direct and prior knowledge of the idea serves as Newman's measure or test of whether the forms which express it are valid. That exactly reverses the Thomist epistemology in which any direct or intuitive knowledge of essences as ideas being impossible for us, we must depend upon the composite entity of form and matter, the existing, objective thing, as the foundation of our knowledge of essences. That reversal, which at first glance may appear inconsiderable, has, in fact, wide-ranging consequences.

The definiteness of the idea may secure for Newman doctrinal conclusions as thoroughly orthodox as St. Thomas's, but though his idealism may be consistent and safe from heterodoxy, the very fact that it is idealism presents difficulties from which Thomist realism is free. These difficulties all descend from the reversal I just mentioned, from placing the idea or subjective image in the ascendency; from making our knowledge of forms dependent from ideas rather than that of ideas from forms; in effect, from reducing form from its status as a metaphysical reality, as the very act of a thing's being "in the flesh," to the status of a simple symbol or economy, a mere shell or outward manifestation of the idea, the husk of a kernel.

The consequence of that reversal and reduction is what I should call the *tyranny* of the idea or of the subjective experience; nor does the orthodox security of a genuine idealism avoid that consequence completely. One way to illustrate what I mean by that tyranny is to point out one major difference between Aquinas's and Newman's concepts of development. St. Thomas does not discuss the principle of development at any length—as a theological concept it post-dated the thirteenth century—but where he does admit the fact of development, he does so in strictly logical terms. For instance, he justifies the *"filoque* clause" on the grounds that it is implicit in the doctrine of the Holy Ghost and can be derived logically therefrom.[34] Development so conceived is a process which can be subjected to the laws of ratiocination. It is something that man does, not something that is done to him. He acquires a species by abstraction; a species is not imposed upon him requiring him to find a mode or form for its expression. In effect, man might be said to "make" the idea; at least we could say that he invents or abstracts it by the power of the agent intellect, and its existence is dependent on his rational choice. Newman admits the existence of this kind of

34. CG, IV, 24, 25. For the whole matter of the similarities and differences between Newman and Aquinas on theories of doctrinal development see Owen Chadwick, *From Bossuet to Newman, the Idea of Doctrinal Development* (Cambridge: Cambridge University Press, 1957), pp. 21–22, 168ff. Vargish comments on the same matter; see p. 41. Also see Pailin, pp. 44ff., for a discussion of development in its nineteenth-century context.

strictly rational development as a special type, and he gives it a special name; it is a *metaphysical* development. He describes it as "a mere analysis of the idea contemplated," and says that it terminates "in its [the idea's] exact and complete delineation."[35] He grants the validity of such a process within certain limits, but his emphasis, as we would expect, lies elsewhere.

It lies, in fact, where we would expect it, on "implicit reason," by which the whole Church, like the "whole man," reasons; and the doctrine of implicit reason transfers autonomy from the reasoning mind to the power of the idea or image which controls the rational process. Thus Newman envisions the Church coming to certain formal dogmatic conclusions, not as though those conclusions were deduced by the devout intellectual work of the Holy Doctors, but rather as though they were imposed upon her by the power of the ideas which the subsequent forms articulate. Thus, he pictures dogmatic development as moving through the whole Church with the power of a river, carrying the crude, unconscious minds of the multitude before it, until, in the last analysis, the theologians of the schools, like the mind of the individual man, can do little more than describe in "explicit" terms what the idea has wrought in the whole body. Thus, as we have seen, an idea "battles to perfection." It will win the battle because of its "chronic vigour,"[36] and it is that same vigor which makes it impossible for men to limit it to logical deductions. The assumption is that the idea has its own life, not only independent of all forms, as we have seen already, but also, and consequently, independent of rational human choices as well. One can no more stop its development than one can stop the motion of a river. In that sense, the supremacy of the idea or image enforces a kind of tyranny on human thought.[37]

35. *Devel.*, p. 52.
36. *Devel.*, p. 203.
37. Development remains a lively topic in Roman Catholic theology, and Newman's essay is generally considered germane to any consideration of the matter. However, it is by no means true that the idea of development has won the day. See, for instance, D. Nicholls, "Developing Doctrines and Changing Beliefs" in the *Scottish Journal of Theology*, XIX (1966), 280–292, for an examination of several contemporary treatments of the idea, pointing to deficiencies in each. See also A. A. Stephenson's review of Walgrave's *New-*

The consequence is the revolutionary aspect of Newman's thought which is implicit in such a work as *Callista*. Because essences are conceived of in subjective terms as though they had an ideal existence before their manifestations as the forms of composite entities, they are therefore conceived of as possessing power to destroy forms as well as to make them. In this respect, the fruit of Newman's genuine idealism is not drastically different from the "Hegelianism" of his liberal contemporaries. A precise concept of the idea and of the relationship between idea and form may, as we have seen, preserve true forms; in that sense it is conservative. On the other hand, the autonomy of the idea leaves no room for that great body of forms, inherited customs of one sort or another, which may not accord with the idea of Church or state strictly defined but which in a realist philosophy may legitimately be regarded as forms or acts of being in their own right. As we have pointed out before, in Thomist thought the very being of a thing is its signature of worth, for its being and its form are inseparable. Thus every institution *exists* and must be judged as an entity in itself, rather than in reference to some idea independent of it.

When the idea or subjective image takes all power to itself, however, everything which is allowed to stand must be justified by its measure. Moreover, since ideas, living as they do in men's minds and nowhere else, are by their nature constantly in motion, either advancing or decaying, stasis is a mere fiction or illusion. Ideas "are ever enlarging into fuller development." Nor will they be stationary in their corruption or dissolution; whether advancing or decaying they move and determine the corresponding development or decay of forms. The great error of conservatism is to ignore this fact; the sober "are indisposed to

man the Theologian in *Theological Studies*, XXII (1961), 688–690. It is interesting to hear a Jesuit from Campion Hall say that he remains "unpersuaded" that Newman's "*Essay*, taken as a whole, is consistent with the immutability of doctrine." (p. 689) For Newman's own defense against similar charges one can consult his correspondence, in particular the letters written in 1851 to Francis Richard Wegg-Prosser (*Letters and Diaries*, XIV, 348–351, 353–354, 360–361, 365–368, 369–373, and 378–379). See also "The Newman-Perrone Paper on Development," ed. T. Lynch, *Gregorianum*, XVI (1935), 402–447.

change in civil matters" for they fear lest by going too far they may precipitate a calamity. What they fail to realize is that preservation of a *status quo* cannot eliminate the danger of "slow corruption."[38] Because ideas control man and his society, man and society, the individual and the Church, are moved willy-nilly by the power of those ideas. Therefore we cannot simply conserve what exists because it exists; the supremacy of the idea and the development it demands will not allow that. Only the idea has the power to preserve those true forms such as the doctrine of the Holy Trinity to which the idea gives birth. We can say that such forms are fixed and immutable, but what we really mean is that they live and are carried forward in the current of the idea. If that same current sweeps away other mutable forms we must simply acquiesce in the loss. Conservatives must learn to defend, not existing entities or institutions *per se* or for their own sake, but that direction of development which has brought these institutions into being and for whose sake, and for that of the seminal idea, they exist.

In fact, as an idea grows and develops, it naturally comes into collision with existing forms which are the products of some contrary idea and development. That is what happened when Christianity developed within the Roman Empire, and we have seen in *Callista* how Newman envisions the idea's triumph over Jucundus and the established order which he represents. That order, Newman shows us, was in decay; but Jucundus, the "sober man," the conservative, failing to grasp that fact and failing to realize that the movement of society is not in society's hands but controlled by the power of ideas, attempts to preserve what exists. His is the old-fashioned, rational mind. He believes that the essence of a thing is inseparable from its embodied form and that existing substances are the foundation of all intellection and the test of all experience.[39] In Newman's view, he is not "spiritually minded." Like the Tory High-Churchmen of Newman's day,

38. *Devel.*, p. 203.
39. In fact, of course, Jucundus is incapable of metaphysical speculation. He does rest his faith in existing facts, however, and it may not be altogether pointless to suggest what kind of metaphysical position he would have endorsed had he been capable of the requisite understanding.

he had not understood that all forms are dominated by the vigor of the idea which shapes them, which they clothe, and that when an idea, like that of Rome, is dead, it is impossible to preserve the forms in which it originally embodied itself. Nor does he realize that when a new idea is in the ascendancy, "it cannot progress at all without cutting across, and thereby destroying or modifying and incorporating with itself existing modes of thinking and operating."[40] Such is the tyranny of the idea; it justifies what exists or attacks it, not on the basis of what it is in itself, as form or act of being, but on the basis of an independent and pre-existent idea of its essence. Such a theory inevitably issues in ideologies of one kind or another, and Newman's theory of doctrinal development is essentially an ideology.

Thus we see that, though Newman safeguards his doctrine of the relativity of forms against the danger of heresy latent in it, he is unable to do so without a considerable narrowing of perspective. He avoids one modern difficulty only by falling into another, for the very force of ideas, which secures the forms that express them, imposes an ideological rigidity on his whole theory of development. The alternative would have been to allow the various doctrines to secure themselves, on the strength of precedent and authority as well as their own reasonableness. The simple question, after all, is, "Is this form, this rite or doctrine, true in itself?" Is God, in fact, a Trinity in Unity? Is our Lord really present in the Sacrament according to the mode of transubstantiation? Was he really, in fact, born of a virgin, and was she both immaculately conceived and, at the end of her mortal life, assumed into heaven? The nineteenth- and twentieth-century liberals maintain that so far as *fact* is concerned each of these questions must be answered in the negative but that each of the doctrines in question may be regarded as a form or symbol (or economy) expressing some general religious principle or other. Newman answers each question positively as to matter of fact, but his emphasis is not so much upon each dogma as such as upon their relationship as forms, symbols, or economies to fixed,

40. *Devel.*, p. 38.

precise ideas of God and of Christianity which are given man by conscience and by revelation. Thus he binds the consideration of each to an ideological estimate of the whole body of dogma. Neither view asks simply, is the doctrine in itself true? Do Scripture, tradition, and reason all warrant our believing it to be true? If they do, then faith and form can never be separated, for the form is the very being of the faith. If we take such a view, we set ourselves free at once both from liberal relativism and from the domination of ideology. Though Newman waged a successful battle against the former danger, he was too closely bound to the conditions of his times to avoid the latter. One safeguard requires another, but the latter was not immediately forthcoming.

PART FOUR

The Consequences

Newman's willingness to distinguish between "faith and form" and his ideological approach to ecclesiastical history which results from that distinction go a long way toward explaining why he was willing to relinquish the "old idea of a Christian Polity," "the tradition of fifteen hundred years," and seek some means of reconciling Catholic teaching and the new civilization. If the very being of an institution derives from its form and if, consequently, the idea of that institution must be abstracted from the existing reality in time and space, the preservation of all meaning and value in society depends upon the preservation of those institutions in which that meaning and value exist. On the contrary, if the idea, and consequently the meaning and value, of an institution is thought of as pre-existing the institution itself, and if the form of the institution is considered merely as an expression of the idea rather than as the source or determiner thereof, it becomes possible to sacrifice the institution with some degree of confidence that the idea can be expressed in another form.

Such a sacrifice inevitably undermines the traditional community, for the latter lives in those common forms—those ceremonies and institutions—which it inherits and in turn passes on. Such a community does not need to scurry about after hard-won spiritual gains in the realm of the idea; it is born to those ideas, for they live in the very institutions which give it its life. What such a community considers basically a waste of time is an effort to justify all its modes of conduct and belief in reference to some body of ideas existing separate from and prior to its inherited institutions. In fact, to live by tradition is not to live by ideas but by existing facts; and where facts are available, what is the need for positing antecedent ideas? The latter is the necessity of the exile, the man who chooses the sea or desert in preference to the city, the "Paradise within thee" in preference to the "easterne riches" or Arlo Hill. The idealist, the historical relativist, even though he may be orthodox in matters of dogma, inevitably lives at the behest of the "spirit afloat," "rising up in the heart." The traditionalist, on the contrary, invariably finds himself "rooted in one dear perpetual place," like the snapdragon in the walls of Trinity College. Since his ideas come by way of the senses and the agent intellect from existing substances and institutions external to himself, he cannot separate his intellectual and spiritual life from its physical and sensible roots. He takes his nourishment, not from the mind, not from the conscience and the heart, but from things as simple as the color and texture of his land, the type of dialect in which he speaks, the kind of manners by which he lives, the styles of architecture which are indigenous to his place, the mode of government to which he is obligated, the religion he has been taught from childhood, and all the vast complexity of customs and prejudices which he takes for granted as a part of the "given" of existence. To cut himself off from these existing facts amounts to a kind of intellectual suicide, for, by doing so, he separates his ideas from the realities, the composite entities and institutions which give rise to them and nourish them. If he should make the Platonists' error of thinking that ideas exist independently of all existing substances and can be apprehended directly by the mind, of believing in effect that the mind is its own place, he may, in pursuit of that error, divorce himself from his sustaining tradition in the name of a myth or fantasy.

That Newman, in spite of his stiff dogmatic conservatism, pursued such an error and did, indeed, divorce himself from the traditional community has been implicit in all we have said. It remains to consider the consequences of that pursuit and that divorce—first, in his role as reformer, as leader of the Oxford Movement; and, second, as literary theorist and man of letters.

CHAPTER XI

The Movement and the Establishment

IN light of what we have already said about Newman's idealism and its consequences, it is interesting that his own interpretation of the Oxford Movement should stress the power—perhaps even the tyranny—of the idea. Viewing the movement in retrospect, he treats it as the development of "one idea," and that "idea, or first principle, was ecclesiastical liberty." In other words, the heart, the very life, of the Oxford Movement was its anti-Erastianism; that idea was responsible for the whole Tractarian development. "The object of its attack was the Establishment, considered simply as such,"[1] for the very "essence" of that Establishment was Erastianism. Therefore, "to destroy Erastianism was to destroy the [national] religion." Hence, Newman concludes that "the movement . . . and the Establishment were in simple antagonism from the first, although neither party knew it; . . . what was the life of the one was the death of the other."[2]

Such language shows Newman's idealist bias very clearly. In attempting to analyze the course, direction, and end of the "movement of 1833," he turns, not to the defense of particular institutions, nor even to the defense, as such, of the whole body of Catholic belief which the *Tracts* had, in fact, espoused, but to the justifying idea from which that defense sprang. The very use of the word *movement* to describe Tractarian activities is indicative of the direction in which Newman's mind works. We have become so accustomed to speaking of the Oxford Movement that we are likely to ignore the term's significance. Newman himself did not use it lightly: "My brethren, you do not bear in mind

1. *Diff.*, I, 101.
2. *Diff.*, I, 105.

that a movement is a thing that moves; you cannot be true to it and remain still."[3] "Ideas have consequences," and once an idea takes possession of the mind, its development is inevitable. We have already examined Newman's views on this subject in general, and it becomes quite clear, in reference to Tractarianism, that the anti-Erastian idea, possessing "vigour," is to be credited with producing those forms of doctrines which the *Tracts* were teaching. We see too that the conflict between the movement and the establishment is to be regarded as an elementary conflict between two different ideas of religion, each with its own formal development and each hostile to the other. In such a view, a certain measure of radicalism or anti-traditionalism is unavoidable, for there can be no compromise or peace between movements produced and empowered by mutually exclusive ideas.

At first glance, such statements appear to contradict a great deal that we know about the Oxford Movement. In fact the movement is generally regarded as a conservative episode in the history of the English Church, and certainly we cannot ignore the fact that Newman and other members of the movement party were all insistent upon obedience to bishops and submission to all the forms of the establishment. How can such obviously conservative and traditionalist teaching be reconciled with Newman's own later view that the whole idea of the movement was in radical, ideological opposition from first to last to the traditions of the national Church? He answers the question for us himself, to the effect that the apparent conservatism of the *Tracts* was accidental rather than essential to their central teaching, the product of the historical circumstances in which the anti-Erastian idea underwent its development rather than something essential to the idea itself. In fact, in Newman's retrospective view, that conservatism might almost be regarded as the fruit of an error on the part of the Tractarians. They believed that the "divinely founded Church," whose liberty they were defending, "was realised and brought into effect in our country in the National Establishment, which was the outward form or development of a continuous dynasty and hereditary power which descended from

3. *Diff.*, I, 129.

the Apostles." Therefore they gave "to that Establishment, in its officers, its laws, its usages, and its worship, that devotion and obedience which are correlative to the very idea of the Church." They taught submission to the bishops and to the *Book of Common Prayer*, for these were the powers with "which it was to cow and overpower an Erastian State."[4] The Prayer Book in particular was "the immediate instrument by means of which they professed to make their way, the fulcrum by which they were to hoist up the Establishment, and set it down securely on the basis of Apostolical Truth."[5]

Thus the teaching of the *Tracts* seemed to be conservative, for they appeared to defend the most venerable institutions of the Church of England—the same institutions indeed which Hooker and the Caroline divines had defended, not in the name of the idea, but of custom and reason. As Newman interprets the movement, however, this conservatism and identity with the High Church past was, as I have indicated, both an accident and an error. The anti-Erastian idea *seemed* to demand a defense of the national Church because the Tractarians mistakenly believed that that Church had its own Catholic idea, its own Catholic life, apart from the establishment. What they came to discover, according to Newman, was that the bishops and the Prayer Book were, after all, no more than forms or developments of the Erastian idea and could be defended on no other terms. The course of the movement and the reaction of the Established Church proved their mistake beyond question. It became quite clear, at least to Newman, that the National Church did not in fact rest on the idea of primitive Catholic Christianity but on that of royal supremacy, and from that moment forward it became obvious that the apparent conservatism of the movement was no more than apparent. As ideas develop, as they "battle into perfection," they separate themselves from those elements which are accidentally attached to them by historical circumstance. As the anti-Erastian idea of the movement struggled to realize itself in the theological controversies of the eighteen-thirties, "it was at

4. *Diff.*, I, 130.
5. *Diff.*, I, 135.

length plain that primitive Christianity ignored the National Church, and that the National Church cared little for primitive Christianity, or for those who appealed to it as her foundation."[6] Henceforth, it became impossible to reconcile the movement with a defense of the English establishment, for experience had proved that there was a radical, an "ideal," opposition between the two.

From following such a line of reasoning, it should be clear enough, by implication, what its opposite might have been. Let us suppose for instance that the movement had not, in fact, conceived of itself as a *movement* but as a simple stasis, a defense of what was, in the face of Whig and Liberal attack. Such, apparently, was the position which men like Mr. Palmer and Mr. Rose wished to take and which Keble himself might have adopted had he remained the leader of the movement. None of these men seems to have questioned the authority of the Establishment in any serious or radical way, for none of them, with the possible exception of Keble, seems to have held to an idea of Christianity which was independent of its established, English form. In that sense, they were like George Herbert, having grown into the English Church and that Church into them. Consequently, for them, the conserving of established forms would never have been regarded simply as accidental to the development of an idea but rather as the very essence of their position.

It is one thing to believe in the bishops and the Prayer Book as institutions in their own right, justifiable on their own terms in light of Scripture, tradition, and reason. It is quite another thing to measure their worth as forms expressive of an idea antecedent to and independent of them, as symbols whereby that idea "was realised and brought into effect in our country" as "the *outward form* or *development* of a continuous dynasty and hereditary power which descended from the Apostles."[7] In the latter view, even when there is no mistake about the truth of the forms, even when they are regarded as the just and necessary expressions of the idea as Newman conceived Roman Catholic forms to be,

6. *Diff.*, I, 152.
7. *Diff.*, I, 130; italics mine.

their defense must still be regarded, in the purest sense, as *accidental* to the defense of the idea. The idea possesses its integrity independently of them, and for that reason true idealism can only be conservative or traditionalist accidentally—when the established forms happen in fact to be the proper embodiments of the idea. In such a view, there is no room for a true conservatism or traditionalism such as that on which Hooker's or Aquinas's philosophy was built, for the latter defends what exists, not with reference to some extrinsic ideal standard, but by appealing to the authority which its own history and its own intrinsic reasonableness bear. Thus we have seen that while Newman defended English bishops because he believed, and only so long as he believed, their existence to be a valid development of the idea of Catholicism, Hooker defended them on the basis of their worth as an institution, not so much with reference to the *idea* of Christianity, but because of the warrant of existing historical facts such as Scripture, Antiquity, the customs of the English realm, and the reasonableness of the institution in its own right.

From Hooker's conservative or traditionalist point of view, a defense of the Established Church can be separated from a defense of the Erastian idea, and though Hooker himself never made that distinction, it seems necessary to do so here in order to show that Newman's anti-traditionalism is really the product of his idealist philosophy rather than, as he assumed, the necessary consequence of Catholic orthodoxy. By the Erastian idea I mean the royal supremacy and the admittedly unchristian view that the Church is to be regarded simply as a department or bureau of the state. On the other hand, by Established Church I mean that complex of traditional Christian institutions, such as the bishops and the Prayer Book, which are inseparable, in fact, from the social, political life of the nation and which are accordingly established—that is they are granted the recognition and protection of both common and statutory law. The latter concept, though it may be perversely interpreted and applied by Erastian legislation as it was in England in the 1830s, is nevertheless clearly distinct from Erastianism *per se* and implies no subjection whatever of Church to state. Historically, it predates the Erastian settlement of the Reformation, for who can consider the relation of Church and state in medieval England without seeing immediately that the English Church in those days, though still in obedience to the Roman Pontiff, was also in every sense of the word an Established Church? It was, in fact, literally established by law; its bishops were as truly lords of realm then as after the Erastian legislation of 1535. Its life was embedded in and dependent upon the customs of the realm just as surely as the customs of the realm were dependent upon the life and authority of the Church. No king could be crowned without the Church to crown him, and the Church depended upon the king's coronation oath and his sword for her temporal peace. Moreover, so far as the membership of the Church was concerned, with very few exceptions, the members of the Body of Christ were likewise the subjects of the crown and vice versa. Indeed, when Hooker defined the Church as the nation in its religious aspect, the nation as the Church in its secular aspect, he was doing little more than describing a state of affairs which had always existed in England and which was in no way simply the fruit of new-fangled legislation in the reign of Henry the Eighth. The ideal is thoroughly medieval, what A. P. d'Entreves calls "the Gelasian doctrine . . . of the distinction and interrelation of two great spheres of human life within one single society—the Christian society, the *respublica christiana*."[8] Aquinas, himself, who could never have been accused of Erastianism, maintained such a doctrine, and, if we strip away the Erastian element, we shall see that the English idea of the Establishment, as it descends from Hooker, Andrewes, and Laud is directly in the Thomist tradition.

Of course the *respublica christiana* is one expression of "the old idea of a Christian Polity," the "tradition of fifteen hundred

8. A. P. d'Entreves, "Introduction," Aquinas, *Selected Political Writings* (Oxford: Basil Blackwell, 1965), p. xxi. The most judicious discussion I know of Newman's position and that of his fellow converts with regard to the old idea of the *respublica christiana* is by Wilfred Ward in his *Life and Times of Cardinal Wiseman* (London: Longmans, Green & Co., 1900), I, 290–307. The only weakness in Ward's treatment is that he tends to see Newman as more conservative than he in fact was. However, that is because he is dealing in those pages with the period of the Oxford Movement rather than with Newman's later life.

years," the vision of creation in which human and divine government is joined, in which angels and men dwell together in a wonderful order. It is that image of the cosmos and of the body politic which, as we have seen, is the staple of English Christian thought until at least the seventeenth century, to which, until approximately the same time, Christian theology and poetry is inextricably linked. As we have shown, that vision is made possible, philosophically, by a realist philosophy in which existing, objective things—angels, men, and beasts; the heavens and the earth; crowns and mitres; rites and doctrines—declare the glory of God; in which the idea or image of God is acquired by abstraction from visible things in a "real world" and in which, consequently, the modern notion of a private or subjective idea or image of God with its radical consequences is impossible. That vision also requires the philosophy of law which Aquinas worked out in the *Summa*, which Hooker adopted almost verbatim, and which, in turn, he passed on to his seventeenth-century, High Church successors. For since both human and divine law are developments from the natural law, and since natural law is "nothing else than the rational creature's participation of the eternal law,"[9] it follows that the governments of Church and state, whatever their diversities of degree and end, have a common origin in the mind of God. Hence, instead of thinking of Church and state as being in opposition to one another, Aquinas, as well as his seventeenth-century English followers, conceives the two as complementary to one another. The same legal principles that justify order and ceremony in the conduct of state affairs also justify the rites and sacraments of the Church. That is not to say that these same principles function in each sphere in the same degree, for Aquinas (and Hooker too, though less adamantly) maintains very stoutly that orders and sacraments are directly of divine institution. However, since human and divine institutions have a common base in the *lex naturalis* and *lex aeterna*, differences in their degree of priority have no tendency to their mutual exclusion.

Aquinas's discussion of the human and divine laws leaves no

9. *ST*, II(1), 91, 2.

question that they rest on a broad, common, natural ground. All law of every kind is "nothing else but a dictate of practical reason emanating from the ruler who governs a perfect community."[10] In fact, reason is essential to the whole concept of law, and an unreasonable law is really a contradiction in terms. Thus, "in human affairs a thing is said to be just, from being right, according to the rule of reason,"[11] and that "rule of reason" is, in fact, no other than the natural law, the "light of natural reason," the *"impressio luminis divini in nobis."*[12] Hence human law, either custom or statute, "has just so much of the nature of law, as it is derived from the law of nature." Any so-called human law which derives from some other source, which is at variance with natural law, is not law at all but "a perversion of law" (*legis corruptio*).[13] Likewise, the divine law, both old and new, must accord with natural law. Notice that Aquinas does not say divine law "flows from" natural law in the way that human law does; that would be to deny its very *raison d'etre*. It was given to man directly by God, both to effect certain ends that natural and human law were incapable of effecting, primarily that of man's eternal beatitude, and also because "of the uncertainty of human judgment."[14] Man derives human law from natural law by the exercise of reason; the divine law, dealing with things inaccessible to unaided reason, must be given directly by revelation.

However, that the divine law does not "flow from" natural law in no way conflicts with the fact that it is in accord with natural law. Indeed, it is impossible that it should not be in accord, for both laws have the law eternal for their source and model. Thus Aquinas argues that the "Old Law was good" on the grounds that it was "in accordance with reason."[15] The old law was "distinct from the natural law, not as being altogether different from it, but as something added thereto." Human law, as we have seen, is distinct from natural law, "not as being altogether different from

10. *ST*. II(1), 91, 1.
11. *ST*, II(1), 95, 2.
12. *ST*, II(1), 91, 2.
13. *ST*, II(1), 95, 2.
14. *ST*, II(1), 91, 4.
15. *ST*, II(1), 98, 1.

it," but as something derived therefrom. Moreover, what in one case is added and the other case derived, whatever their differences in subject matter, are both in accord with reason. Therefore we see that divine law and human law, though by no means identical, are nevertheless, harmonious and complementary. Both are grounded in nature and reason and, of course, nature and reason are from God. "For just as grace presupposes nature, so must the Divine law presuppose the natural law."[16] Moreover, the same conditions apply to the new law as well as the old, for the new law was given not to contradict but to complete the old. Consequently, in so far as the old law is in accord with nature and reason, so also is the new. In fact, there are some respects in which the new law is closer to natural law than the old law was, for, like the natural law, the new law, instead of being a set of external commandments, is a rule "instilled into man." The difference between the two is again the difference in mode of receiving them, not in their source. Both are from God and both accord with the law eternal, but where natural law is instilled in man as "a part of his nature" the new law is "added on to his nature by a gift of grace."[17]

It is interesting to consider Aquinas's practical applications of these general legal principles, for they show clearly the distinction between his position and Newman's. Newman, as we have seen, thinks of the Apostolic priesthood as ordained exclusively by the divine law and of the interests of that priesthood as in many instances hostile to those of secular rulers. Aquinas, on the other hand, argues for the "Sacrament of Order" in the Church by drawing analogies from nature as well as glory. In fact, the principle of order or hierarchy applies in every province of creation because God, wishing "to produce His works in likeness to Himself, as far as possible, in order that they might be perfect" impressed "this natural law on all things, that last things should be reduced and perfected by middle things, and middle things by the first." The principle applies in the human body, in the body politic, in the structure of the universe, in the order of

16. *ST*, II(1), 99, 2.
17. *ST*, II(1), 106, 1.

angels; and "that this beauty might not be lacking to the Church, He established Order in her so that some should deliver the sacraments to others, being thus made like to God in their own way, as co-operating with God."[18] Of course, the power of the Sacraments, and, consequently, the peculiarly holy authority of bishops and priests, is something "added" by divine law to natural reason; but the whole direction of Aquinas's argument here is to show that what is added is in accord with the principles of nature and reason, for both the natural and divine ordinances produce in God's works a likeness to Himself. Thus it follows, as we have suggested, that the rule of bishops and the rule of princes, the authority of the Church and that of the state, rest on common ground in the eternal law, and though the end of divine government differs in degree from the end of human government, the two contribute to and depend upon one another.

At first glance, this distinction of ends seems to undermine the principle of harmony for which we have been arguing and to militate against any kind of established religion, even a non-Erastian one. Certainly Aquinas is insistent that the end of human society is eternal beatitude and that that fact necessitates not only the divine law and the priesthood but also the subordination of the human to the divine authority. If the "possession of God" were an end which "could be attained by the power of human nature, then the duty of a king would have to include the direction of men to it." Since however, that end surpasses our natural reach, the "government of this kind pertains to that king who is not only a man, but also God, namely, our Lord Jesus Christ" and to the "royal priesthood [which] is derived from Him."[19] Therefore, says St. Thomas, the "ministry" of spiritual things is entrusted "not to earthly kings but to priests, and most of all to the chief priest, the successor of St. Peter, the Vicar of Christ, the Roman Pontiff. To him all the kings of the Christian People are to be subject as to our Lord Jesus Christ Himself."[20] In this aspect of his argument, St. Thomas seems to be main-

18. *ST*, III (Supplement), 34, 1.
19. St. Thomas Aquinas, *On Kingship*, trans. Gerald B. Phelan (Toronto: The Pontifical Institute of Mediaeval Studies, 1949), pp. 60–61.
20. *On Kingship*, p. 62.

taining a radically different position from that of Hooker and the English High-Churchmen. Of course, in so far as the identification of the Christian priesthood with the papacy is concerned, that difference is undeniable, but if we examine the application of Aquinas's principle, we see that the divergence is not so great as it at first appears to be.

In fact, the "subordination" of king to Pope has, in practice, the effect of exalting not only the divine but also the human authority and demanding their dependence on one another. That is because the "life by which men live well here on earth is ordained, as to its end, to that blessed life which we hope for in heaven."[21] Hence it follows that human government makes a necessary contribution to divine government, and we must not forget that Aquinas, like Hooker, always thought of state and Church as one body, two complementary spheres of action in one commonwealth. That body, obviously, cannot attain its ultimate end, the possession of God, without the authority of divine government to direct it. On the other hand, it cannot attain its human end, which is happiness, without the authority of human government.[22] Moreover, since the two ends are both of God's institution, and since they contribute to one another, it follows that the supremacy of divine authority in no way obviates the necessity of the human but rather makes that necessity even greater. In fact, the two ends can scarcely be separated, for "the beatitude of heaven is the end of that virtuous life which we live at present." Since the king's task is to promote the good of this present life, it follows that his human government contributes directly to the divine end. Therefore, "he should command those things which lead to the happiness of Heaven and, as far as possible, forbid the contrary."[23] Hence the doctrine of subordination of king to Pope seems to lead, in practice, to a theory of their harmonious labor in guiding the *respublica christiana* to its proper ends.

It should be clear by now that the Thomist conception of law and the consequent justification of the Christian commonwealth

21. *On Kingship*, p. 63.
22. *On Kingship*, p. 64.
23. *On Kingship*, p. 64.

provide philosophical foundations for a conservative or traditional defense of established orders both in Church and state. In fact, it is one great virtue of the natural law system that it makes possible a defense of institutions such as the bishops and the Prayer Book as valid in their own right rather than simply as developments of an idea. Since, as we have seen, natural reason is the measure of all law, the test which ought to be applied to any legal institution, human or divine, is whether it accords with right reason. Actually that is a very simple test, but an idealist bias of Newman's sort makes it virtually impossible of application. Beginning as he does with the assumption that all institutions are the developments of ideas, it is almost impossible for him to see each institution in itself. Aquinas, on the contrary, begins with individual institutions—orders, sacraments, kingship —and, by examining the reasonableness of each, demonstrates its harmony with the *lex naturalis* and, ultimately, with the *lex aeterna*. The latter view necessitates a conservative approach to existing institutions, for nothing which is justified by its accord with natural law can be jettisoned on any grounds whatever, certainly not in the name of an idea which may be no more than a fiction or fantasy. When Newman says he abandoned a defense of the English Establishment because the *idea* of the movement required that abandonment, the proper Thomist response would be that if that Establishment was in accord with the divine and natural law, if it met the test of reason, if it was, therefore, *true*, no idea could prevail against it. Of course, St. Thomas might not have found that the English establishment, in fact, met those tests, but that is another matter altogether. His conclusions might have been much the same as Newman's in the same circumstances, but the difference between their respective modes of arriving at those conclusions would obviously have been great. Between the radicalism of the idea and the conservatism of the law is a great gulf fixed, and devotion to the former makes defense of the Christian commonwealth, the traditional political and spiritual order of Christendom, all but impossible.

These considerations return us to our point of departure, Newman's *Letter to the Duke of Norfolk*. There, as we have seen, he admits the existence and the virtue of a distinctively Christian civilization of the sort which St. Thomas's thought both assumes and endorses and which the old High Churchmen of England had defended with no less zeal than they had defended the Faith itself. Such a civilization rested on "the traditions of the old Empire" which "have been retained . . . [and] maintained in substance, as the basis of European civilization down to this day, and notably among ourselves." For though England divorced itself from the Church of Rome, and though "the king took the place of the Pope," the "old idea of a Christian Polity was still in force."[24] For reasons which we have already cited—namely, according to Newman, the fragmentation of thought and opinion consequent upon intellectual development in modern society— "the theory of Toryism," the idea of the *respublica christiana* "came to pieces and went the way of all flesh."[25] Though Newman, with part of his mind, regrets that loss, nevertheless he is prepared to accept it as inevitable and, in some respects, good; and from what we now know of his departure from the Caroline tradition, of his sympathy with the "spirit afloat" in the nineteenth century, of his subjectivist and idealist epistemology, of the vast discrepancies between his philosophical principles and the traditional Thomist ones, of the essentially modern "character of mind" which informs his theology, we can easily understand why he was not altogether out of sympathy with Toryism's departure—why his regret for the past was only partial. Indeed, the very phrase, "the way of all flesh," if we are to take it literally, suggests that in Newman's view the old civilization was not, for all its worth, sacrosanct. Moreover, from what we now know of his philosophical principles it is easy to see why he holds out a certain sympathy to the new intellectual activity to which he attributes the fragmentation.

Since that sympathy is only implicit in his *Letter to the Duke of Norfolk*, it is interesting to examine another discussion of the same matter in which Newman's own civilization is not directly in question and in which he is discussing the course of social his-

24. *Diff.*, II, 262.
25. *Diff.*, II, 268.

tory in more or less general and, to him, universally applicable terms. I have reference to his *History of the Turks*, in particular the lecture on "Barbarism and Civilization." The latter is distinguished from the former by the very intellectual activity to which Newman attributes the destruction of Christian polity. The unity of a state consists in the fact that the individuals who constitute the body politic participate "in some common possession."[26] In a barbarous state that "common possession" is an object of the "imagination," in a civilized state, an object of the "sense."[27] By an object of the imagination he means an objective, palpable structure of things such as the pomp of court and cathedral which can be held as image but which is not subject to thought. By an object of the sense he means, evidently, the idea which the mind alone can grasp. In short, the barbarous society takes the forms of things as it finds them and lives by devotion to those forms. The civilized society, in which the intellect is at work, delves beneath the forms to discover the ultimately "unimaginable" idea or subjective understanding of the essence on which the forms depend and of which they are economies.[28]

These distinctions can be applied quite easily to Newman's remarks in his *Letter to the Duke of Norfolk*, for when he proceeds to illustrate what he means by the common possession of a barbarous society, it is clear that he includes those very forms which are the staples of the old Christian order of England. He mentions in particular the two institutions which, taken in conjunction, constitute for St. Thomas, the two great spheres of harmonious activity in the traditional Christian polity—the Pope's political power (the temporal authority of the Church in guiding the commonwealth to its supernatural end) and the divine right of kings (the authority of the state in guiding that same commonwealth to its temporal happiness and helping prepare it thereby for its heavenly ends). Both institutions, says Newman, flourished "when Europe was semi-barbarous." Such institutions cannot flourish when societies become civilized, for the new activity of the intellect makes assent to such objective structures

26. *HS*, I, 161.
27. *HS*, I, 162.
28. *HS*, I, 170.

impossible; "the divine right of the successors of the English St. Edward received a death-blow in the philosophy of Bacon and Locke."[29]

Thus the new, earnest, intellectual young men of the Oxford Movement rise to replace the old-fashioned Tory High-Churchmen; the idea or image of Church and state implanted in the conscience and the heart usurps the ancient hegemony of visible realities in the world of sense; essence comes to dwell in thought rather than in the form of the existing reality; and law, deprived of its metaphysical authority, ceases to bind heaven and earth, the invisible and the visible, in a single harmony. The very terms, *barbarism* and *civilization*, suggest that Newman has more than a little sympathy for the modern state of affairs, and if we apply what he says about the Turks to what he says to Norfolk and Gladstone about the condition of England in 1875, we can see how that sympathy applies. He grants that the exercise of reason and the consequent advance of civilization has its distinct disadvantages, that it may even lead eventually to the dissipation of political greatness. Barbarian societies—and we begin to see that what Newman means are closed, traditional, religious societies like that which the "old idea of a Christian Polity" represented—"have the *prestige* of antiquity and the strength of conservatism." They "remain in the circle of ideas which sufficed their forefathers; the opinions, principles, and habits which they inherited, they transmit." Hence, they preserve stability and order whereas, when "thought is encouraged, too many will think, and will think too much." Thus "an endless variety of opinion is the certain though slow result,"[30] and under the pressure of such variety "the common bond of unity in the state" eventually collapses.[31] Such a collapse is an evil; but, apparently, the possibility of it is worth the risk of breaking with the past, for it attends upon the advance of civilization which is itself, in Newman's view, a good. "Civilization is that state to which man's nature points and tends."[32]

Thus it appears that the new intellectual life "during the last

29. *HS*, I, 170.
30. *HS*, I, 173.
31. *HS*, I, 174.
32. *HS*, I, 164–165.

seventy years," which has undermined the "tradition of fifteen hundred years," is in itself an unmistakable good and also the state "to which man's nature points and tends." It is as inevitably attendant upon the development of the human race as the consequence of sunlight on the earth's surface, and the loss attendant upon it, however painful in itself, must be accepted with a good grace. That loss "was in the nature of things." Newman insists indeed that nothing, "not a hundred Popes could have hindered it," and one suspects a considerable embarrassment on Newman's part with the *Syllabus* of 1864, which had obviously been designed to hinder it and which Newman is professedly defending. "The Pope has denounced the sentiment that he ought to come to terms with 'progress, liberalism, and the new civilization.' I have no thought at all of disputing his words. I leave the great problem to the future."[33] That may be damnation with faint praise; in any event, Newman seems to be expressing a view more nearly his own in hoping that the future will find some mode of dealing with what is both inevitable and good in the new order.[34]

These indications of why Newman is prepared to "make terms" with "the new civilization" are further illuminated by some of his remarks in correspondence with T. W. Allies. In these letters Newman again makes the distinction between barbarism and civilization, remarking that "certain ages, i.e., the ages of barbarism, are more susceptible of religious impressions than other ages; and call for, need, the visible rule of Religion." That is the case because "a ruder people asks for a strong form of religion, armed with temporal sanctions, and it is good for it; whereas other ages reject it, and it would be bad for them."[35] The present, clearly, is one of those "other ages," and Newman says that "a medieval system now would but foster the worst hypocrisy—not because

33. *Diff.*, II, 268.

34. The following statement to Ambrose Phillipps de Lisle is typical of several comments in the correspondence of 1865: "As to the Encyclical, without looking at it doctrinally, it is but stating a *fact* to say that it is a heavy blow and a great discouragement to us in England. There must be a re-action sooner or later—and we must pray God to bring it about in His good time—and meanwhile to give us patience." (letter dated February 13, 1865, in *Letters and Diaries*, XXI, 415).

35. *Letters and Diaries*, XIX, 422.

this age is worse than that, but because imagination acts more powerfully upon barbarians, and reason on traders, *savants*, and newspaper readers."[36] Consequently, he says quite frankly: "I do not see my way to hold that 'Catholic Civilization,' as you describe it, is *in fact* (I do not say in the abstract), but in fact, has been, or shall be, or can be, a good, or *per se* desirable."[37]

These remarks leave little doubt that, with regard to the Christian order of the English establishment, Newman was, in fact, antitraditional; that his "farewell to Toryism" was not altogether mournful, but that he interpreted the loss of the old order as a necessary attendant upon what he conceived to be the advance of the intellectual life of the civilization. They also suggest that his enmity to the establishment is not simply identical with his anti-Erastianism, for he grants that the old civilization was common both to Pope and king. What Newman has said, however, about the anti-Erastian idea of the Oxford Movement may prove to be applicable in a general way to the whole question, for it should be clear that, whether the old order is attacked by the Oxford Movement or by the movement of civilization generally, no matter how diverse these two may be, their common term is movement, and movement, as we have seen, presupposes a moving idea. The primary difference between the tractarians and old High-Churchmen was that the former *moved* under the impulse of the idea while the latter *stood* in the defense of the established order. The former *thought*; indeed their point of origin was the noetic and consequently reforming atmosphere of the Oriel common room. The latter simply acted on the basis of an inherited system. The former were "civilized," the latter "barbarians." For a while, accidentally, the two parties found themselves defending the same ancient institutions, but as the Tractarian mind moved forward, the *idea* (anti-Erastianism, according to Newman,) gradually set itself free from allegiance to the Establishment and pursued the course of its own proper development. Similarly, "during the last seventy years," other

36. *Letters and Diaries*, XIX, 423.
37. *Letters and Diaries*, XIX, 421.

ideas have given their impulse to other movements—ideas and movements which in themselves are vastly different from Tractarianism but which like Tractarianism have come into inevitable conflict with the "medieval system." Thus the Round Table has dissolved, and God proceeds to fulfill himself in *many* ways.

One question, however, remains; and it is a question which a believer in Thomist philosophy and in the virtue of the old civilization is obliged to ask: why should the operation of intellect lead *necessarily* to the fragmentation of thought? I suggested earlier that the proper Thomist defense against the radicalism of idealist thought is to test the worth of established institutions, not in reference to some general idea of Church and state but to their own intrinsic reasonableness. Now, if there is such a thing as natural law, and if all true institutions, both human and divine, derive their truth from their agreement with that law, there seems to be no reason why the exercise of reason should in any way threaten those institutions. In fact, the contrary should be the case; for if the Thomist (and Caroline) view is correct, those institutions, so far as they are human, were established, as law, by the operation of reason and, so far as they are of direct divine institution, can be seen to be in accord with reason. In fact in such a view to say that a thing is traditional and ought to be defended as such is virtually equivalent to saying that it is rational and ought to be defended as such; for no institution which is irrational, which is out of accord with natural reason, can last long enough to become traditional, to be established. In other words, the natural-law philosophy allows no grounds whatever for a distinction of Newman's sort between the barbarian and the civilized or between objects of imagination and objects of sense and intellect. The validity of divine right or of the temporal power of the papacy rests on the reasonableness of those institutions, and since what is reasonable is, ipso facto, true, those institutions have to be defended in the name of truth itself.

It thus becomes clear that, when Newman is prepared to jettison those institutions in the name of "civilization" or intellectual advancement, he clearly means something different by intellect and reason from what Aquinas means. That difference is not far to seek; in fact, it is implicit in all we have been saying about Newman's idealism, subjectivism, and individualism and about his view of the relationship between faith and form. However carefully and successfully these modern "isms" may be restricted in the name of orthodoxy, the restrictions never completely obliterate their original philosophic force. No matter how definite Newman may be in his doctrine of conscience, the fact remains that the function of the conscience is subjective and that, though every man's conscience apprehends the same divine truth, the modes of apprehension may differ widely enough to lead different men in the direction of mutually exclusive ideas. No matter how explicit Newman may be that ideas are fixed and definite and clearly distinct from nebulous principles, still ideas lack the firmness and stability—the objectivity—of rational abstractions and of law. Thus, though Newman's safeguards may protect orthodox doctrine in a strict sense, they leave the way open for the divergence of opinion and belief in secondary matters which seems necessarily to attend a subjective epistemology and an idealist philosophy.

The exact nature of Newman's position, his subtle but vast distance from Thomist conservatism, emerges, ironically, at a moment in the *Letter to Norfolk* when he attempts to equate his own position with that of St. Thomas. He is defending his own doctrine of conscience against the liberal perversion of that doctrine; the latter, as we have seen, amounts to little more than a purely emotional and private judgment in religious matters. Conscience, rightly considered, is the "internal witness of both the existence and the law of God."[38] As modern liberals use the term, it means little more than an instinct for doing what one likes. It follows that, while in the modern view conscience will be coming in conflict repeatedly with all forms of established authority, in the orthodox view those instances of conflict will be few, the exception rather than the rule. Then Newman proceeds to suggest that, in fact, established orders are established on the dictates of conscience, rightly considered, and that therefore the internal and the external power are intimately related and can-

38. *Diff.*, II, 248.

not, theoretically, conflict with one another. Had we followed Newman only thus far, we would see already that he is attributing to conscience, in relationship to positive law of one kind or another, the authority and the function which St. Thomas assigns to natural law or natural reason. It is therefore no surprise to discover that Newman has, in fact, stated that equation in so many words. " 'The natural law,' says St. Thomas, 'is an impression of the Divine Light in us, a participation of the eternal law in the rational creature.' . . . This law, as apprehended in the minds of individual men, is called 'conscience.' "[39]

Here, however, we come to an exceedingly important point of distinction; for if Newman had read Aquinas closely, he would have seen that St. Thomas assigns the apprehension of the eternal law not to the conscience but to the reason, and the differences between the two faculties is vast. At the heart of that difference lies the fact that reason proceeds according to the laws of the syllogism which all men hold in common and thus possesses a kind of universal validity, whereas conscience is by its very nature subjective and individual. Thus, though Newman insists on a strict construction of the doctrine of conscience, the fact that he gives to conscience rather than to reason the power to establish institutions and sit in judgment on their disestablishment amounts to sacrificing the objective and independent authority of those institutions. It amounts, in fact, as we would expect, to submitting all establishments to the ultimate power of the idea or subjective image which the conscience apprehends and which moves of its own power to develop itself according to its own nature. Conscience and natural law are not the same; the infused or imprinted idea and the acquired species are not the same; neither, therefore, do those forms which the idea generates and sustains and which live by the endorsement of the conscience have the same validity and durability in themselves as those establishments which are the constructs of reason and of law.

One must not leave the false impression that Newman was a revolutionary. I have used the term *radicalism* to describe his

39. *Diff.*, II, 247.

mode of thought, but it is perfectly clear that that radicalism is never translated into religious or political activism.[40] In fact, his distaste for the revolutionary spirit of his times is manifest at numerous points in his published work, as well as in his correspondence. On the other hand, I think it is fair to say that his disapproval of political and social revolution is in the same category as the various safeguards with which he defends his doctrinal orthodoxy—a refusal to take his characteristic modes of thought to their logical conclusion. His essay on Lamennais offers an interesting explanation of his attitudes on this matter, for in it we see him making a last-minute retreat from Lamennais's rebellion.

It is obvious that the two had a great deal in common. Lamennais's fight against Gallicanism corresponds in many respects to the Tractarians' war with Erastianism. Both take up arms against a "law Church," and both, in the process, find themselves in antitraditionalist roles. Newman feels obliged to abandon the defense of the English establishment, and that abandonment produces, as we have seen, an attack upon aristocratic, Tory, High-Church interests. Lamennais, when the Three Days' Revolution came, "believing that the Church Catholic was equal to any emergence or variety of human society . . . desired her to throw herself upon the onward course of democracy, and to lead a revolutionary movement, which in her first ages she had created."[41] The two positions are clearly similar, and yet Newman obviously does not care for Lamennais's course of ac-

40. Newman's politics have not been given such careful treatment as they deserve. The principal work on the subject is Terence Kenny's *The Political Thought of John Henry Newman* (London: Longmans, Green & Co., 1957). See also Alvan S. Ryan, "The Development of Newman's Politics," *The Review of Politics*, VII (1945), 210–240. Ryan's conclusions seem to support my contention that Newman's position is ultimately an antitraditional one: "In terms of his political thought, Newman's attitude involves no diminution of loyalty to the Church, though such was the charge of those who called him a minimizer. Instead, it signifies Newman's recognition that any practical solution of the problem of Church and State in England, at least, involves an acceptance as he says of 'liberal principles,' or a principle of pluralism." (p. 237) Ryan also suggests the interesting possibility of similarities between Newman's conception of society and Maritain's "New Christendom" (p. 239).

41. *Essays*, I, 156.

tion. The question is why he does not; and in the answer lies his escape from the revolutionary consequences of his philosophy.

According to Newman, "the elementary error" in Lamennais's position is that "he does not seem to recognize, nay, to contemplate the idea, that rebellion is a sin."[42] Notice that the fault is a moral, not an intellectual, one, and I think it is safe to say that Newman's safeguard against the dangers of radicalism is a moral rather than an intellectual safeguard. The real deficiency in Lamennais's position is not, apparently, in what he was attempting to do—at least Newman never challenges that, and we know enough of the latter's thought by now to see that he would have been sympathetic with much of Lamennais's anti-Gallicanism—but with the way in which he was attempting to do it. His choices were not, ultimately, moral or conscientious. On the contrary, "he is thoroughly political in his views and feelings" and not altogether "scrupulous."[43] Moreover, he was impatient, and we know that a great deal of heresy is nothing more than truth advanced by a rebellious faction before the time for its development is ripe.[44] "He has a keen perception of the truth that Almighty power has promised empire to the Church; but, like Jeroboam, he cannot bear to wait God's time."[45]

Newman's own mode of action with regard to the *Syllabus of Errors* illustrates the opposite course of action with reference to the truth, the application of the safeguards of scrupulosity, patience, and charity. Newman too has a "keen perception of the truth," or rather of what on account of his subjectivism he takes to be the truth—that the Christian *respublica*, the "old idea of a Christian Polity," the "tradition of fifteen hundred years" is dead. Yet he bows to the *Syllabus* in respect for papal authority, with a kind of instinctive piety, trusting in God's direction of all human affairs and hoping for a better resolution of difficulties in

42. *Essays*, I, 157.
43. *Essays*, I, 161.
44. Newman makes this point in several different contexts. For one statement of it, see *Ap.*, p. 232.
45. *Essays*, I, 160.

the future. The word *piety* in its true sense may express the crucial concept here. It implies respect for authority primarily on moral as opposed to intellectual grounds, and it constitutes one basis for a conservative habit of mind. "Pius Aeneas" respected his father and the household gods of Troy and attempted to defend the Trojan "idea" on the strength of that piety. And, indeed, piety has great strength; in fact it is one of the gifts of the Holy Ghost, and it shapes the mind and heart of man. Indeed it is a correlative of holy charity, and its very presence in the soul precludes forever the possibility of revolution. Piety instills the virtue of obedience in every instinct of our lives and makes us subject to the "powers that be." In one sense, therefore, it is the strongest of all safeguards against heterodox religion or revolutionary politics.

On the other hand, it still seems just to say that in Newman's case this safeguard was not rational or philosophical. No one thing is any other thing, and piety is not sound reason. Therefore it cannot perform sound reason's tasks; and though piety may teach us to be subject to the "powers that be," only reason can persuade us that "the powers that be are ordained of God." When reason, or, in Newman's case, conscience, seems to say that a great many of the "powers that be"—divine right, the temporal power of the Pope—are not ordained of God but are the relics of a barbarous past, no amount of piety can defend these customs and institutions indefinitely. It is one thing to counsel patience and to trust in the slow movement of civilization's progress under God. It is quite another thing to defend what is established, to defend it absolutely and without compromise, on the grounds that in itself it is reasonable and therefore of God. The former mode of thought constitutes no final defense, for though piety, as a gift of the Spirit and a habit of mind, may save our souls from the damning corruptions of rebellious thought, it cannot ultimately preserve institutions because it does not, cannot, speak to the question of their truth or falsehood. Thus, for all its strength, in one sense it provides no ultimate safeguard of a traditional civilization.

It is for this reason, I believe, that in our own time, in the revolutionary developments in the Church of Rome subsequent to the Second Vatican Council, Newman has become the darling of a new generation of Modernists, of men who wish now to effect what the *Syllabus* of 1864 delayed. Some of these modern theologians may lack Newman's piety, but I think they are correct, as Loisy and his followers were, in recognizing that Newman, in spite of his own stiff doctrinal orthodoxy, is their intellectual ancestor. Their espousal of his theories of development bring home to us the rather striking consequence of what Newman admitted so quietly in his *Letter to the Duke of Norfolk*, the "hereditary Earl Marshal of England," in 1875. Without fanfare, and in what might be regarded as a minor publication, the most important Catholic theologian of the nineteenth or twentieth centuries, either by Anglican or Roman standards, declined to defend the great inheritance of Christian civilization. Toryism "came to pieces and went the way of all flesh." All the king's horses and all the king's men could never put it together again. In effect, Newman relinquished all defense of the world that St. Thomas and Dante had built, that Chaucer, Spenser, Hooker, Shakespeare, Donne, Herbert, Andrewes, Laud, and even Milton had inhabited; a world which was still a reality and still defensible in the era of the Restoration and in the eighteenth century and to whose defense Dryden, Swift, Pope, and Doctor Johnson committed their lives and talents. Newman gave away the great tradition of English poetry, theology, politics, and law. In effect, he said that the world which the Church had built the Church no longer could or should defend. If we consider it carefully, those few paragraphs in 1875, representing as they do the mature fruit of Newman's social and political thought, take on enormous importance; for if the orthodox giant of the modern Church was not able or willing to defend that great tradition, who else may hope to? Perhaps it could only have been defended by Thomism, and the revival of Thomism in the Church was not to begin for another four years.[46] That revival has borne fruit in this century, and many of us have knowledge as a consequence

46. It is ironic that the same Pope who made Newman a cardinal issued, in the same year, 1879, the encyclical (*Aeterni Patris*) which led to the revival of Thomist studies in the twentieth century.

which was inaccessible to Newman. But, in the meantime, the damage has been done and, in part, by the one man who might have been able, had his philosophy been sounder than it was, to prevent it. After all, the radicalism that stems from idealism, though it may be safeguarded by piety, is radicalism, all the same.

CHAPTER XII

The Desert and the City

THE literary consequences of Newman's philosophy are closely akin to the social and political ones. Just as we may regard him as the one man above all others in the last two centuries who might have offered Europe sound theological and philosophical grounds for the defense of Christendom, so we may likewise regard him as the one person in the same period who was in a position to deliver modern poetry from the bondage of subjectivism which secular Romantic thought imposed upon it. As he failed in the one area, so he failed in the other, for he had "made terms," philosophically, with the very evils he might have combatted.

To understand Newman's relationship to modern literature, we must recollect that the problems attendant upon his philosophy have to do primarily with attitudes toward nature, toward the *visibilia*. Moreover, since literary symbols are drawn from the external world, differing attitudes toward nature necessarily affect the metaphysical status of those symbols. For our purposes, we may distinguish between two contradictory ways of understanding symbols, and these, as we might expect, spring from the two modes of vision with which we have been dealing from the outset: the objective or realist mode of the Thomist and the Caroline schools and, in general, of western Christendom; and the subjective or idealist mode of Patristic and of "modern" thought, to which Newman belongs. With specific reference to the question of symbolism, we might say that the mind is objective or realist to the extent that it assumes the meaning of a symbol to reside in the external object or institution itself; that it is subjective or idealist in so far as it believes that the mind (or the conscience, or the "implicit reason" of the "whole man") must bestow meaning on the external object. Or, to put it another way, the orientation of the poetic mind is objective and realist to the extent that it finds the tenor within the vehicle, subjective or idealist to the extent that it feels compelled to impose the tenor upon the vehicle. Therefore we might say that the subjective mind rests the power of symbol-making in itself, while the objective mind remains largely passive and assumes that symbols come to it, ready made, as realities in the visible world, replete with their meaning and independent of the mind that perceives them.

It should be clear from these distinctions that the doctrine of the economy belongs to the subjective or idealist category so far as literature is concerned. The rich lands of Pro-Consular Africa have no meaning for Jucundus beyond the fact that their produce furnishes his table. To Agellius, however, after Saint Cyprian has instructed him, they are seen to be an economic or symbolic representation of Paradise. In the latter case, it is the mind of the perceiver which either bestows or discovers the meaning within the symbol; the physical, external object does not convey its significance in itself, in its own sensible qualities. In fact, all Newman's comments on nature as a sacramental system—those discussions which we have already alluded to in which nature is understood to be a parable awaiting proper interpretation—all of these suggest the same basic approach to literary symbol and to the role of nature as a source of symbol. Meaning dwells not in what is beheld but in the eye of the beholder; or, as Carlyle says, the poet is the new priest, for he bestows new meaning on the outworn forms of earth and of human society. For the same reason, Shelley makes poets the unacknowledged legislators of the world, and Coleridge links the secondary or poetic imagination, by analogy, through the primary imagination, with the "eternal act of creation in the infinite *I Am.*" In each case, the role of the poet as creator is stressed heavily, and necessarily so; for the subjective approach to the meaning of symbols places the responsibility for that meaning squarely upon the mind of the poet. He cannot be simply a receiver of meaning already given.

Of course, it might be possible to argue that there is a middle ground between these two positions, but, granting that possibility, I think we shall see that what appears at first glance to be a third alternative belongs finally to either the subjective or objective category. Suppose, for instance, that the symbol does, indeed, possess meanings in itself but that those are not visible to the intellect except under certain circumstances. To draw an analogy from purely physical sight, we might take the instance of a physician and a layman examining the x-ray picture of a human lung. The picture reveals certain things, diseased tissue perhaps, which are clearly recognizable to the doctor but which the layman does not "see." Of course he does actually see them in one sense, but he lacks the training necessary to grasp what is before his eyes. In that case, we might say that the meaning of the picture is objective, contained obviously within the picture itself, but that so far as the apprehension of that meaning is concerned, at least from the layman's point of view, the mode of vision is subjective; that is, the meaning exists for the beholder in direct relationship to the beholder's power of apprehension.

A similar situation exists with regard to all special or arcane knowledge. Both the man who knows the Anglo-Saxon language and the man who does not see the same symbols, the same words in a given sequence; but the meaning of those symbols is evident only to the trained intellect. Similarly, with all mysteries and symbolic rites, both sacred and secular; the initiates and non-initiates see the same symbols, but whereas one comprehends their significance, the other remains blind to it. Thus Clement and Origen argue that the meaning of symbols in Holy Scripture is only available to the gnostic who has been initiated into those economic mysteries. That is not to say that the sacred symbols have no objective meaning in themselves, but it still places the realization of that meaning in the mind of the reader. The same distinction can also apply to the images which secular poets use. To the poetic mind in its purest state of objectivity, the meaning of a symbol is manifest to all that behold it. To the poetic mind in a pure state of subjectivity, the symbol possesses in itself no meaning at all and depends for its power as a symbol on the imaginative powers of the poet and the reader. But for the poetic mind in a middle state of the sort we have been describing, the symbol may possess meaning in itself which will be invisible except to the initiate, to the intellect which, either because of prior knowledge, or because it understands the "mystery," or simply because it is in a heightened state of awareness, possesses capacities of vision which the lay mind lacks.

Therefore we might say that in the middle state the mind of the poet is in essentially the same condition which we have hitherto described, following Herbert, as one of paraphrase. In that condition, the poet is neither simply the perceiver or the reflector of given meanings nor the creator or imposer of meanings previously nonexistent but the inventor (in the old sense) or discoverer of meanings which are present in the symbol but hidden. As I suggested earlier, however, this middle state may not finally prove to be clearly distinct from the purely subjective or idealist one, at least not so far as epistemology is concerned. Or, to put the matter another way, we might say that *metaphysically* the middle ground we have been describing belongs to the objective or realist concept of nature: the meaning is actually in the symbolic object, whether it can be seen there by the untutored intellect or not; but that *epistemologically* the middle ground belongs to the subjective or idealist mode of vision, for though the meaning is present actually, its existence depends for all practical purposes not on the object in itself but on the imaginative and interpretative powers of the beholder. So long as that dependence exists, the autonomy of the mind is preserved and the virtual independence of the poetic imagination from reality external to itself. Epistemologically, the difference is only in degree, not in kind. On the contrary, the objective or realist mode of poetic vision is bound to, dependent upon, the external reality which it beholds; just as in the Thomist theory of intellection the intelligible species, the images of reality which actualize the intellect, are dependent upon sense images and, through those, upon the external, objective reality which causes those images. The objective mind can neither make a hell of heaven nor a heaven of hell, nor can it be the inventor or discoverer of the paradise within. Rather, it must take and enjoy or suffer what is given it. It is Aristotle's mimetic imagination, and we should not forget that the *mimesis* of reality is quite distinct from either the *creation* or *invention* of reality, whatever differences may exist be-

tween the latter two. Though we may grant a common metaphysical basis for both the *mimetic* and *inventive* modes of vision, still, in so far as we are concerned with the mind qua mind,
the great epistemological boundary falls between those who seek
reality within, in the mind's operations, and those who seek it
externally to themselves.

Since Newman shares the "modern" predisposition to a
subjective mode of vision, it is not surprising that his comments
on symbolic literature should reflect that bias. The foregoing
reference to Aristotle's theory of mimesis immediately calls to
mind Newman's early essay "Poetry, with Reference to Aristotle's
Poetics." Blanco White accused Newman of Platonizing, and the
charge is just: for Newman, in effect, converts Aristotle's objective and realist conception of the poet's function into an inventive (or creative) and idealist conception. For instance, he is not
willing to allow Aristotle's emphasis on plot or fable to pass at its
face value. "It is one thing," he argues, "to form the *beau ideal*
of a tragedy on scientific principles; another to point out the actual beauty of a particular school of dramatic composition."[1] The
former is what Aristotle has done when he insists upon plot, but
the "actual beauty" of Greek tragedy, its "charm," does "not or-
dinarily arise from scientific correctness of plot." That "beauty"
arises, rather, from "characters, sentiments, and diction," and
plot or action "will be more justly viewed as the vehicle for in-
troducing the personages of the drama, than as the principal object of the poet's art."[2]

It should be obvious at first glance that such a statement exactly reverses Aristotle's meaning, and in the very subjective direction that we have mentioned.[3] Interestingly, Newman refers
to "the economy of the fable,"[4] and we see at once that he is
bringing the economic principle to bear upon literary theory.
From Aristotle's point of view, it makes sense to insist upon plot,

1. *Essays*, I, 1.
2. *Essays*, I, 2.
3. Cf. Norman Friedman, "Newman, Aristotle, and the New Criticism: On
the Modern Element in Newman's Poetics," *PMLA*, LXXXI (1966),
261–271.
4. *Essays*, I, 1.

for actions contain their meaning in themselves. The history of the Theban line is a symbol in the objective sense; all that is required of the poet is the mimesis of a story, for the story is a symbol in which the significance is self-contained and obvious. In fact, from Aristotle's point of view, it would be foolish for a poet to imitate an action in which there was either no significance at all or in which the meaning was hidden; rather, it must be an action "of a certain magnitude," an action which is, in itself, a ready-made symbol or set of symbols. In no sense is such an action an economy as Newman uses the term. It does not exist in possible isolation from its meaning, nor does it require or even allow us to treat the sensible as no more than an economical vehicle for the intelligible. Whatever we apprehend of universal significance in the fall of Oedipus is finally inseparable from the story of that fall. Aristotle is not concerned with spiritual qualities in the realm of idea, nor does he conceive of plot as in any sense the shadowy or partial embodying of those qualities by way of condescension to the feebleness of human perception. The latter is what Newman was evidently looking for in Aristotle and what he forces the Philosopher to say. Newman's emphasis is upon "the very spirit of beauty [which] breathes through every part of the composition."[5] The plot is an economical or sacramental representation of that spirit and hence must be interpreted subjectively rather than objectively. Plot is not what Aristotle says it is but rather "the outward framework most suitable to the reception of the spirit of poetry."[6]

Newman's interpretation of the *Poetics* is not simply a product of his youth; we find him maintaining basically the same subjective view of literary symbol in his university lectures in the eighteen-fifties. We should not be surprised at the fact, for we have already seen that such views are in accord with the entire direction of his thought. In his opening lecture to the new School of Philosophy and Letters, he argues that the great works of literature, "the classics," are, in their secular function, analogous to "the lives of saints, and the articles of faith, and the cate-

5. *Essays*, I, 4.
6. *Essays*, I, 7.

chism" in the Church.[7] Both are "instruments" of education in their respective fields, for both are economies. The classics represent economically the spirit of civilization; hagiography, the creeds, the catechism, represent, economically, the spirit of the Church. The implication is that Homer, Sophocles, Virgil, or Shakespeare set out to impose upon some story of their arbitrary choosing the spirit or idea of civilization that they held, subjectively, in their minds. There is no suggestion that their stories have their own inherent interest and significance and are worth telling or dramatizing for their own sakes. It is interesting to note Newman's employment of the word *classics* here and to recall Arnold's similar use of it in his theory of touchstones. For both, poetry must serve ends beyond itself, and Arnold agrees with Newman that poetry is finally an economy for the spirit of civilization. The principal difference between the two is that Arnold equates civilization with religion while Newman keeps them distinct; however, that difference is theological or doctrinal rather than philosophical or esthetic. Both agree that the ultimate meaning and, consequently, the "real" worth of poetic symbol is as a vehicle for spirits or ideas which dwell not in things or stories but in the mind.

In his lecture on "Literature," the second in the series delivered to the School of Philosophy and Letters, Newman makes his point even more explicitly. In fact, he states in so many words the view that we have here been attributing to him. "In other words, Literature expresses, not objective truth, as it is called, but subjective; not things, but thoughts."[8] It is essentially "personal" in that thoughts or ideas belong to the person, and the symbols exist to convey those thoughts. Here we see how the subjective view of symbolic meaning in poetry joins itself to the principles of wholeness and individuality which we have considered above. The disposition of the whole and unique man, his "thoughts" in the broadest sense, are the subject matter which plot and symbol exist to convey: "It is the fire within the author's breast which overflows in the torrent of his burning, irresistible eloquence; it is

7. *Idea*, p. 256.
8. *Idea*, p. 274.

the poetry of his inner soul, which relieves itself in the Ode or the Elegy; and his mental attitude and bearing, the beauty of his moral countenance, the force and keeness of his logic, are imaged in the tenderness, or energy, or richness of his language."[9] On the other hand, scientific study is "objective" because it deals with "things" not "thoughts" and takes the external world not as a vehicle for or economy of invisible ideas or spirits which lie beyond it but as an end in itself. In matters of science, the object remains the object, the story remains the story, so to speak, "even were there no individual man in the whole world to know [it] or talk about [it]." "Such, for instance, would be Euclid's Elements; they relate to truths universal and eternal; they are not mere thoughts, but things: they exist in themselves, not by virtue of our understanding them, not in dependence upon our will, but in what is called the *nature* of things, or at least on conditions external to us."[10]

These distinctions remind us of Newman's comments on the differences between poetry and science in his essays on the Benedictine Schools, and, interestingly, those were being written at approximately the same time as the university lectures. He calls Benedictine monasticism "the most poetical of religious disciplines,"[11] and implicit in the comment is the assumption that some religious disciplines are not "poetical." That implication is reinforced in the university lecture on literature where he says that theology is objective or subjective, scientific or poetic, in accordance with the way in which it is treated. Mathematics is invariably objective and scientific; by its nature it cannot be otherwise. But other disciplines vary depending on how they are treated: "What is true of mathematics is true also of every study, so far forth as it is scientific; it makes use of words as the mere vehicle of things, and is thereby withdrawn from the province of literature."[12] We recall that Aristotle's emphasis upon plot, upon the objective, external aspects of tragedy, is just such a withdrawal so far as Newman is concerned. The *Poetics* attempt "to

9. *Idea*, p. 279.
10. *Idea*, p. 274.
11. *HS*, II, 385.
12. *Idea*, p. 274.

form the *beau ideal* of a tragedy on scientific principles"; Newman prefers a subjective or "poetic" treatment in which the plot or symbol is regarded, not as a *thing* possessing its own objective or external value, but as a sacramental representation of "the fire within the author's breast." Just so, the beau ideal of theology may be set down in terms of either scientific or poetic principles; "Thus metaphysics, ethics, law, political economy, chemistry, theology, cease to be literature in the same degree as they are capable of a severe scientific treatment." On the contrary, and this is clearly preferable to Newman, theology, like "Law or Natural history," can be "treated by an author with so much of colouring derived from his own mind as to become a sort of literature; this is especially seen in the instance of Theology, when it takes the shape of Pulpit Eloquence."[13]

Aristotle's work is again introduced as an example of the scientific or objective treatment of symbols. Aristotle, says Newman, invariably moves in a scientific rather than a poetic direction, "for even though the things which he treats of and exhibits may not always be real and true, yet he treats them as if they were, not as if they were the thoughts of his own mind; that is, he treats them scientifically."[14] In light of such comments, we understand what Newman means when he says that the badge of Benedictine theology was poetry, that of medieval, Scholastic (Aristotelian) theology, science. In a poetical theology, man approaches the doctrines and rites of religion not as "things" but as economies; he understands them "to be vast, immeasurable, impenetrable, inscrutable, mysterious; so that at best we are only forming conjectures about them, not conclusions, for the phenomena which they present admit of many explanations, and we cannot know the true one."[15] The latter, of course, is always the case with economies or sacraments, for they open upon an invisible world which reason can never fully map or explore. The Church uses them as the poet uses plot and character, not for their inherent worth but as vehicles for invisible realities in the realm of the

13. *Idea*, pp. 274–275.
14. *Idea*, p. 275.
15. *HS*, II, 387.

idea. In such a view, meaning can never simply be fixed in a symbol.

On the other hand, the objective or scientific approach to theology "investigates, analyzes, numbers, weighs, measures, ascertains, locates, the objects of its contemplation." That sort of approach is possible because, as we have said, it assumes the objective significance of the symbolic object: "the play's the thing," not some vast invisible drama beyond the apprehension of our senses and our reason. The latter may, does, exist, but our knowledge of it cannot transcend its local name and habitation, cannot divorce itself from the sense images of the real world. Thus the "aim of science [or a scientific approach to theology] is to get a hold of things, to grasp them, to handle them, to comprehend them"[16] and that is altogether fitting if one believes that the truth lies in those *things*. Poetry on the other hand, according to Newman's distinction, always transcends the thing, passes to that moment when the light of sense goes out; for the purpose of literary symbols is to convey what lies in the mind and heart of the poet just as the purpose of religious symbols and of the whole natural order is to convey economically what lies in the mind of God.

Thus Newman considers both Patristic and Benedictine theology to be "poetic." We have seen enough already of his study of the Alexandrian Fathers to understand why he should give *them* that label, and he finds many of the same principles at work in Benedictine monasticism. For instance, while the scientific or objective approach to theology always results in systems such as the *Summa*, Benedictine theology, as befits the poetic mode, is "not an Order proceeding from one mind at a particular date, and appearing all at once in its full perfection . . . ; but it is an organization, diverse, complex, and irregular, and variously ramified, rich rather than symmetrical . . . like some great natural growth." In short it is a "development," a history, a sort of biography, "according to the idea," in which the various doctrines and institutions exist as economies in the gradual working

16. *HS*, II, 386.

out of an ultimate aim, rather than as objective realities, complete in themselves, to be analyzed and incorporated into a fixed system. Newman speaks of Benedictine theology's growing "spontaneously," of its shaping itself "according to events, from an irrepressible fulness of life within," of its moving with "a silent mysterious operation."[17] In all those respects it is a "poetical" theology according to Newman's categories, for its shifting forms are the symbols of the life within and that life is the thing of ultimate importance. The new, scientific theology which St. Anselm fathered and of which St. Thomas is the flower was of a totally different mind and character, and we are not surprised to discover that Newman, the master of pulpit eloquence, the autobiographer and historian, prefers the old school to the new.

In that regard it is interesting that he traces a connection between Oxford, especially the "Oxonian theology" of Keble, and the Benedictine centuries. Keble and his contemporaries "thought little of science or philosophy," and, Newman adds, it is scarcely "too much to say that the Colleges in the English Universities may be considered in matter of fact to be the lineal descendants or heirs of the Benedictine schools of Charlemagne."[18] Though Newman necessarily submitted himself as a Roman Catholic to the "scientific" terminology of the *Summa*, there is no indication that he ever abandoned what he learned from Keble in the eighteen-twenties and thirties about poetry and the theological use of poetic symbol. The principles of Keble's Tract Number Eighty-nine, "On the Mysticism Attributed to the Early Fathers of the Church," remain the basis of Newman's poetics. There Keble explains and defends at great length the principle of economical, sacramental, or mystical interpretation of Scripture as it was practiced by the Fathers, and he defends them against the rationalistic, scientific and therefore, from Newman's and Keble's point of view, "unpoetic" approach to theology: "We must not be startled, though we find ourselves compelled to own, that modern and ancient theology are to a

17. HS, II, 388.
18. HS, II, 466.

great extent irreconcileable." When Keble refers to modern theology, he appears to be thinking of work like that of Paley, and,
though he does not mention the Schoolmen, one suspects he
would identify them with the moderns as opposed to the ancients.
So vast, in fact, is the gulf between the two that if modern
"notions are right, the Fathers are indeed 'mystical' in a bad
sense."[19]

Keble, of course, does not think so. For him, as for Newman,
the subjective, poetic approach to philosophy opens for us the
vision of an invisible, ideal world which an objective, realist
epistemology hides from our sight. If "God's visible ordinary
works" are viewed simply as *things*, merely as realities in themselves, we shall never get past them to that which is truly real.
Therefore we must learn to view each visible thing as "a standing
type or symbol"—Newman would have said "economy"—of
things invisible. Thus in Holy Baptism water is the symbol or
"pledge" of God's "great *invisible* work."[20] As we learn to read
the visible world symbolically, we come to see that the forms and
forces of the visible creation "make up between them 'a new
heaven and a new earth,' and . . . complete the proof, that 'the
first heaven and the first earth' are to be regarded both generally
and in their parts, as types and shadows of those which are out
of sight."[21] Like Newman, Keble identifies such a view as "poetical." The Bible and the Fathers agree, against the moderns, in the
"studied preference of *poetical* forms of thought and language, as
the channel of supernatural knowledge to mankind." In fact
poetry is a gift of great importance to religion, for it is the poetic
mode of vision which makes it possible for man to reach a
knowledge of God while he is still in the physical creation.
Poetry, says Keble, has the power "to make the world of sense,
from beginning to end, symbolical of the absent and unseen."[22]

19. No. 89, p. 9 (Vol. VI). All references to the *Tracts for the Times* are
to the "New Edition" (London: J. G. & F. Rivington, 1838–1841). Since
pages in this edition are numbered by tract rather than by volume, all citations are to the individual tracts.
20. No. 89, p. 29 (Vol. VI); italics mine.
21. No. 89, p. 170 (Vol. VI).
22. No. 89, p. 185 (Vol. VI).

In that capacity it becomes—as opposed to science and to the objective mode of vision—the *ancilla* to Christian theology and prophecy.

Moreover, Keble agreed with Newman that modern "poetry is our mysticism." His dedication to Wordsworth, his lectures from the Oxford chair of poetry, his "Life of Sir Walter Scott"[23] leave no doubt that he shared Newman's sense of similarity between the theology of the Fathers and Romantic poetry. Notice that he attributes to Wordsworth that same conception of symbolism and that same idea of the poetic function which he finds in Scripture and the Fathers. Wordsworth's gift, "whether he sang of man or of nature," has been to direct men's attention, not to the object or thing before them, as the scientist would do, but "to lift up men's hearts to holy things." Wordsworth is "a chief minister [notice the metaphoric implications of the term] not only of sweetest poetry," the language of the senses, "but also of high and sacred truth,"[24] the vision of the invisible world of which sensible objects are the symbols. This symbolic vision of invisible things is holy and consequently must be approached with reserve or with what Keble here calls "modesty." " 'Holy things for holy persons' ";[25] again the emphasis is upon point of view, upon the necessity for subjective apprehension. The objective or scientific mentality feels no compunction about submitting all *things* to analysis in the broad light of day, but true poets, like the Fathers, know that what the world takes for *things* are really mysterious symbols and, consequently, must be treated with awe and reverence. Thus poets may "hint at very many things" rather than taking "pains to describe and define them." The latter is St. Thomas's way rather than that of St. Benedict. Poets, on the contrary, are "under no necessity to delineate in minute detail."[26]

Keble devotes a great deal of attention to theories of inspiration and to the question why the poet writes. In this area of

23. In *The British Critic*, 1838.
24. *Keble's Lectures on Poetry, 1832–1841*, trans. Edward Kershaw Francis (Oxford: The Clarendon Press, 1912), I, 8. Hereafter cited as *Lectures*.
25. *Lectures*, I, 74.
26. *Lectures*, I, 77.

thought he is constantly echoing Newman's statement that poetry is "the fire within the author's breast which overflows in the torrent of his burning, irresistible eloquence."[27] Keble, for instance, maintains that poetry is an aid and relief to minds oppressed by intense feeling; utterance provides relief from our emotional burden.[28] He develops the view at considerable length in his essay on Scott, whose work, says Keble, illustrates the principle that *"poetry is the indirect expression in words, most appropriately in metrical words, of some overpowering emotion, or ruling taste, or feeling, the direct indulgence whereof is somehow repressed."*[29] In such a statement Keble obviously owes something to Wordsworth's "spontaneous overflow of powerful feelings," but his language is curiously modern; so modern, in fact, that Meyer Abrams calls him a "proto-Freudian."[30] However, as Abrams also sees, Keble's position finds its explanation in the link between theology and poetry, and in this respect Keble is a much more complex esthetician than Wordsworth. For instance, if we consider the matter for a moment, we can see that poetry considered as the "overflow of powerful feelings," or as the outpouring of the "fire within the author's breast," as the "indirect expression in words . . . of some overpowering emotion" presents an analogy to the creation. Neither Newman nor Keble draw that analogy as such, but it is implicit in what they say on the subject of poetry generally, and also on the poetic or subjective approach to theology.

That analogy might be stated as follows: the creation is to God what the poem is to the poet. Thus we read nature as a vast symbol of the fire within its Author's breast, just as we read a poem, not for the details of objective plot, but for what the poem shows us of the author's mind and heart, his subjective impressions, his innate or infused ideas. Therefore Keble also rejects a mimetic or objective view of the poet's role, for the poet's con-

27. *Idea*, p. 279.

28. *Lectures*, I, 20–23.

29. John Keble, *Occasional Papers and Reviews* (Oxford: James Parker and Co., 1877), p. 6. Hereafter cited as *OPR*. Italics Keble's.

30. *The Mirror and the Lamp* (New York: W. W. Norton & Company, 1958), p. 147. Hereafter cited as "Abrams."

cern is not with the visible creation but with God who lies behind it; and, as the poet writes, he gives utterance to his internal,
subjective, in a sense unutterable, apprehension of those realities.
Keble prefers the word *expression* to *imitation*, "for the latter
word clearly conveys a cold and inadequate notion of the writer's
meaning."[31] The adjective *cold* suggests, as it does for Newman,
the external and the rationalistic. The Fathers, on the contrary,
were warm, expressive poets, for they read creation, not scientifically, but as a poem; and having thus apprehended through her
symbols the "good land" beyond her and having filled their
souls "even to overflowing, with the highest and greatest objects,"
they were able by "sacramental signs" to assist the Church "to
find and use, every where and always, means effectual, though
indirect, for realizing to herself those objects, and bringing them
near."[32]

The reference to "sacramental signs" brings us to the whole
question of the sacraments as illustrative of the subjective-objec-
tive, poetic-scientific distinction which Newman and Keble
make. Generally speaking we tend to think of the Protestant
view of the sacraments as subjective, the Catholic as objective.
The former takes the objects, the water, oil, bread and wine,
not as literal vehicles for the grace they convey but rather as
symbols of realities which have their literal existence elsewhere
and which are merely represented by the physical objects. Thus
when Protestants look at bread and wine in the Eucharist,
their doctrine forces them to think of the real, but altogether invisible, body and blood of Christ, which is to be apprehended
subjectively, in the conscience and in the heart, rather than objectively in the consecrated bread and wine. The Catholic doctrine, on the contrary, considers Christ's body and blood as objectively, "substantially," present under the accidents of bread
and wine. Thus the thing itself, the object which the physical
senses apprehend, retains its reality and importance. It can be
weighed, measured, and analyzed. The most remarkable aspect of

31. OPR, p. 8.
32. OPR, p. 16.

Thomist sacramental theory is its scientific objectivity—the minute, painstaking examination of exactly how the substance of bread and wine is altered while the accidents are preserved. To the subjective mind, the poetic mind as Newman conceives it, such particularity, such cold, scientific objectivity, no doubt seems scandalous; yet it preserves, as Newman's subjectivism does not and cannot, the integrity and autonomy of the physical creation. Newman never denies the Real Presence (far from it); but in his view the sacraments are only a particular instance, a special case. The bread and wine are symbolic of God in a mystical or poetic sense, just as all created things are; but in the special case of the bread and wine, or of the water or the oil, when these elements are duly consecrated by Holy Church, the signs become effectual, bringing into the visible world the things they signify. The doctrine of the Real Presence and its necessary consequence, the objective presence of Christ on the altar, are therefore particular and, one might almost say, arbitrary modifications of the general rules of symbolic or economic relationships. The sacraments, in other words, are a particular instance of the economy, in which the sign bears a direct and fixed rather than an indirect and fluctuating relationship to the *invisibilia* it signifies.

One consequence of the difference between the characteristically Protestant and Catholic views of the sacraments is that for most Protestants the sacramental rite is considered to be "expressive," in Newman's or Keble's sense, while the Catholic concept of it is mimetic. If Christ is only present invisibly and, consequently, if our apprehension of Him is internal or subjective, the poetry known as the rite or drama of the Mass comes to be conceived as the "spontaneous overflow of powerful feelings," in which the "plot," like the bread and wine, exists primarily as a vehicle for invisible realities perceivable only as ideas in the mind. If, on the other hand, Christ's body and blood are objectively present, at a given time on a given altar, passive there, under the accidents of bread and wine, to breaking, chewing and drinking, it becomes clear immediately that the "reality" lies outside ourselves and that we must approach it with reverence and with attention to precise, minute detail, just as great narrative and dramatic poets approach the traditional stories which are the subjects of their poetry. Thus the heart of the Mass is the rehearsing what our Lord said and did, not because those words and acts exist simply as promoters for subjective apprehension or religious emotion, but because, like the consecrated elements, they have the "reality" objectively in themselves.

Newman, I repeat, would never have denied that reality, but again we see that his beliefs were sounder than his philosophy and that his safeguards, though effective in preventing doctrinal heterodoxy, did not secure him against the epistemological emphases which characterize those heresies. His fullest development of the theory of the Real Presence before his entering the Church of Rome was in "Tract Ninety," and there we see clearly that his thought moves in a direction which is almost the exact opposite of Aquinas's. Newman's argument hinges on the proposition that since "we do not at all know what is meant by distance or intervals absolutely," we cannot really speak absolutely about "presence."[33] To be "*really* present" may not mean the same thing as to be "*locally* present"; to the Protestant or secular objection that " 'CHRIST is not really here, because He is not locally here,' " Newman answers, " 'He is really here, yet not locally.' "[34] He proceeds to argue that the presence of spiritual or invisible things is "*sui generis*" and consequently not measurable by our spatial and temporal conceptions of presence.[35] Likewise, where "locomotion is the means of a material presence; the Sacrament is the means of His spiritual Presence."[36] In the latter distinction, we see how far Newman is from Thomist realism. Aquinas would never divide the real from the local, for since Christ is present under the accidents of bread and wine, He is, though still at the Father's right hand, also present locally where those accidents inhere in Him as their substance. Consequently, it is impossible to argue that Christ's coming to us when we communicate is under a mode which is *sui generis*. After all, from the objective or realist point of view, to insist on "presence" without "locality" is simply to equivocate.

33. No. 90, p. 53 (Vol. VI).
34. No. 90, p. 54 (Vol. VI).
35. No. 90, p. 55 (Vol. VI).
36. No. 90, p. 57 (Vol. VI).

Of course Newman, when he entered the Church of Rome, was obliged to accept the doctrine of transubstantiation, but it seems fair to say that he never really embraced the "spirit" or the full, objective ramifications of the dogma. As we have seen from passages in the *Apologia,* though he accepted the dogma on the basis of the Church's infallible authority, he never shows any particular interest in or enthusiasm for the philosophical propositions implicit in the dogma per se. Such a mode of acceptance is altogether honest and, on its own terms, completely satisfactory; however, it evades the intellectual issue altogether. It is clear from the whole context of Newman's work, moreover, that he can accept the fruits of scientific and objective theology on the basis of ecclesiastical authority without ever foregoing his own subjective or poetic approach. He tells us that he found in the Church of Rome, not a "book theology," but a "living system." The distinction reminds us immediately of the difference as he sees it between the systematic theology of the Schools and the organic life of the Patristic and Benedictine tradition. A living system, like a human being, holds truth, subjectively, in itself. Thus, once the true Church embraces a doctrine such as that of transubstantiation, whatever its origin, that doctrine ceases to be an objective, external reality to be handled scientifically and becomes instead a part of the progressive economy of the living being. In 1838 Newman says that Anglican theology " 'supposed the Truth to be entirely objective and detached, not' (as in the theology of Rome) 'lying hid in the bosom of the Church.' "[37] Transubstantiation, once the doctrine is hid within that bosom, loses its objective, detached, scientific (we might say its "notional") character. In approaching it, Newman no longer has to concern himself with the plot but with the mind or soul of the poet, who is in this case Holy Church, which uses the plot merely as an external economy for subjective truth.

All along we have been considering Newman's "character of mind"—his scepticism, his idealism, his individualism, and his radicalism—as indications of his modernity. We may now add to that list his subjective view of symbols. In fact a great many

37. *Ap.,* p. 106.

contemporary critics agree that the shift from *mimesis* to *expression* is the most distinctive feature of nineteenth- and twentieth-century poetry and poetic theory. M. H. Abrams, for instance, taking the mirror as his symbol of the objective view, the lamp as his symbol of the subjective, argues that the former was "characteristic of much of the thinking from Plato to the eighteenth century; the second typifies the prevailing romantic conception of the poetic mind." The mirror, as a metaphor, compares "the mind to a reflector of external objects," the lamp "to a radiant projector which makes a contribution to the objects it perceives."[38] The assumption, obviously, in the metaphor of the mirror, is that the light of truth is to be found outside the mind; in the metaphor of the lamp, that it lies within. The former asthetic position is clearly the corollary of a realist philosophy and of a certain basic confidence in nature and right reason; the latter of a subjective or idealist philosophy and of the corresponding scepticism about man's ability to see God "plainly" in the "living busy world." The poetic mind, conceiving itself not as "a reflector of external objects" but as a "radiant projector," is the mind exercising itself as an autonomous interpreter of reality, independent of the object and its limitations, whether it thinks of itself as a pure creator of meaning or simply as an inventor or discoverer. To such a mind the demands of reality are distinct from those of locality, for such a mind is ultimately its own place.

C. S. Lewis also argues that such a mind is "modern." He points to the "medieval and Renaissance delight in the universe," a pleasure which rose from contemplation of what Lewis calls the "model," the great, harmonious order of the cosmos.[39] One thinks, for instance, of Hooker's or Andrewes's or Donne's pleasure in the vast theocentric creation which they describe, and it should be clear that such delight assumes from the outset the objective reality of that creation. In the presence of a given reality, of a plot which bears significance in itself, of the Body and Blood of Christ under the local accidents of bread and wine, the mind is passive in its joy, set free from the chore of self-

38. Abrams, p. vi.
39. *DI*, p. 203.

expression, of discovering or creating and imposing meaning on external objects conceived as potential symbols. Consequently, Lewis suggests, "the man of genius then [in the Middle Ages or the Renaissance] found himself in a situation very different from that of his modern successor. Such a man today often, perhaps usually, feels himself confronted with a reality whose significance he cannot know" or which, he suspects, may have no significance, objectively, in itself.[40] Thus the modern man of genius, and Newman is a case in point, is obliged either "to discover a meaning, or, out of his own subjectivity, to give a meaning—or at least a shape—to what in itself had neither."[41] (And, as we have seen, meaning and shape, meaning and "form," are finally inseparable.)

Lewis's comments all hint at a cause-and-effect relationship between subjectivism and philosophical scepticism. That relationship has been implicit in everything which we have said about Newman's mode of vision and is clearly a factor in the whole question of what constitutes "modernism." Subjectivism in all its manifestations, especially in its view of nature and of symbols, accommodates itself to scepticism in a way that Thomist and Caroline realism cannot. When a man comes to distrust nature and right reason, he naturally falls back, in his search for religious certitude, upon subjective apprehension. If he is convinced by orthodox dogma that there must be a "good land" but cannot discern it in what his senses and his reason convey to him of the external, objective world, he seeks it instead in an invisible realm present directly, in ideas or subjective impressions, within the mind, relegating external reality to the category of an economy or a set of symbols which depend for their meaning on the operation of the mind. If he is convinced that God *must* be present but cannot believe that he is locally, sensibly present in the world, he falls back upon a theory of presence sui generis.

Thus, as Lewis suggests, the modern man feels obliged to find his meaning elsewhere than in the world as it is; in fact having found subjectively whatever meaning he attains to, he must in

40. *DI*, pp. 203–204.
41. *DI*, p. 204.

turn impose that meaning upon the external world. On the contrary, "the Model universe of our ancestors had a built-in significance. And that in two senses; as having 'significant form' (it is an admirable design) and as a manifestation of the wisdom and goodness that created it. There was no question of waking it into beauty or life."[42] Because Newman, in spite of his Catholicism, is a modern man, he must "wake" his world if it is to live and have beauty. Until the lamp of his conscience lights the landscape, it remains in impenetrable shadow; without the perceptive power of the gnostic, economies are opaque. So long as the whole civilization believes that the creation "shows God plainly," there is no need for the category of gnostic or initiate, for no man need be a creator or inventor of nature's symbolic meaning. All mirrors are alike; lamps differ in their intensity and some are never lighted. When the light of sense goes out, however, mirrors are no more good.

These considerations draw us full circle, to the "old idea of a Christian Polity"; for it should be clear that the loss of objectivity in theology and poetry is related, whether as cause or effect to the dissolution in England, and in Europe generally, of a closed, traditional, Christian community. The process of secularization, the growing scepticism about the validity of natural law and rational judgments, was also probably, in part, an effect of the social change, for the primary consequence of "modernization" was to deprive European civilization of any common consent or intention as to the meaning of symbols.

Again Aquinas's doctrine of the sacraments is helpful by way of illustration, for what applies to the relationship between the sacraments and the Church applies, by analogy, to the relationship between symbols and the traditional society in which the meanings of those symbols inhere. The link in each case is the *word*. According to Thomist definition, the words by which the Eucharist is instituted constitute the form of the sacrament; the bread and wine is the potential matter. It is by the word that the transubstantiation is effected, and without the word

42. *DI*, p. 204.

there can be no sacrament. "Consequently it must be said that all the aforesaid words belong to the substance of the form; but that by the first words, *This is the chalice of My blood,* the change of the wine into blood is denoted, as explained above . . . in the form for the consecration of the bread."[43] The words of institution derive from Christ an "instrumental power," a "created power," which produces "the sacramental effects."[44]

Immediately a philosophical problem arises; since "sensible things [the matter of the sacrament, the bread and wine] and words are of different genera, for sensible things are the product of nature, but words, of reason; it seems that in the sacraments, words are not required besides sensible things." St. Thomas's answer is that in the sacraments, "words and things, like form and matter, combine in the formation of one thing, in so far as the signification of things is completed by means of words, as above stated." As a matter of fact, the sensible thing can never function adequately as a sign or image without the addition to it, the fusion with it, of the "significant" power of words; the words "determine the signification of the sensible things." By way of illustration St. Thomas points to the relationship between words and water in Holy Baptism; "for water may signify both a cleansing by reason of its humidity, and refreshment by reason of its being cool." If the sensible thing were used without the word, if the child were sprinkled with water by a silent priest, there would be no determination of meaning and the sacrament would be worthless; "but when we say, *I baptize thee,* it is clear that we use water in baptism in order to signify a spiritual cleansing."[45]

However, the use of these significant words, in the objective, realist, Thomist view, is never a private or individual affair. The meaning of words is not privately determined, and the validity of a sacrament depends not simply upon the use of words but of those particular words with that particular signification to which the whole Church is universally committed. If a priest attempts

43. *ST,* III, 78, 3.
44. *ST,* III, 78, 4.
45. *ST,* III, 60, 6.

by "addition or suppression to perform a rite other from that which is recognized by the Church, it seems that the sacrament is invalid: because he seems not to intend to do what the Church does."[46] Moreover, the Church's common consent to these determinate words, which are the forms of her sacraments, binds her together in a body, for as St. Augustine has said, *"It is impossible to keep men together in one religious denomination, whether true or false, except they be united by means of visible signs and sacraments,"* and that they be so united, "in the name of the one true religion" is necessary for salvation. "Therefore sacraments are necessary for man's salvation,"[47] and primarily in their relationship to that union in charity which is the bond of the Church.

It should be clear that what applies to the relation between the sacraments and the Church applies analogously to the relationship between other images and human society; "for spiritual life has a certain conformity with the life of the body: just as other corporeal things have a certain likeness to things spiritual." Therefore, just as union in the ecclesiastical community is necessary to man's salvation, so, in nature, man attains perfection, not in isolation, but "in regard to the whole community of the society in which he lives."[48] As the Church is united in assigning certain meanings or significations to those "effective signs" which are essential to our salvation and to the common life of charity in the body of Christ, so in the "corporeal life" the human community unites in assigning meanings, determinate words, to sensible things, establishing thereby an order of signs or symbols by which the world is waked "to beauty and life." It follows that the human community can no more live without common symbols than the Church can live without the supernatural bond of the sacraments.

In a healthy society, the pomp of kingship provides just such a body of symbols; such too are the robes of various offices, regal

46. *ST*, III, 60, 8.
47. *ST*, III, 61, 1. Italics in original; Aquinas is quoting from St. Augustine (*Contra Faust.*, XIX).
48. *ST*, III, 65, 1.

and academic, the tackle and gear of the various trades, the livery of servants, the badges of subordination and fealty of all sorts, family coats of arms, and all the other images, each of which is a union of word or meaning on one hand, of the sensible thing on the other, the joining of form or act-of-being with matter for the purpose of signification where the whole society is united in its intended meaning. Of course in a Christian society like that of medieval Europe the very sacraments themselves, particularly those such as marriage, ordination and consecration which affect the human community in its public or political aspect, by establishment of social bonds and by the institution of authorities, serve as uniting symbols in the corporeal society. Thus, in a closed, traditional, Christian community it comes about that through union with the word almost all the sensible things of common experience are transformed into symbols which both receive their meaning from the corporate society in which they inhere and at the same time give meaning and unity to that society. Flowers, trees, colors; earth, air, fire, water; the configuration of the heavens and indeed the whole vast structure of the created universe—all those become symbols, unions of words and matter.

It is in such a community that the objective mode of vision, the mimetic or realizing imagination, the mirror, is at home. It is when the traditional community breaks up, when there is no longer common consent to the meaning of sensible things, that the objective mode of vision becomes impossible and each individual man must rely upon his own ability to impose meaning. Therefore we can see that the apparent disappearance of God from His creation, the increasing difficulty in believing that the creation shows God "plainly," is a process which coincides closely with the collapse of the traditional community. The secularization of Europe and the fragmentation of Europe are the corollaries of one another, two sides, as it were, of the same coin; and herein lies a great mystery which is implicit in all Eucharistic theology, not least in Aquinas's. The Church has never been able to discuss the sacraments except in terms of the life of the body, nor salvation except in terms of the Church and her sacraments. The individual believer, considered simply as an individual, is an impossibility. The meaning of the image, the life of the community, and the life of the individual are all bound up together, and when the ecclesiastical community is fragmented the validity of the sacrament is impaired or lost and the individual perishes. The same conditions appear to apply in the secular community where fragmentation and deracination, the symbolic "departure from Oxford," destroy the images of civilization and force individual human beings into spiritual isolation and desiccation. Hooker's profound sense of God's presence in all His works is not Hooker's alone but the common possession of his civilization in its consent to the meaning of its various signs. Newman's sense of God's absence from His works is his alone, for though all modern men may share that sense, there is no community in a negation. The common possessions of a fragmented society are atheism, the consequent failure of all symbols, and, for the individual, various forms of loneliness, neurosis and damnation.

Caught in such desparate circumstances, what must man do? W. H. Auden sees that question as a key to the whole phenomenon of Romanticism in which "the City," which for the traditional Christian community was the locus of a common imagery and itself the bond of peace, becomes, on account of secularization and fragmentation, "the Trivial Unhappy Unjust City, the desert of the average from which the only escape is to the wild, lonely, but still vital sea."[49] The sea is the theater of personal choice where, by suffering, the individual attempts to achieve for himself, at whatever cost, the salvation, the wholeness, which the city once gave. In a true community, says Auden, "I always precedes We." However, "In a closed traditional community this fact is hidden, because the I is only potential."[50] The point might be debated. In that mysterious union of I and We in the traditional community it becomes all but impossible to say which takes the precedence. Indeed, the very unanimity of consent to traditional images, or, in the Church, the bond of the sacraments, makes the distinction impossible. Of course, Auden himself

49. W. H. Auden, *The Enchafèd Flood* (New York: Vintage Books, 1967), p. 25. Hereafter cited as "Auden."
50. Auden, p. 30.

speaks as a *deraciné*, and once the uprooting and fragmentation happen, it becomes impossible to speak of the original union accurately. In fact, that union, being a mystery in the literal sense, lives in the fusion of word and sensible matter which constitutes the image or sacrament, and our difficulty in articulating the principle of that union is akin to our difficulty in explaining the union of Word and flesh in the Incarnation.

In any event we may let the matter rest there, for Auden does agree that "in a closed traditional community this fact [that *I* always precedes *We*] is hidden, because *I* is only potential." However, "the further civilization moves towards the open condition," the alternatives become "*either* personal choice and through the sum of such choices an actual community *or* the annihilation of personality and the dissolution of community into crowds."[51] Since the sea is the place for that personal choice, part of which involves the new role of the mind in creating images, most of the heroes of literature since 1798, set sail. Thus we return to the theme of exile, the departure from Troy or Oxford, the farewell to the "old orthodoxy of England," to the "old idea of a Christian Polity," to the "tradition of fifteen hundred years." Newman cuts himself loose from the traditional community of the English High-Church party, which, at least in his eyes, has become the "Trivial Unhappy Unjust City" in order, through personal choice, to forge for himself new symbols of religion or, which amounts epistemologically and poetically to much the same thing, to seek out ancient or foreign symbols. In either case the common consent of the body to the union of word and thing is lost. Though "no desert father," Newman, like St. Clement, found the desert in the city, "set up the grave in the house." There may be a great deal of difference between the ancient, unconverted, still pagan city and the modern apostate one, but neither Clement's Alexandria, Agellius's Rome nor Newman's Oxford are completely hospitable to the Christian vision of the world. Before a common consent to the meaning of symbols is established and again after it is lost, the individual, the "modern man" in whatever age, the exile, must impose his

51. Auden, pp. 30–31.

own subjective meaning on the creation. Aquinas and the Schoolmen, Hooker and the Carolines, belong to an altogether different
kind of world. So also do the great poets of the traditional
Christian community from Dante to Milton and even perhaps to
Doctor Johnson. The nineteenth century brought back the desert
and the beast and, therefore, necessarily, the exile and the wan-
dering hero.

Because it was the collapse of the traditional Christian community which brought the exile back into prominence, it is
normal to think of him as a secular or antichristian figure. Indeed
most of the modern wanderers, from Wordsworth to Joyce, have
been in quest of a mode of vision which is at best a modification
of, at worst an out-and-out attack upon, the previously established, now, presumably, exhausted or disproved Christian mode.
It may be arguable that Newman's accomplishment has been to
make an orthodox "modernism," a genuinely Christian deracination, possible; that he embraced and "redeemed" a mode of
vision and a set of philosophical principles which for a century
and a half have served as grounds for heresy and apostasy.[52] In
other words, according to such reasoning, Newman has done for
modern thought what Aquinas did for Aristotle: saved for Christianity philosophical verities which had previously been wedded
to an untenable theology or atheology. On the other hand, we
must not forget that not all philosophies lend themselves with
equal ease to Christianization. In fact, as we have already suggested, Aquinas was able to Christianize Aristotle by taking his
arguments to their logical conclusion, whereas Newman achieved
an orthodox modernism only by securing modern thought against
the consequences of its full development. In fact, from all we
have seen of Newman's *mind* in the preceding pages, his efforts
to make peace between "Catholic teaching" and the "new civilization" must finally be regarded more as a liability than as an
accomplishment, and the question which naturally suggests itself
is whether any system of philosophy or theory of society can be

52. This is essentially what Erich Przywara argues in his "St. Augustine and
the Modern World," *Augustine*, pp. 249–286. It is also the assumption of the
theologians who admire the work of the Second Vatican Council and who
consider Newman to be their theological and philosophical predecessor.

found which accords so well with the truth of Christian doctrine (and therefore with the deepest needs of man) as does the *Summa* and its legacy, both Scholastic and Caroline, and as does the traditional hierarchy of medieval Christendom.

The answer is that probably no such system and no such theory can be found; and if that negative is a just one it seems to follow that what is now widely regarded as Newman's peculiar achievement may prove in the long run to be an index of his peculiar failure; namely, that he did not set his face resolutely against the whole course of modern thought. He was in a uniquely good position to have done just that, for he was unquestionably the most prominent, the most influential, the most nearly saintly theologian of the past two centuries. It seems to me to have been his great failure that in relinquishing the "old idea of a Christian Polity" and in attempting to defend orthodox dogma without also defending the civilization which that dogma and its vision had brought into being he omitted to bring to modern thought and modern literature what he alone could have brought, what no one else in his century or ours has been in a position or had the strength to bring—a thoroughly traditional Christian philosophy of nature and society.

Index